# THE LIVES OF THE

# English Rakes

# THE LIVES OF THE

# English

# Rakes

## Fergus Linnane

**PORTRAIT**

Copyright © 2006 by Fergus Linnane

First published in 2006 by **Portrait**
an imprint of
Piatkus Books Ltd
5 Windmill Street
London W1T 2JA
e-mail: info@piatkus.co.uk

**The moral right of the author has been asserted**

*A catalogue record for this book is available from the British Library*

ISBN 0 7499 5096 X

**Picture credits** The following images in the plate sections are © Getty Images:
Lady Castlemaine, Bertie, Daisy Brooke and Lillie Langtry. All other images are
from the author's private collection.

Data manipulation by
Action Publishing Technology Ltd, Gloucester

Printed & bound in Great Britain by
William Clowes Ltd, Beccles, Suffolk

# Contents

For my sister, Lorna

# Preface

When Graham Greene wrote *Lord Rochester's Monkey*, his biography of the Restoration rake and poet, in the early 1930s, he was advised that the only way it could be published was as a limited edition for private circulation. Otherwise he and his publisher would probably be prosecuted for obscenity. This was because Rochester's poetry was regarded as too indecent for general circulation – at the British Museum and the Bodleian Library his works were hidden away and could be seen, if at all, only by special request. Greene showed the manuscript to his publisher, Heinemann, who turned it down. He wrote later that he 'hadn't the heart' to offer it elsewhere after this discouraging response, and so the book was not published until 1974.

Greene complained of the 'almost Victorian atmosphere' of the early thirties when he wrote his book, yet he too suffered from an almost Victorian reticence, preferring bowdlerised versions of the poems to what he called the 'hotter' ones now regarded as authentic. His version of 'The Debauchee' is feeble:

> I send for my whore, when for fear of a clap,
> I dally about her, and spew in her lap ...

The original has so much more force, and not just because of the obscenity that Greene rejected:

> I send for my whore, when for fear of a clap,
> I spend in her hand, and I spew in her lap . . .

Earlier Sir Sidney Lee's essay on Rochester in the old *Dictionary of National Biography* (begun in 1882) had set the tone:

> The sentiment in his love songs is artificial whenever it is not offensively obscene. Numerous verses of gross indelicacy which have been put to his credit . . . may be from other pens. But there is enough foulness in his fully authenticated poems to give him a title to be remembered as the writer of the filthiest verse in the language.

This attitude persisted for longer than we might think. As late as 1958 Donald McCormick in *The Hell-Fire Club* said of the Psalms the members Potter and Whitehead wrote for the club's revels, 'none . . . are fit for publication'.

There has been no attempt at a comprehensive history of the English rakes since E. Beresford Chancellor's six-volume *The Lives of the Rakes*, published in 1925. That work too suffered from the extreme reticence of the age. While this study is by no means comprehensive, it is the product of a franker age.

Some rakes were among the major political figures of their times, but to avoid the text becoming unwieldy I have avoided politics as far as possible. Also to avoid interrupting the flow I have continued the stories of the mistresses of Charles II and Edward VII after the monarchs' deaths in an appendix, 'The Royal Mistresses'.

I have modernised spelling in most cases, and grammar in some.

# Introduction

Rake. A loose, disorderly, vicious, wild, gay, thoughtless fellow; a man addicted to pleasure.

(Dr Johnson's *Dictionary*, 1755)

Rake. A dissolute man, esp. one in fashionable society; roué.

(*Collins Dictionary*, modern)

THE LONG HEYDAY OF THE ENGLISH RAKE lasted roughly from 1660, when Charles II returned from exile, until the death of George IV in 1830. There was a brief revival of some aspects of rakish behaviour among the cronies of Edward, Prince of Wales, in the second half of the nineteenth century. After that, what later became known as Victorian values made such behaviour largely unacceptable.

The first attribute of the rake was cold hedonism rather than grand romantic passion. He was usually a cynical exploiter of women, often a reckless gambler, sometimes a touchy egoist quick to take offence and to seek redress in duels. He could be a good friend and a bad enemy. He was often aristocratic and sometimes rich.

There were of course womanisers and bullies in other countries, but there was widespread acceptance that the English rake was the most cynical, heartless and brutal of the type. He spent his life in a frenzy of sexual pursuits, gambling, drinking, duels and brawls. He treated his equals with cold disdain and his inferiors with dangerous contempt. The French historian Hippolyte Taine in his *History of English Literature* (1863) recalls a story about a friend of the Cavalier poet Richard Lovelace, who 'decoys a young innocent girl, makes her drunk, spends the night with her in a brothel and departs, leaving her there in payment of the bill, and rubs his hands on learning that she has been imprisoned and has gone out of her mind and died'. This little story has most of the elements of the typical rakish episode: a heartless aristocrat, innocence ruined and cast aside, an almost fiendish delight in causing pain.

Bishop Burnet,* who knew them both, wrote a similar story about the two most prominent rakes at Charles II's court, the Duke of Buckingham and the Earl of Rochester: the Earl seduced a miser's pretty young wife, persuaded her to steal her husband's money, and when he had finished with her passed her on to Buckingham. When he tired of her they sent her packing. The miser, bereft of money and wife, hanged himself. Buckingham and Rochester treated the whole thing as a joke.

The concept and behaviour of the rake changed over time. The rough manners of the seventeenth century softened during the course of the next hundred years. We can see this in the lives of two eighteenth-century figures, the extraordinary Colonel Francis Charteris (1675–1732) and the Duke of Queensberry (1724–1810). Charteris was a brute, known as the Rape-Master General of Britain. He was sentenced to death for rape but used his wealth and his high-born contacts to bribe his way out. Queensberry was a great charmer and seducer who died in old age in a bed covered with love letters, some from women he had never even met. In another sign of change, men were less ready to fight to the death. The duelling so common at the court of Charles II gradually died

---

\* Burnet was a controversial and ambitious cleric who alienated Charles II and his brother James, among others. He eventually became a Dutch citizen, a favourite of William III, and accompanied him to England in 1688 as royal chaplain. In 1689 he was appointed Bishop of Salisbury. He published *History of My Own Time* in 1724–34. His enemies thought him a time-serving hypocrite.

out, partly because of that king's opposition. Of course not every-thing had changed, as illustrated by Jesse in his biography of George Selwyn. Queensberry wrote to his friend Selwyn in 1766 of another rake, Viscount Bolingbroke, 'Bully' to his friends: 'Bully is appearing again in society, and swears that he will seduce any innocent girl whatever. I do not doubt that he will.'

The circle of hangers-on and toadies around George, Prince of Wales, later George IV (1762–1830) displays rakishness in its final decay. The Prince himself was its finest flower, selfish, mean-spirited, vain and vindictive to a degree. He dropped friends and lovers without a qualm, often with the most insulting and hurtful brush-offs. Leigh Hunt summed him up: 'This Adonis in loveliness is a corpulent man of fifty … a libertine over head and ears in debt and disgrace, a despiser of domestic ties, the companion of gamblers and demireps, a man who has just closed half a century without one single claim on the gratitude of his country or the respect of authority.' His frankness cost him a two-year prison sentence.

Edward VII, known as Bertie, was like Charles II a man domi-nated by his love of beautiful women, lazy and pleasure loving. It could be said that some of his mistresses, particularly Lillie Langtry, were more rakish than he. But some of the men in his circle were rich and idle, with nothing to do but spend their time in an end-less pursuit of pleasure.

It has been suggested that rakes were often the products of unhappy childhoods, had lost their fathers early, or had dominant mothers, and that this explained their later behaviour. Perhaps. If there are common causes I think they might be boredom and spleen. These were men who were easily bored. Lord Rochester wrote to a friend: 'The world, ever since I can remember, has been so insupportably the same, that 'twere vain to hope there were any alterations.' There speaks the true voice of a man who craves wilder music and stronger wine. One thinks of the Don Juan myth, of men who were the victims of impulses almost beyond their control.

# Part I

# Charles II:
# A Merry Monarch

# Prelude

THE RETURN FROM EXILE OF CHARLES II in 1660 brought
back colour and glamour to a moribund court and pleasure to a nation starved of both. It was the end of 11 years
of Puritanism, years in which secret police prowled the streets and
a blight descended on all public pleasures. Theatres and brothels
were closed, dancing and music – except for hymns – were forbidden, drink and sex were frowned on. In rare cases fornication
became a capital offence. The bears in the bear-baiting pits were
shot, not to end cruelty but to rob people of this very popular
spectacle.

With the King came a group of young aristocrats who had
shared his hard times and now shared his free and easy attitude to
sex and morals. Together they set the moral tone of the age, one
which continued to influence the behaviour of people in the
upper reaches of society until well into the reign of Victoria.

Charles, says the historian Macaulay, was 'addicted beyond
measure to sensual indulgence'. We know the names of 13 of his
mistresses – among them some of the greatest beauties of their
time – but there were also many one-night stands with actresses
and whores and indeed anyone who caught his roving eye. Consequently there were innumerable bastards, about a dozen of
whom he acknowledged and five of whom were created dukes. He
was undoubtedly a rake in his appetite for sex, drink and disreputable companions, but unlike some of the wilder spirits at his

court he was kind-hearted and genuinely loved women; he treated them as his intellectual equals, although according to the Earl of Clarendon in his *History of the Rebellion and Civil Wars in England* he mostly talked to them about 'that purpose he thought them all made for'. This was unfair: he discussed politics with them, which unfortunately led to claims that they were running the state. He was physically equipped to be a great lover, as Lady Castlemaine, herself an expert, told a friend. Rochester wrote of him: 'His sceptre and his prick are of a length . . .'

There is a little story about the King that shows him at his worst and best. He was a keen follower of the turf, and rode a winner at Newmarket in 1671. When he attended the races the entire court accompanied him, sometimes three times a year. The King was even more than usually unbuttoned on these occasions, joining in the revelry of his young friends at inns, calling on his fiddlers to accompany obscene ditties. One night Rochester and one of Charles's mistresses, probably Nell Gwynn, played an outrageous trick on the King. Charles agreed to go with them to a brothel – the London bawds would follow the court to Newmarket with their loveliest girls. In his disguise as Old Rowley which he used on these occasions the King went to the brothel, chose a girl and went to a room.

The girl had been briefed by Rochester, and picked the King's pocket. When he was ready to leave he called for Rochester and was told that he had already left. He then found that his money was gone, and that he could not pay the bill. Neither the bawd nor the girl knew who he was, which of course was the point of the trick. When he asked if he could pay later the bawd refused – she had met his kind before. Eventually the King took a ring from his finger, and the bawd very reluctantly, as it was late, roused a sleeping jeweller in the town to value it. The story goes that the jeweller recognised a royal jewel, and asked the bawd who it belonged to. 'A black looking, ugly son of a whore, who had no money in his pocket and was obliged to pawn his ring.' The jeweller went to the brothel, knelt before the King and returned the ring. The bawd and her girls and servants, we are told, fell to their knees. The King instantly forgave them and asked 'whether the ring would not bear another bottle'. It seems he also forgave Rochester. As Cephas Goldsworthy recounts in *The Satyr, An Account of the Life and Work, Death and Salvation of John Wilmot, Second Earl of Rochester,* 'The King was delighted by the prank. Until the end of his days he never tired of repeating the story, weeping with laughter.'

While he did not himself fully deserve the description, Charles attracted to his court young men who were indeed full-blown rakes. Although he could see through them he was too easy-going to make more than token efforts to restrain their bad behaviour. Witty repartee, in men and women, eased his boredom and melancholy. John Wilmot, Earl of Rochester, the quintessential Restoration rake, was banished from court from time to time for his malicious behaviour, and just as often forgiven and recalled. As Bishop Burnet says, the King, who did not always love him, loved his wit.

Charles shared certain attributes with these young men. After the trauma of his father's execution he suffered military defeat and humiliation and long years of privation in exile. He was 30 in 1660, cynical and disillusioned. His deeply sensual and pleasure-loving nature balked at the thought of official duties and the tedium of affairs of state. (Although, when his attention was engaged, he could surprise his advisers with his capacity for work. He was also a deep schemer, and needed to be — Parliament kept him short of money and he remained afloat with secret payments from the French King, Louis XIV, almost universally regarded as England's prime enemy.) He had sailed through a sea of troubles and come safely to shore, and he wanted only to enjoy himself. What he mainly asked of his courtiers was that they should amuse him, and cause him as little trouble as possible.

This love of the quiet life made him vulnerable to emotional blackmail. His women learned that tears and tantrums would usually get them what they wanted. One of them, the Frenchwoman Louise de Kéroualle, would threaten suicide when she was not getting her way. When told yet again that she was dying, Charles exclaimed: 'God's fish! I don't believe a word of all this; she's better than you or I are, and she wants something that makes her play her pranks over this. She has served me so often so, that I am sure of what I say as if I were part of her.' Another mistress, Barbara Villiers, whom he made Countess of Castlemaine and Duchess of Cleveland, and very wealthy, was given to screeching tantrums and bled the state white. She once made him get down on his knees to beg forgiveness, although he may have done it light-heartedly, and she bullied him into appointing her a Lady of the Bedchamber to his wife Catherine. When the Queen found out her nose bled and she fell to the ground in a fit of hysterics.

Although she later learned to put up with Charles' mistresses, even supping in Barbara's apartments, Pepys reported a tart exchange between the two women. Barbara commented on the length of time the Queen had spent with her dresser: 'I wonder your Majesty can have the patience to sit so long a-dressing.' Catherine replied: 'I have so much reason to use patience that I can well bear with it.'

Lady Castlemaine was the dominant mistress of the early years of Charles's reign. She produced a string of bastards, some of them the King's, and saw other mistresses come and go. If there was such a thing as a female rake, surely it was she. She was, by general agreement, one of the great beauties of the age. Pepys was embarrassingly smitten by her. In a dream he was 'admitted to use all the dalliance I desired with her'. Sir Peter Lely, the dominant British portraitist of the period, probably painted her more often than anyone else, and he is said to have remarked that it was 'beyond the compass of art to give this lady her due, as to her sweet and exquisite beauty'. She became a key symbol for the decadence of the court, and was known to be so debauched that observers watched her closely, searching for signs that what we would now call her lifestyle was beginning to ruin her looks.

The King's own elaborate sex life was hardly an encouragement to continence at his court. His sexual education began during the Civil War when he was 14. His beautiful and wealthy former nurse, Mrs Christabella Wyndham, performed the service, as women in her position sometimes did. However, while such sexual instruction might be tolerated or even expected if discreet, she scandalised society by kissing him enthusiastically in public. Two years later he had his first recorded love affair, with Marguerite Carteret, who was four years his senior. In 1648 his mistress Lucy Walter, 'brown, beautiful and bold' in the words of the diarist John Evelyn, gave birth to a son, later the dim and doomed Duke of Monmouth. Although Lucy was free with her favours Charles never questioned the paternity.

On the eve of the Restoration Barbara Villiers took over, although she was no more monogamous than Charles. According to Rochester and others her lovers included the Duke of Monmouth; the Earl of Chesterfield; the warrior John Churchill, later Duke of Marlborough; Ralph Montagu, ambassador to the French court; Henry Jermyn, Baron of Dover; the playwright William Wycherley; Charles Hart the actor; and Jacob Hall the rope-dancer, one of the King's three official acrobats. Hall, a man of magnificent physique, was reportedly able to imitate the seemingly impossible sexual contortions in Aretino's *Postures*,[*] something that would have endeared him to Castlemaine. Having sex with the King's mistress might be thought dangerous, but Charles was all-forgiving — when he discovered Jermyn's affair with Castlemaine he merely banned him from court for a while. Castlemaine herself could be a terror. When a young man named John Ellis boasted that he had succeeded the King in her affections, she hired thugs to castrate him. Pope refers to the incident in 'A Sermon Against Adultery':

> Who push'd poor Ellis on th'imperial whore?
> 'Twas but to be where Charles had been before.
> The fatal steel unjustly was applied
> When not his lust offended, but his pride.

Servants were fair game; she was said to have seduced the running footman who accompanied her coach:

[*] A series of erotic illustrations accompanying text by the Italian poet Pietro Aretino.

> She through her lackey's drawers, as he ran,
> Discerns love's cause, and a new flame began ...
> Full forty men a day have swiv'd this whore,
> Yet like a bitch she wags her tail for more.

And Rochester, who as a royal attendant had lain sleepless by the King's bedside as he enjoyed her, and had also seen her letting herself go in the lowest brothels in London, wrote:

> When she has jaded quite
> Her almost boundless appetite ...
> She'll still drudge on in tastless vice,
> As if she sinned for exercise ...

She was notoriously greedy and extorted huge sums from the King by raucous emotional blackmail. Burnet called her 'enormously vicious and ravenous'.

In 1670 the King decided he wanted a quieter life with his other mistresses. The 'lewd Imperial Whore' Castlemaine was pensioned off with the title of Duchess of Cleveland, and Charles told her: 'Madam, all I ask of you for your own sake is, live so for the future as to make the least noise you can, and I care not who you love.' She had obtained enormous sums by various means including whoring, much of which went to her lover John Churchill. Charles had once caught him in her room, and muttered: 'I forgive you, for you do it for your bread.' He was equally forgiving when shown love letters between Castlemaine and Jacob Hall. He merely handed them back to her and advised her to be more discreet. But discretion was not really in her nature: when Hall was imprisoned for building a rope-dancing booth at Charing Cross without permission, she used her influence to get him freed. Gramont* said that 'out of gratitude he did not disappoint the Lady's expectations in any way'.

---

* Count Philibert de Gramont, whose *Memoirs* (1713) are an amusing account of the amorous intrigues of Charles's court. They were actually written by Count Anthony Hamilton.

Charles gave Castlemaine the fairy-tale palace of Nonsuch, in Cheam, an affair of gilded domes and magnificent decorations. Almost immediately she had this national treasure pulled down and sold the materials and the land. She accepted bribes for using her influence with the King, including one of £10,000 (equivalent to more than £1,000,000 today) from a syndicate which wanted to win a contract to collect taxes. They didn't get it, but she kept the money.

In 1676 she went to live in Paris where she had affairs with the English ambassador Ralph Montagu and the Archbishop of Paris, who was described as 'her principal gallant'. Another lover, the French king's servant the Marquis de Chatillon, a good-looking but impecunious young man, may have profited by the liaison, as she was generous to her lovers. She found time to have an affair with an actor and highwayman named Cardonell Goodman, nicknamed Scum, who was found guilty of trying to poison two of her children.

The other main mistresses of the King are well known. 'Pretty, witty' Nell Gwynn was a virtually illiterate actress who had learned the ways of the world serving drinks in her mother's low tavern and as an orange girl in the theatre. These girls sold fruit, and sometimes themselves, to theatre-goers. Their leader at the Theatre Royal was the notoriously promiscuous and impudent Orange Betty Mackarel, called 'the giantess Betty Mackarela'. She could hold her own with the wits in the pit, 'hot at repartee with Orange Betty'. The leader of the orange girls at Drury Lane Theatre was Orange Moll. Pepys liked to gossip with her, and picked up some interesting titbits about Nell Gwynn's career before she became the King's mistress:

Sir W. Pen and I had a great deal of discourse with Moll: who tells us that Nell is already left by my Lord Buckhurst, and that he makes sport of her, and swears that she hath had all she could get from him: And Hart, her great admirer, now hates her; and that she is very poor, and hath lost my Lady Castlemaine, who was her great friend also; but she is come to the House [the theatre] but is neglected by them all.

Nonsuch Palace. This national treasure was given to Lady Castlemaine by Charles II. She had it pulled down and sold off the materials.

Nell was introduced to the King by Buckingham when she was 17. After he had been to see her act he suggested to Charles that as he had enjoyed her performance and that of the King's Players he should leave them a handsome tip. The King explained that he did not carry money, but offered to borrow some from his friends. She is reported to have retorted: 'Odd's fish, what kind of company have I got myself into?' No wonder the King found her irresistible. About two years later, in 1670, she was pregnant by him. Bishop Burnet wrote of her:

> Gwynn, the most indiscreet and wildest creature that ever was in court, continued to the end of the King's life in great favour, and was maintained at a vast expense. The Duke of Buckingham told me, that when she was first brought to the king, she asked only five hundred pounds a year: and the king refused it. But when he told me this, about four years after, he said she had got of the king about sixty thousand pounds. She acted all persons in so lively a manner, and was such a constant diversion to the king, that even a new mistress could not drive her away. But after all he never treated her with the decencies of a mistress, but rather with the lewdness of a prostitute; as she had been indeed to a great many: and therefore she called the king her Charles the third. Since she had formerly been kept by two of that name.

Nell's main rival was the Frenchwoman Louise de Kéroualle, who was a Catholic. When an angry mob stopped Nell's coach at Oxford, having mistaken her for Louise, she put her head out of the window and called: 'Pray, good people, be civil – I am the Protestant whore.' She had great fun at de Kéroualle's expense, amusing the King with her imitations. 'If me taut me was one bad woman me would cut mine own trote.' Occasionally Louise was unwise enough to bandy words with Nell. On one occasion Nell appeared at Whitehall richly dressed, and Louise, who had been made Duchess of Portsmouth, said, 'Nelly, you are grown rich, I believe, by your dress. Why woman, you are fine enough to be a queen.' Nell replied, 'You are entirely right, madam, and I am whore enough to be a duchess.'

The dismissal of Villiers had not greatly improved Charles's finances. Louise de Kéroualle had a taste for splendour. She had a total of 24 rooms and 16 garrets at Whitehall. They were redecorated three times – 'amazing luxury', exclaims Antonia Fraser in *King Charles II*. She had a taste for expensive objects including French tapestries, clocks, silver, Japanese cabinets and pictures which had originally belonged to the Queen. In fact Evelyn described her apartments as having 'ten times the richness and glory' of the Queen's.

The King, always strapped for cash, was hard put to support two duchesses. Nell Gwynn did not come cheap, either. It was said that in one five-week period Charles gave away £100,000, most of which went to the two duchesses. Nell got £20,000, to their fury. They invited her to dinner, and were not sorry when she nearly choked to death on a napkin. The King stood aside from the constant in-fighting in his seraglio.

Finally, Charles had a fling with the supercharged beauty Hortense Mancini, Duchesse de Mazarin, one of the five famous, lovely and wayward nieces of the French statesman Cardinal Mazarin. He had known and courted her when he was in exile. She was famous for a string of amours with both men and women, and she liked to dress as a man, as Elizabeth Hamilton recounts in *The Illustrious Lady*. She soon slipped into the bed vacated by Castlemaine. Perhaps the quiet domestic charms of Louise were palling, and Charles wanted someone more like the dangerous and reckless Barbara Villiers. The affair, which began in the winter of 1675, was short-lived. In 1677 Hortense began a very public flirtation with the Prince de Monaco, and Charles dismissed her. He seems to have largely made do with Louise and Nell from then on. The poet Andrew Marvell regretted the episode:

> That the King should send for another French whore
> When one already hath made him so poor.

The curtain came down on this particular period of rakishness on

2 February 1685. As the King was dressing, his servants noticed that he had become incoherent and could not finish his sentences. He gave 'the dreadfullest shriek' and collapsed unconscious into a chair, where he remained insensible for hours while physicians tried to resuscitate him. They finally succeeded by clapping a warming pan to his head, and the King looked round, bewildered. 'What is the matter with me?' he asked, and his brother the Duke of York told him: 'You have had a fit, sir.' He lay dying for several days, with the Queen and the Duchess of Portsmouth taking it in turns to sit by his bedside. With weary politeness he apologised for being 'an unconscionable time a-dying'.

His brother asked whether he would like him to fetch a Catholic priest and he replied: 'For God's sake, brother, do, and please to lose no time.' When the priest came Charles converted to the Catholic faith, and regretted he had left it so long. At last, when he knew the end was near, he asked his attendants to draw up the curtain and open the window so that 'I may behold the light of the sun for the last time'. Many in the crowd that gathered outside the palace grieved for the popular King. He had strolled among them, unafraid and approachable, often to be seen walking briskly in St James's Park with his pet dogs, or feeding the ducks in the canal. Not until George III became king would the public again have a monarch with whom they could so readily identify.

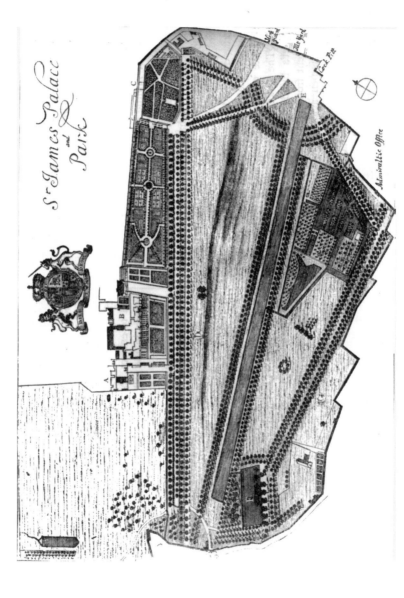

St James's Park in Charles II's time. The king, who was fond of exercise, would walk there briskly with his dogs or feed the ducks in the canal.

# Rochester: So Idle a Rogue

THE TWO MOST PROMINENT RAKES at the Stuart court were the Duke of Buckingham, Charles's friend since childhood, and the Earl of Rochester. Both were members of a group of young courtiers known as the Wits, although Buckingham's age — he was already 32 at the time of the Restoration — made him an exception.

Even more spectacularly debauched was John Wilmot, second Earl of Rochester. He was described by Burnet in *Some Passages in the Life and Death of John Earl of Rochester* thus:

> His manners were those of a lawless and wretched mountebank; his delight was to haunt the stews, to debauch women, to write filthy songs and lewd pamphlets; he spent his time in gossiping with the maids of honour, broils with men of letters, the receiving of insults, the giving of blows ... Once with the Duke of Buckingham he rented an inn on the Newmarket Road and turned innkeeper, supplying the husbands with drink and defiling their wives ...

The easy-going ways of the King — what Antonia Fraser in *King Charles II* calls his 'laxity' — gave a moral lead to the Merry Gang, as the poet Andrew Marvell called the 'fast set' of rakes who surrounded him. The group included Henry Jermyn, Lord Buckhurst, Harry Killigrew, Sir Charles Sedley and the playwrights William Wycherley and George Etherege, and their antics have for ever coloured the reputation of Charles's court. But it was Rochester who above all others left upon it the stamp of rakishness. We see him now as above all a poet who expressed the pathos of life and loss and inconstancy:

### Love and Life

All my past Life is mine no more,
The flying hours are gone:
Like transitory Dreams giv'n ore,
Whose images are kept in store,
By Memory alone.

The Time that is to come is not,
How can it then be mine?
The present Moment's all my Lot,
And that, as fast as it is got,
Phyllis, is only thine.

Then talk not of Inconstancy,
False Hearts and broken Vows;
If I, by Miracle, can be
This live-long Minute true to thee,
'Tis all that Heav'n allows.

However, to what Antonia Fraser in *King Charles II* calls 'his own gaping generation' he was a drunken rogue, an obscene wit and satirist, if one of genius. We are conscious of a tragically short life – he was 33 when he died – but his contemporaries had to live from day to day with his actions, which 'ranged from the merely foolish to the genuinely criminal'.

As James William Johnson states in *A Profane Wit, The Life of John Wilmot, Earl of Rochester*, he was known for his excesses as 'the Mad Earl' . He lived his own legend to such an extent that a century later Samuel Johnson wrote of him:

Thus in a course of drunken gaiety and gross sensuality, with intervals of study perhaps yet more criminal, with an avowed contempt for all decency and order, a total disregard to every moral, and a resolute denial of every religious obligation, he lived worthless and useless, and blazed out his youth and his health in lavish voluptuousness, till at the age of one and thirty, he had exhausted the fund of life, and reduced himself to a state of weakness and decay.

Yet there was something irresistible about his wit and charm. Burnet wrote in *Some Passages in the Life and Death of John Earl of Rochester*: 'His conversation was easy and obliging. He had a strange vivacity of thought and vigour of expression. His wit had a subtlety and sublimity both, that were scarce imitable.'

In the Davy Manuscripts in the British Library is an example of this wit. It records a meeting between Rochester and the scholar and divine Isaac Barrow:

His lordship, by way of banter, thus accosted him: 'Doctor, I am yours to my shoe tie.' Barrow, seeing his aim, returned his salute as obsequiously, with 'My Lord, I am yours to the ground.' Rochester, improving his blow, quickly returned it with 'Doctor, I am yours to the centre'; which was as smartly followed by Barrow, with 'My Lord, I am yours to the antipodes': upon which Rochester, scorning to be foiled by a musty old piece of divinity (as he used to call him) exclaimed, 'Doctor, I am yours to the lowest pit of hell!' on which Barrow, turning his heel, answered, 'There, my Lord, I leave you.'

Rochester's father, the first Earl, was a Cavalier soldier who accompanied Charles into exile. He died in exile in 1658 when his son was 11, and the boy was brought up by his devout and high-minded mother, Anne. He was intellectually precocious and at the early age of 12 he was sent to Oxford University. The alternative was a public school such as Eton, which the delicate boy might have found rather challenging, if not intellectually. Incidentally, there is a story that links Rochester to Eton; if literally untrue, it is true to the spirit of his nature. The story goes that in 1665 the King and Rochester were in their cups and arguing about who was the ugliest man in London. Charles suggested his ally the Earl of Lauderdale. Rochester offered to go out into the streets to find someone uglier, and came back with a clergyman named Richard Allestree, who won the contest. Allestree protested at this humiliation and although Rochester and his cronies laughed, Charles felt for him and appointed him Provost of Eton.

Allestree was indeed appointed Provost in 1665, but he was known to all concerned, being a Royalist who had fought in the Civil War and a chaplain to the King, so the story is probably at least exaggerated. However, that it was accepted at the time tells us a lot about Rochester.

At Oxford Rochester had as tutor Robert Whitehall, a minor poet and bon vivant, who introduced the boy to drink and, it has been suggested, to whores. It has also been suggested that it was at Oxford that Rochester got his first dose of the pox. Whitehall is said to have 'doted' on him, although whether there was a sexual relationship is not known. However, he lent Rochester his academic gown 'for night-time explorations at inns, taverns and brothels'. Disguises and sexual adventures became life-long passions. Burnet suggested that Rochester's later use of disguise was 'sometimes to follow some mean amours, which, for the variety of them, he affected'. At other times 'merely for diversion, he would go about in odd shapes'.

While Rochester was at Oxford the world was changing, very much in his favour. In September 1658 Oliver Cromwell died. His son Richard briefly held the reins of state, before falling out with the army and resigning. General Monck, commander of the army in Scotland, marched south and started the benign revolution that brought back the King. For aristocrats such as Rochester, horizons had suddenly widened.

In the autumn of 1661 when Rochester was 14 he was given a Master of Arts degree, receiving it from the Earl of Clarendon, his mother's cousin and Chancellor of the University, and a man he would later betray. His title, refused by the Puritans, had already been restored to him, and the King granted him the considerable income of £500 a year (about £48,000 in today's money). The boy set off on a Grand Tour of the Continent accompanied by Sir Andrew Balfour, a classical scholar who influenced his reading. He returned in 1665, aged 18, carrying a letter to the King from his sister Henriette, Duchesse d'Orléans, whom Rochester had met in France.

His visit to Whitehall to deliver the letter may have been his introduction to the court. He was now said to be a graceful and well-shaped person, tall, if not a little too slender. His witty sallies were appreciated, and Charles and others were attracted. The King, so easily bored, was prepared for the moment anyway to shrug off his excesses because of his entertainment value. Rochester was also welcomed by the King's mistress Lady Castlemaine, his distant relative. Although he was only 18 the Merry Gang made him the boon companion of their drinking and wenching, one of them, Harry Savile, becoming an intimate and life-long friend. It was, wrote the poet and playwright John Dryden, 'a very merry, dancing, drinking, laughing, quaffing and unthinking time'.

Savile, though several years older, was the member of the Merry Gang closest to Rochester. He was another heavy drinker, witty and charming and attractive to women. Pepys claimed that he had a love affair with the Duchess of York, wife of the King's brother. Like Rochester, he would die young of syphilis.

Later portraits of Rochester suggest a slight sexual ambiguity: the wide-lipped sensuous mouth, the large, well-developed nose, that almost insolent, challenging gaze. In his play *The Man of Mode* his friend Etherege described the poet, in the character of Dorimant: 'I know he is a Devil, but he has something of the Angel yet undefac'd in him'. This halfway stage between innocence and experience appealed to both men and women.

To what extent the bad behaviour of Charles and Buckingham sanctioned the gross misconduct of their young admirers is debatable. That these young men indulged in behaviour that was often disgusting and sometimes criminal is not in question. Hester W. Chapman writes in *Great Villiers*: 'Hovering about Buckingham like a ring of poisonous dragon-flies were Sedley, Buckhurst, Etherege and Rochester – young men who were delicately discriminating in their aesthetic appreciations as they were bestial, predatory and violent in their pursuit of pleasure.'

Sir Charles Sedley and the playwright Sir George Etherege were close friends. Commenting on the stage and its patrons at this period, the Victorian writer Dr John Doran said of them, 'Two more atrocious libertines than these two men were not to be found in the apartments at Whitehall, or in the streets, taverns and dens of London. Yet both were famed for like external qualities ... ' Sedley was another womaniser, whose technique was, said Buckingham, like 'witchcraft'. Rochester described his powers of seduction as 'his prevailing, gentle art'.

Sedley and his crony Charles Sackville, Lord Buckhurst, were notorious for a scrape they got into at the appropriately named Cock tavern in Bow Street. They had been drinking and eventually stripped off and stepped on to the balcony. Samuel Pepys describes how they exposed themselves to the onlookers, Sedley acting

> all the postures of lust and buggery that could be imagined, and abusing of scripture and, as it were, from whence preaching a mountebank sermon from that pulpit, saying that there he had to sell such a powder as should make all the cunts in town run after him. And that being done he took a glass of wine and washed his prick in it and then drank it off; and then took another and drunk the King's health.

A large angry crowd gathered and eventually stormed the tavern. The two men, who narrowly escaped lynching, were brought before the courts. The Lord Chief Justice told Sedley that it was because of wicked wretches like him 'that God's anger and judgments hang over us'. However, he had not broken any law, and was bound over to behave well or forfeit £5,000 (about £500,000 today), a threat he ignored.

It wasn't the last scrape Sedley and Buckhurst got into together.

In October 1668 they ran about the streets showing their backsides, got into a brawl with the Watch and were held in jail overnight. On this occasion the King intervened and the constable was given a ticking-off from the Lord Chief Justice for detaining them.

Lord Buckhurst was a Gentleman of the King's Bedchamber. He was one of Nell Gwynn's first lovers, and for a time she left the stage to live with him. As Goldsworthy says in *The Satyr*, after a bad start he became a distinguished public servant, 'a generous, good-natured man, so shy that he scarcely ever spoke unless fuelled by alcohol'. Perhaps he was more than a little drunk the day he was warned that there were highwaymen on the road ahead of him. He overtook a tanner called Hoppy on the road and killed the innocent man on the spot. He and his companions took Hoppy's money and later explained that they thought he had stolen it.

A remarkable fact about these fashionable profligates was their literary achievements. Most of them were writers of more than amateur talent. Buckingham's play *The Rehearsal*, a clever parody of Dryden, was a success. Killigrew was a minor playwright, William Wycherley a successful one. Etherege too wrote for the stage. His first play, *The Comical Revenge, or Love in a Tub*, was a critical and financial success, and he went on to more or less invent the satire on contemporary manners, a form exploited by writers from Vanbrugh and Congreve down to Oscar Wilde. He was a dandy, and – inevitably, given the company he kept – a profligate and womaniser. He was known as 'Gentle George'. Buckhurst wrote light-hearted verse, the best remembered of which is the ballad 'To All You Ladies Now on Land'. It was written at the beginning of the first Dutch war, and has the grace of the best poetry of the period:

> Then if we write not by each post,
> Think not we are unkind;
> Nor yet conclude our ships are lost
> By Dutchmen or by wind:
> Our tears we'll send a speedier way,
> The tide shall bring them twice a day.

Sedley too was a talented writer, the author of fine lyrics and translations. During a performance of one of his plays the theatre roof fell in, injuring him. A sycophantic friend remarked that the play was so full of fire it had blown up author, theatre and audience. Sedley replied: 'Nonsense! It was so heavy it brought down the house and buried the poet in his own rubbish.'

In spite of their touchiness these men could all laugh at jokes made at other people's expense, and Rochester had an unhappy gift for waspish wit. When he found it getting laughs from this glittering company he was encouraged to go ever further into dangerous territory. Eventually of course he went too far, and was banished – if only temporarily – for obscene satires on the King himself.

Dazzled as he was by his literary friends, Rochester began to imitate them in other ways. Aping Etherege he became a dandy, preening for hours at a mirror before appearing languid and heavily scented at court. Women jaded with the endless round of court affairs were always pleased to see a new and pretty face, and Rochester was soon being welcomed into 'the most select of boudoirs and the most coveted of beds'. It seems paradoxical that Restoration rakes spent much of their time in brothels when sex was so freely available with high-born women at court. But the quick couplings with the trollops of the taverns made a change from all the bowing and scraping, the elaborate courtesies that preceded fornication at court, and they had the allure of cheap music or perfume, a quick assault on the senses. And in an age of rampant sexual disease there was an added thrill of danger, though as we shall see, sex at court was no safer.

Perhaps the laxity of sexual manners at court made Rochester think he could get away with an act of outrageous folly. In the spring of 1665 he was banished from court and committed to the Tower after attempting to kidnap an heiress. Elizabeth Malet was a witty, intelligent beauty with a fortune of £2,500 (about £250,000) a year. The King, worried by Rochester's extravagance and debts, suggested she would make a good match. At first the flirtatious girl encouraged Rochester, then changed her mind. She had many suitors, and wanted to 'choose for herself'. Feeling he

had been made a fool, Rochester decided to force himself on Miss
Malet, who was in effect under the King's protection. One night as
she returned home with her guardian from supper with one of the
maids of honour, Frances Stewart, a gang of armed men sent by
Rochester ambushed her coach at Charing Cross. The heiress was
dragged to another coach and driven away, with Rochester following. The furious King had him pursued and taken to the Tower.
Pleading with the King for his release, Rochester cited 'inadver-
tence, ignorance of the law and passion'. He said he would choose
death ten thousand times rather than incur the King's displeasure.
Charles made at least a show of punishing the young rascal, keeping him kicking his heels in the Tower for three weeks before
releasing him. For a time Rochester withdrew from the court.

That summer the Great Plague was raging in London, killing
one in four, and Rochester may have decided that joining the war
against the Dutch was no more dangerous than staying in the capital. It was a good moment for a practical display of loyalty and the
18-year-old volunteered to serve in the navy. In a battle at Bergen
he 'distinguished himself by uncommon intrepidity', in the words
of Samuel Johnson in his *Lives of the English Poets*. A curious
episode on Rochester's ship, the *Revenge*, was to have a lasting
effect on him. Other young aristocratic adventurers had rushed to
join the Bergen expedition in the hope of glory and booty. With
Rochester were Edward Montague and 'another gentleman of
quality' named Wyndham. Both men had premonitions of death,
and Rochester and Wyndham made a formal agreement that if
either of them was killed he would appear to the other as a ghost
or spirit, to inform him about the eternal state. The expedition was
ambushed, and although it escaped without losing a single ship –
and without any glory or booty – 400 men were lost, four of them
on the *Revenge*. Among them were Montague and Wyndham. Burnet wrote in his *Life* of Rochester:

> Mr Montague, though he had such a strong presage in his mind of
> his approaching death, yet he generously stayed all the while in the
> place of greatest danger. The other gentleman signalised his courage

in a most undaunted manner, till near the end of the action, when he fell on a sudden into such a trembling that he could scarce stand, and Mr Montague going to him to hold him up, as they were in each other's arms, a cannon ball killed him outright, and carried away Mr Montague's belly, so that he died within an hour after.

Wyndham never appeared to Rochester, 'which was a great snare to him, during the rest of his life'. He had questioned his own atheism, and seemed to have it confirmed. But a conflict remained, and Graham Greene in *Lord Rochester's Monkey* thought that it was that conflict which produced the poet. During the action he behaved with courage, and 'a person of honour' told Burnet that 'he heard the Lord Clifford, who was in the same ship, often magnified his courage at that time very highly'.

That summer Rochester was at sea again, under the command of Sir Edward Spragge, as the fleet headed for an even greater disaster. In the first week of June there was a four-day battle in which the British fleet lost 6,000 men killed, 3,000 prisoners taken, and eight ships of the line sunk.

> He went aboard the ship commanded by Sir Edward Spragge the day before the great sea fight of that year: almost all the volunteers on the same ship were killed. Mr Middleton (brother to Sir Hugh Middleton) was shot in the arms. During the action, Spragge, not being satisfied with the behaviour of one of the captains, could not easily find a person that would cheerfully venture through so much danger, to carry his commands to the captain. This Lord [Rochester] offered himself to the service, and went in a little boat through all the shot, and delivered his message, and returned back to Sir Edward, which was much commended by all that saw it.

Rochester returned to London in October 1666, after the Great Fire had reduced much of it to smouldering rubble. The fire had begun on 2 September in Pudding Lane, and when it subsided five days later an area roughly one and a half miles by half a mile containing about 13,000 houses, inns and public buildings had gone.

John Evelyn had watched the fire from the south bank of the Thames, and felt as though he was witnessing the destruction of Sodom, or Judgment Day.

Rochester returned to court a war hero. The delighted King gave him a reward of £750 and Rochester sought relief from the painful memories of war in a series of pranks. Among the pretty young women around the court who caught his eye was Anne Temple. Anthony Hamilton, author of *Memoirs of the Comte de Gramont*, thought her vain and rather stupid, but she had a good shape, fine teeth and languid eyes. Rochester amused himself by attempting to seduce her. To her aid came the formidable Lady Dorothy Howard, a maid-in-waiting to the Duchess of York. This 'intelligent and virtuous' woman, admired by Pepys and Evelyn, knew all about Rochester, and tried to warn young Temple. Rochester responded by spreading malicious rumours that Howard was a lesbian and wanted Temple for herself.

One man who seems to have accepted Rochester's version was Anthony Hamilton. He says Temple 'loved all sorts of sweets, as much as a child of nine or ten' and that Howard tried to seduce her by plying her with 'sweet-meats and all kinds of syrups'. After she returned from riding one day hot and tired, she was invited to rest in Howard's chamber where she could undress and relax. As she did so, claims Hamilton, Howard kissed and fondled her. 'Of course you look as charming as an angel in your riding habit, but there is nothing so comfortable as a loose dress and being at one's ease; you cannot imagine, my dear Temple,' she continued, embracing her, 'how much you please me by this free, unceremonious conduct.'

According to Hamilton, Howard used the opportunity to pour out malicious gossip against Rochester. Describing in detail his seduction technique, she supposedly said:

Lord Rochester is undoubtedly the most witty man in England; but he is also the most unprincipled. He is nothing but a danger to our sex; and that to such a degree that no woman listens to him three times without irretrievably losing her reputation ... In the meantime nothing is more dangerous than the creepy way he lays hold of your mind. He applauds your taste, submits to your feelings, and even though he himself does not believe a single word of what he is saying, he makes you believe it all. I wager that from the conversation you have had with him, you thought him one of the most honourable and sincerest men living. For my part I cannot imagine what he means by the attentions he pays you. Of course your accomplishments are more than enough to excite everyone's adoration and praise. But even if he had been lucky enough to gain your affections, he would not know what to do with the loveliest creature at court; for a long time his debauches have depended on favours of all the common street-walkers. Just think, my dear Temple, what horrid malice possesses him, to the ruin and confusion of innocence! A wretch, to have no other reason in lavishing attentions on Miss Temple than to give a greater verisimilitude to the calumnies with which he loaded her!

To press her point, Howard then sang to her some satiric verses Rochester had composed about another court beauty, but substituted Temple's name. 'It worked; the credulous Temple no sooner heard her sing the lampoon than she firmly believed it to have been written about herself; and in the first transports of her rage, wanting nothing more than to deny the fictions of the poet. "Ah! my dear Howard," she said, "I can bear it no longer."'

Howard's chamber adjoined one of the Duchess of York's bathrooms, and lying unseen in the bath, listening to all this, was another young court beauty whom Rochester had succeeded in seducing, Sarah Cooke. She stayed, with the water growing ever colder, until she could go to Rochester and tell him what she had seen and heard.

Rochester soon took his revenge. One evening Howard and Temple went walking in the Mall, wearing masks having swapped clothes so they could pretend to be each other. Rochester, who had been warned of this by Sarah Cooke, accosted them with his fellow reprobate Harry Killigrew. Rochester spoke to Howard, pretending he mistook her for Temple, and Killigrew spoke to

Temple as though she was Howard. He rebuked her for disparaging Rochester, one of the most honourable men at court, and warned her off her attempts on the virtue of the young and innocent Temple.

Miss Temple rushed back to her room and tore off Howard's clothes in shock and revulsion. Howard followed and tried to comfort the naked girl. A matron of the bedchamber arrived to find them in this apparently compromising situation, and ordered Howard out of the room. When the dust settled Howard kept her job, Sarah Cooke was dismissed and Rochester was banished again. Rochester never forgave Howard, and seven years later slandered her as Doll Howard in the lampoon 'Signor Dildo'. Incidentally, Anne Temple married the middle-aged widower Sir Charles Lyttelton and had 13 children.

While this was going on Rochester was still courting Elizabeth Malet. About this time she gave an amusing and surprisingly ribald account of her suitors to William Ashburnham, Cofferer of the King's Household, who passed it on to Pepys: 'My Lord Herbert would have her – my Lord Hinchingbrooke was indifferent to have her – my Lord Jo. Butler might not have her – my Lord of Rochester would have forced her; and Sir [Francis] Popham (who nevertheless is likely to have her) would kiss her breach to have her.'

This was probably deliberately meant to deceive. According to Johnson in *A Profane Wit*, she was carrying on a secret correspondence with Rochester in the latter months of 1666. If she had doubts about his affections he eased them by dropping his mistress Sarah Cooke, and he had even temporarily given up drinking. And besides, he was a handsome young man. Miss Malet decided she loved him after all, and they were married soon after Christmas in 1666. In spite of Rochester's continued sexual adventures and declining health the marriage was fairly happy. Rochester had inherited a modest country estate at Adderbury, north of Oxford, and they had good times there. Elizabeth retired from court into private life, raising their four children and managing the estate. There she waited for him, often impatient, perhaps angry, but always in the end forgiving.

Rochester was living a double life, as a country gentleman and as a roaring boy raising hell in the brothels and taverns of London or later in the arms of his mistress, the actress Elizabeth Barry, and spreading malicious gossip and libels at court. The writer and antiquarian John Aubrey says in *Brief Lives* that 'in the country he was generally civil enough' but he used to declare that when he got to Brentford on the way into London 'the devil entered into him and never left him until he came into the country again.' He was often in trouble with what he called his Whore Pipe:

> Was ever Mortal Man like me,
> Continually in Jeopardy,
> And always, silly Prick, by thee!
>
> There's not a petticoat goes by
> But from my cod-piece out you fly,
> Not to be held 'twixt Hand and Thigh.
>
> I never felt a soft, white Hand
> But Hector-like you strutting stand
> As if the World you would command.

These episodes left a bitter taste. He loved his wife but could not be constant to her, and his conscience tortured him:

> Absent from thee I languish still,
> Then ask me not, when I return?
> The straying fool 'twill plainly kill
> To wish all day, all night to mourn.
>
> Dear, from thine arms then let me fly,
> That my fantastic mind may prove
> The torments it deserves to try,
> That tears my fixt heart from my love.

When wearied with a world of woe,
To thy safe bosom I retire,
Where love and peace and truth does flow,
May I contented there expire.

Lest once more wandering from that Heav'n,
I fall on some base heart unblest;
Faithless to thee, false, unforgiven,
And lose my everlasting rest.

It was to the country he retired to write his 'libels' during periods of banishment or illness. One of his best sources of scandal was a court footman whom Rochester dressed in a red coat to look like a court guard, and provided with a musket. Posted outside the apartments of certain high-born women involved in 'intrigues', the footman recorded the comings and goings from various bedchambers. Rochester used his spy's reports as the basis for some reckless lampoons. In fact Rochester often caused offence; eventually, says Greene in *Lord Rochester's Monkey*, he became the King's worst critic. Once the King suggested that his courtiers should compose his epitaph, and promised he would not take offence, however acerbic the results. Rochester cannot have helped his cause with this offering:

We have a pritty witty King
Whose word no man relies on,
Who never said a foolish thing
Nor ever did a wise one.

The King even more wittily riposted that his words were his own, whereas his acts were his ministers'.

Reflections on the King and his court which would have ended most careers usually earned Rochester only temporary banishment. The Royalist politician Sir John Coventry was less lucky. During a parliamentary debate about proposals to tax playhouses he had asked 'whether the King's pleasure lay among the men, or women that acted'. This tactless remark, a comment on Charles's affairs with Nell Gwynn, Moll Davis, Mary Knight and other actresses, was resented by the King's supporters. Sir Thomas Sandys, possibly acting for the King's bastard son the Duke of Monmouth, recruited a gang of thugs to punish him. Some nights later Coventry's coach was ambushed by 'near twenty persons armed, horse and foot'. They wrapped him tight in his cloak so he couldn't fight back, 'and others cutting and mangling his face with a knife, in a barbarous manner, when he could make no defence of himself . . . '

At times Rochester's effrontery was breathtaking and dangerous, in view of what happened to Coventry. He was drinking one night with the King and his humourless brother the Duke of York. With them were Monmouth, 'who was almost feeble-minded', the strikingly ugly Duke of Lauderdale and Dr Alexander Frazier, an incompetent and ignorant royal physician. The King asked for an example of his extempore verses, and Rochester asked what the subject might be. Present company, said the King. 'I daren't,' said Rochester, 'I'll only offend you.' The King promised he would not take offence.

> Here's Monmouth the witty,
> And Lauderdale the pretty,
> And Frazier, that learned physician;
> But above all the rest,
> Here's the Duke for a jest,
> And the King for a grand politician.

The King is said to have been delighted; the others were not, particularly when a copy of the verse was posted up in public. Perhaps it was fortunate Rochester died before the Duke of York came to the throne.

It seems that whatever his straits he almost never used his wife's fortune, which was now his in law. In 1667 his own fortunes improved slightly when the King appointed him a Gentleman of the Bedchamber. This carried a salary of £1,000 a year for life (more than £100,000 today), but it was seldom paid. The duties were intermittent but onerous. He had to spend every night for a week in each quarter sleeping in the King's bedchamber. He slept on a pallet bed by the King's side, if he slept at all. The King had a collection of clocks, which chimed throughout the night; he also had several spaniels in his bed, and one of his mistresses or perhaps a strumpet smuggled in through secret passages by his pander William Chiffinch. (The dozen Gentlemen of the Bedchamber could not help knowing the King's sexual habits and preferences.) If the chief Gentleman of the Bedchamber, the Groom of the Stole, was absent, Rochester had to dress the King, and wait on him if he ate in private. This intimacy, instead of binding him to the man who was his benefactor in so many ways, left him bitter and disillusioned. Charles was a father figure to him, and inevitably there was something of the love–hate relationship that often exists between father and son. Even the King's easy-going ways began to pall. Rochester would eventually portray Charles as the king Bolloximian in the treasonous satire *Sodom*.

## Syphilis and spleen

Almost 20 when he married Elizabeth Malet, Rochester lived only 13 years more, years filled with much of the stuff of his legend. As Graham Greene points out in *Lord Rochester's Monkey*, these years are difficult to chronicle. 'They are full of fantastic stories and impersonations ... ' Perhaps they can be told only impressionistically, as he must have lived them. He confessed to being more or less drunk for five years. Boredom and spleen, disappointment with himself and the world, and a slow death from syphilis, drove him to drink. As his mind darkened his verse went from indecent to obscene. Yet he was capable of writing some of the most tender lyrics in the language: 'The Imperfect Enjoyment', a poem of about 1670, has a rare frankness and intimacy, and treats love with a dignity sadly lacking in later works:

Naked she lay clasped in my longing arms,
I, filled with love and she all over charms,
Both equally inspired with eager fire,
Melting through kindness, flaming in desire:
With arms, legs, lips close clinging to embrace,
She clips me to her breast, and sucks me to her face.

The nimble tongue (love's lesser lightning) played
Within my mouth, and to my thoughts conveyed
Swift orders, that I should prepare to throw
The all-dissolving thunderbolt below.
My fluttering soul, sprung from the pointed kiss
Hangs hovering o'er her balmy brinks of bliss.

But while her busy hand would guide that part
Which should convey my soul up to her heart,
In liquid raptures I dissolve all o'er,
Melt into sperm, and spend at every pore;
A touch from any part of her had done't,
Her hand, her foot, her very look's a cunt.

Smiling, she chides in a kind murmuring noise
And from her body wipes the clammy joys;
When with a thousand kisses wand'ring o'er
My panting bosom, and – 'Is there no more?'
She cries. 'All this to love and rapture's due;
Must we not pay a debt to pleasure too?'

Soon after his arrival at court Rochester became one of the leaders of a club of aristocratic rowdies called the Ballers. They met at a brothel in St James's run by a notorious bawd known as Mother Bennet, the widow of a baker. The members danced naked with Bennet's girls and indulged in other forms of sexual exhibitionism. Act II of Rochester's playlet *Sodom* gives some idea of what went on:

A Dance – Six naked men and six naked women appear and dance. In their dancing the men do obeisance to the women's cunts, kissing and tonguing them often. The women in like manner do ceremony to the men's pricks, kissing the glans, quidling and dandling their cods, and so fall to copulation, after which the women sigh, the men look simply and so sneak off.

Pepys spent a lively evening with the Ballers in May 1668, and his description gives us a rare glimpse of how those rich and privileged young men let their hair down. He went to Vauxhall pleasure gardens where he met Harry Killigrew, 'a rogue, newly come back out of France but still in disgrace with our Court', and other members of the group. He stayed with them to supper in one of the arbours for which the gardens were noted, scenes of assignations and rapes. He called the group 'as very rogues as any in the town, who were ready to take hold of every woman that came by them', and said their bawdy talk made his head ache. They described a typical night at the brothel of 'my Lady Bennet' and how they had danced naked with her girls, and 'all the roguish things in the world'. Pepys was an experienced seducer, as he frankly admitted, and it is difficult to imagine what 'roguish things' made him so censorious. However, he justified his presence, just as he justified reading pornography, as something a man should do once. 'But Lord, what loose cursed company was I in tonight; though full of wit and worth a man's being in for once, to know the nature of it and their manner of talk and lives.'

Rochester had other diversions. One was a feud with another club, known as the Farmers because some of the duties of customs officials had been farmed out to them, including the prevention of the importation of illegal goods into the country. Rochester had been importing dildoes from the continent, where as Henry Blyth notes in *The High Tide of Pleasure*, 'they were widely in use, particularly in nunneries'. Perhaps tired of the demands being made on him, he supplied them to certain ladies of the court. For some reason the wives of the Farmers objected.

Another incident that saw Rochester banished for a time

occurred when the King dined with the Dutch ambassador on 7 February 1669. As usual there was heavy drinking, and one of the guests, Harry Killigrew's father, offended Rochester. Tom Killigrew, a theatre manager, playwright and Groom of the Bedchamber, could be as malicious as the young Earl. When the dense Duke of Monmouth asked Killigrew what he would give to be as young as Monmouth himself, Tom replied that he would be content to have as little wit. He insulted the King by referring to the royal mistresses and saying that 'one prick in our day costs more maintenance than a thousand concubines in Solomon's'. At the dinner Killigrew directed this 'mirth and raillery' at Rochester and apparently made a remark about the Earl keeping his wife in the country. According to Pepys the Earl boxed Killigrew's ears in the presence of the King, 'which do give much offence to the people here at the Court, to see how cheap the King makes himself ... ' Some courtiers were shocked the following day to see the King promenading in public with Rochester. Pepys was distressed that the King should consort with 'so idle a rogue'.

However, after the young Earl was involved in another drunken brawl at the Tower, Charles decided on reflection that it would be a good idea if he went abroad for a brief spell. Rochester was given a face-saving quasi-diplomatic mission with his friend Ralph Montagu, who had been appointed ambassador to Louis XIV. Rochester apologised to the elder Killigrew's son Harry, and went to Paris, with a letter from the King to his sister, the Duchesse d'Orléans. It shows that Rochester was still in favour. 'Pray use him as one that I have a very good opinion of,' the King wrote. 'You will find him not to want wit, and did behave himself in all the Dutch wars as well as anybody, as a volunteer.'

It was the French king who punished Rochester for his bad behaviour in Charles's presence. When Rochester accompanied Montagu to meet Louis, the Sun King refused to let him kiss his hand, saying explicitly that he would not countenance those who brawled in the presence of a king. He added that no one frowned on by 'the King his brother of England' would find favour with him. Rochester never forgot this insult from the premier monarch of Europe. In 1676 he portrayed Louis as Tarsehole, the King of Gomorrah, in the final version of *Sodom*.

Shortly afterwards he had revenge of a sort for this snub, although over another matter. Rochester went to the theatre with Lord Cavendish. A group of seven or eight of Louis's personal guards were sitting nearby, and one of them insulted Cavendish, who struck him. The guards then attacked Cavendish, who was stabbed with swords at least seven times. He was rescued by his Swiss servant, who picked him up and threw him into the orchestra pit. Rochester had saved himself by fleeing from the scene.

Montagu complained to Louis, and the French king threatened to hang all the guardsmen involved. He was shocked that 'such a thing should happen to be done by his officers to any strangers, much more to the English and to people of that quality'. Cavendish recovered, the guards were punished and Rochester had the satisfaction of seeing the King's chagrin.

Johnson notes in *A Profane Wit* that Rochester took a keen interest in Paris's sexual underworld, including 'such French sexual variations as transvestism, paedophilia and male homosexual societies'. Throughout his adult life Rochester showed an interest in homosexuality. A poem of around 1673 which has been attributed to him describes the daily routine of a debauchee:

I rise at eleven, I dine about two,
I get drunk before seven, and the next thing I do,
I send for my whore, when for fear of a clap,
I spend in her hand, and I spew in her lap;
Then we quarrel and scold, till I fall fast asleep,
When the bitch growing bold, to my pocket does creep.
Then slyly she leaves me, and to revenge the affront,
At once she bereaves me of money and cunt.
If by chance then I wake, hot headed and drunk,
What a coil do I make for the loss of my punk!
I storm, and I roar, and I fall in a rage.
And missing my whore, I bugger my page...

Back in England Rochester was soon in trouble again. Having sat on a committee which drew up a law against duelling – in fact he helped draft the statute – he became embroiled in a feud which was to cause him considerable loss of face.

John Sheffield, the Earl of Mulgrave, was a year younger than Rochester, and his envy of Rochester's glittering career and talents made him a lifelong enemy. He would eventually become Duke of Buckingham after George Villiers died without an heir, he had wealth and the esteem of Princess Anne, the future Queen. But in Rochester's circle of wits and gallants he was regarded as a laughing stock. His pride was a byword at court, and Rochester lampooned him as 'My Lord All-Pride'. He called him 'goggle-eyed', a reference to Mulgrave's hyperthyroid condition, 'splay-footed' and a 'looby'.

> Bursting with pride, the loathed impostume swells,
> Prick him, he sheds his venom strait, and smells;
> But 'tis so lewd a scribbler, that he writes,
> With as much force to nature as he fights . . .
> And with his arm, and head, his brain's so weak
> That his starved fancy is compelled to rake,
> Among the excrements of others' wit,
> To make a stinking meal of what they shit.

John Macky wrote of Mulgrave in his *Memoirs of the Secret Service*: 'Very proud, insolent and covetous, and takes all advantages. In paying his debts unwilling; and is neither esteemed nor beloved: for notwithstanding his great interest at Court, it is certain he has none in either Houses of Parliament, or in the country.'

In November 1669 Mulgrave challenged Rochester to a duel. According to Mulgrave's memoirs, written fifty years later, he was informed that 'Rochester had said something of me, which, according to his custom, was very malicious.' He sent a friend, Colonel Edmund Ashton, to deliver his challenge to Rochester, who denied making the remarks. Although, says Mulgrave, he accepted that Rochester was telling the truth, he insisted that the duel go ahead anyway. 'The mere report, though I found it to be false, obliged me (as I then foolishly thought) to go on with the quarrel; and the next day was appointed for us to fight on horseback, in England a little unusual, but it was his part to choose.'

Knowing the King's strong feelings against duelling, Mulgrave spent the night lying low at Knightsbridge. The King heard of the planned fight and sent a guard to prevent it. Unable to find Mulgrave, he arrested Rochester. The Earl gave his word that he would not escape, then slipped away. The frustrated King asked the House of Lords to intervene – both men were of course peers. The Lords instructed the Usher of the Black Rod to arrest the two.

On the morning of the duel, 23 November, Rochester turned up with a Lifeguardsman as second. This was not the man he had originally named, and Colonel Ashton objected to the 'arrant Lifeguardsman whom nobody knew'. Seconds often joined in the fight, and Ashton didn't like the look of the burly guardsman. He probably also objected on class grounds. And the guardsman was mounted on a large cavalry horse, while Mulgrave and Ashton were less well mounted.

Mulgrave says that after Ashton objected to the guardsman and his mount, they all agreed to fight on foot. 'But as my Lord Rochester and I were riding into the next field in order to it, he told me that he had first chosen to fight on horseback because he was so weak with a certain distemper that he found himself unfit to fight at all in any way, much less afoot.' He claims he told Rochester that they would look ridiculous if they returned without fighting, and Rochester hoped that he would not take advantage by fighting a man in such a weak condition. Mulgrave agreed to call off the duel as long as the seconds would be witness to the fact that it was Rochester who had withdrawn. 'Seeing through Mulgrave's ploy and amused by it, Rochester said he would take the full onus', according to Johnson in *A Profane Wit*. According to Mulgrave, Ashton 'thought himself obliged to write down every word and circumstance … in order to spread everywhere the true reason of our returning without having fought'. With scarcely veiled malice Mulgrave adds that the episode 'entirely ruined his [Rochester's] reputation as to courage (of which I was really sorry to be the occasion) though nobody still had a greater as to wit ... '

The two men were taken before the House of Lords. Mulgrave promised not to engage in a duel with Rochester, who told the House: 'I have never been angry with the Earl of Mulgrave, and I have no reason to believe that he was so with me; for his lordship hath always carried himself so gently and civilly toward me.'

The whole episode had been a farce worthy of a Restoration comedy, but Rochester really was ill, almost certainly with a venereal disease. Johnson speculates in *A Profane Wit* that he may have been infected with syphilis without knowing it, and his rackety way of life would have made any temporary recovery slow and uncertain. Bouts of disease, drunken sleepless nights, the need always to be on his mettle in the company of other wits and literary talents took their toll.

Venereal diseases were fashionable if painful, and not to have been poxed was to lack a rakish credential, almost as if one were still a virgin. After catching a dose from a courtesan, probably Moll Hinton, Rochester's friend Buckhurst sent her a sum of money and a gentle caution: 'A Little Advice and a great deal of Physic may in time restore you to that Health I wish you had enjoyed a Sunday night instead of — your humble suffering servant.'

Gonorrhoea might be cured, but there was no remedy for syphilis.[*] Called variously the Great Pox, the Spanish Pox, or the French Pox, it was treated from about 1496 with highly toxic mercury: 'A night with Venus, a lifetime with Mercury' was a popular

---

[*] Condoms provided some protection against syphilis but they were not widely used. First manufactured in the seventeenth century, they were used to prevent infection rather than pregnancy. They were usually made from sheep's intestines. They caught on in court circles. Burford attributes to Rochester a pamphlet of 1667 entitled *A Panegyric Upon Cundum*, praising their efficacy against both disease and pregnancy: 'happy is the man who in his pocket keeps a well-made cundum ... nor dreads the Ills of Shankers or Cordes or Buboes dire'. As a contraceptive it prevented: 'big belly and the squalling brat'. He recommended it 'not only for the chaste Marriage Bed but the Filthiest Stews and Houses of Kept Dames'. But it is not clear that he used them.

adage. Mercury was already in use to treat skin diseases, and the early symptoms of syphilis included open sores, so it was natural to use the poison in an attempt to cure the disease. It was administered orally or applied in ointments to rashes, scabs and ulcers. Patients would be sweated in hot tubs, breathing in the mercury fumes. A particularly disgusting side effect was prolific drooling, the 'stinking salivation'. Goldsworthy in *The Satyr* notes that 'some quacks insisted on the loss of four pints of saliva on the first day'.*

Death through kidney and liver failure was not uncommon. Other patients died of heart failure, poisoning and dehydration. Some committed suicide. Mercury could also be injected into the nose and genitals. Side effects included loss of teeth, gum ulceration, bone deterioration, nausea and diarrhoea.

VD was rife at court. Dryden claimed that Charles II caught a venereal disease from Lady Shrewsbury, and his mistress Louise accused the King of infecting her. Charles's brother the Duke of York, later James II, handed down 'the diseases of love' to some of his many children. Pepys wrote that Dr Alexander Frazier, physician-in-ordinary, 'was helping the ladies at court to slip their calves, and great men of their Clap'. In *Brief Lives* John Aubrey recalled that the playwright Sir William Davenant 'got a terrible clap of a black handsome wench that lay in Axe Yard, Westminster . . . which cost him his nose'. Davenant got little sympathy, Aubrey writing that 'with which unlucky mischance many wits were too cruelly bold . . . ' There was a club for men who had lost their noses to the infection, according to Ned Ward. He says in his *History of the London Clubs*:

---

* Isaac Pewsey was a syphilitic driven mad by the mercury treatment. A servant named Mary Hill told a court in 1698 that she had heard her mistress, Sara Pewsey, cry out 'What, will you murder me?' She ran into the parlour of the house in Mile End Green, Stepney, to find Isaac 'twisting and squeezing his wife's hands over a cane chair'. Sara was heavily pregnant, but Pewsey kicked her all the way from the parlour into the kitchen. During salivation he would call Sara, who tried to look after him, 'bitch, whore . . . without any provocation or cause'. Once during his salivation he 'did . . . throw a basin of nasty spittle on her . . . which stunk so intolerably that the maid could hardly come near her to help her off with her clothes' (Linnane, *Encyclopedia of London Vice and Crime*).

A Merry Gentleman who had often hazarded his own Boltsplit, by steering a Vicious Course of Life among the dangerous Rocks of Venus, having observed in his Walks through our English Sodom, that abundance of both sexes had sacrificed their Noses to the God of Priapus, and had unluckily fallen into the Ethiopian Fashion of flat Faces, pleased himself with the Opinion it might prove a very comical Sight for so many Maimed Lechers, Snuffing old Stallions, young unfortunate Whore-Masters, poor Scarified Bawds and Sallivated Whetstones, to show their scandalous Vizards in a Nose-less Society.

The mercury treatment was given in the sweating houses of Leather Lane off Holborn, where a Frenchman named Fourcade, one of the King's surgeons, offered mercury baths. A Dr Fourcard, presumably the same man, a specialist in venereal diseases, was sent by the King 'post-haste to Newmarket to help out' with treating courtiers for the pox in June 1675. The baths were used by wealthy and noble sufferers. Rochester himself wrote to his wife from Fourcade's in October 1669, where he was being treated for difficulty in urinating: 'From our tub at Mns Fourcard's this 18th of Octob: Wife, our gut has been gripped [his urinary tract had been squeezed between thumb and forefinger] and we are now in bed so that we are not in a condition of writing either according to thy merit or our desert ... '

So when he was challenged by Mulgrave he had recently undergone this painful and weakening treatment. In 1669, after suffering the initial phase of the disease, Rochester seems to have had a remission for about a year before suffering its secondary and tertiary stages. Later he would suffer the progressive symptoms – failing sight, 'pissing of blood', swollen lymph glands, skin eruptions and weakness.

When the disease raged through him he thought of Adderbury and his loving wife. He wrote to her:

Dear Wife,

I recover so slowly, and relapse so continually, that I am almost weary of my self, if I had the least strength I would come to Adderbury, but in the condition I am, Kensington and back is a voyage I can hardly support; I hope you excuse my sending you no money, for till I am well enough to fetch it myself they will not give me a farthing, & if I had not pawned my Plate, I believe I must have starved in my sickness, well god Bless you & the children whate'r becomes of yr humble servant, Rochester

However, he was usually capable of bouncing back when he seemed at his lowest ebb. In August 1670 he caught 'a more virulent form of the pox' from his latest mistress, a girl named Foster. And he had other troubles. His pension from the King was six years in arrears. He hung around the court in the hope of getting some of it, but in vain. He was 23, an alcoholic, fatally ill although he didn't know it, and broke.

## Debauchery at Woodstock

In September 1671 Rochester attended a banquet for a French envoy from Louis XIV. The envoy later reported to Louis that although King Charles was present the whole company got uproariously drunk. Some days later, he was dining at Garraway's Coffee House with Harry Killigrew and others when he suddenly complained about his eyesight and left, riding off to Woodstock Park in Oxfordshire. Holding as he did the title of Game Keeper of Oxfordshire and Ranger of Wychwood, he thus had the privileges of Woodstock Lodge, the half-timbered royal hunting lodge. It was here that he entertained his louche friends, indeed he seems to have spent time with his wife there only once. Adderbury, to which he went seldom now, still represented peace and the opportunity to write; Woodstock was just London in the country, with the same round of drinking and whoring. Harry Savile referred to 'the sobriety of Adderbury and the debauchery of Woodstock'. It was also a place where he went to have treatment for venereal disease, a good reason not to invite his wife there.

He also retired into the country to write his satires. Burnet said of such exercises: 'He laid out his wit very freely in Libels and Satires, in which he had a talent of mixing his wit with his malice, and fitting both with apt words, that men were pleased to be tempted with them: from thence his composures came to be easily known . . . '

On this occasion he worked on 'A Ramble in Saint James's Park', an obscene attack on many targets, including Foster, the girl who had poxed him. The first-person narrator goes to the park after 'Much wine had passed with grave discourse/ Of who fucks who'. He recounts a mock history of the park:

> But though Saint James has the honour on't
> 'Tis consecrate to prick and cunt . . .
> When ancient Pict began to whore
> Deluded of his assignation
> (Jilting it seems was then in fashion)
> Poor pensive lover in this place
> Would frigg upon his mother's face
> Whence rows of mandrakes tall did rise
> Whose lewd tops fucked the very skies
> Each imitative branch does twine
> In some loved fold of Aretine
> And nightly now beneath their shade
> Are buggeries, rapes and incests made.

The park is the venue for a long list of fornicators: 'Great ladies, chamber maids and drudges . . . divines, great lords and tailors, prentices, poets, pimps . . . do here arrive, and here promiscuously swive.' Foster is depicted as the narrator's mistress Corinna, 'infinitely vile', the 'proud bitch' on whom he vows vengeance.

> When your lewd cunt came spewing home
> Drenched with the seed of half the town
> My dram of sperm was supped up after
> For the digestive surfeit water . . .

There is more than a hint of self-loathing in all this, but far from mending his ways the Earl was back in London early in 1672 and in trouble. During a performance at the Theatre Royal he dropped a piece of orange peel from his box into the pit below. It hit Dick Newport, another member of the Ballers, who angrily vaulted into the box and struck Rochester. They both drew their swords and wounded one another. Rochester was cut in the stomach and Newport in the shoulder, but neither wound was serious. The Duke of Monmouth, who was present, arrested them and made them promise to drop the quarrel.

Rochester had been absent from his wife for some months, at least partly to conceal his illness. They were reunited in June 1672, and she soon knew only too well about his venereal disease – by March 1673 she was being treated for it herself. Little was known or understood about the nature and progress of venereal diseases, and Rochester probably thought himself cured before going back to his wife. They met at Woodstock for a change, and although by this time Lady Rochester knew about his affairs with other women their marriage entered on one of its happiest periods.

During this stay he seems to have composed a searing satire about two of the King's mistresses – Rochester's own relative 'Cousin Barbara' Villiers, Duchess of Cleveland, and Mary Knight – and two of Castlemaine's lovers. The 'Sodom' referred to is an area of London brothels known as Little Sodom, frequented by both Cousin Barbara and Rochester:

> Quoth the Duchess of Cleveland to Councillor Knight
> I'd fain have a prick knew I how to come by't
> But you must be secret and give your advice
> Though cunt is not coy, reputation is nice.

> Knight:

> To some cellar in Sodom your Grace must retire
> Where porters with black pots set round the coal fire
> There open your case, and your Grace cannot fail
> Of a dozen of pricks for a dozen of ale . . .

Duchess:

Then give me the key that unlocks the back door
I'd rather be fucked by porters and carmen
Than thus be abused by Churchill and German [Jermyn]

Rochester's hypocrisy towards Cousin Barbara is many layered. He had lain on his pallet bed while the King satisfied himself with 'the lewd imperial whore'. He had gone disguised as a porter to Little Sodom for 'low amours', and may even have seen her involved in just such a sodomitic scene as this. Surely it is not pressing probability too far to guess that he took part. But by 1672 there is a strong element of disgust in his attitude to female sexuality.

Disgust was a strong motivating force for writing the farce known as *Sodom*, of which Rochester is generally accepted as the author, at least of the earliest version. Johnson in *A Profane Wit* says it dates from 'not earlier than July 1672'. Sodom is the court of Charles II, with which Rochester had become ever more cynically disillusioned. He takes the basic idea of Aristophanes' farce *Lysistrata*, where women deny intercourse to men, and reverses it. In *Sodom* men refuse to have intercourse with women, who have infected them with sexual diseases. Bolloximian the King of Sodom (Charles II) issues an edict giving men freedom to have sex with each other, and himself 'swives' his male courtiers 'in their fundaments'. Clitoris (Louise de Kéroualle) winds up Cuntagratia, the Queen, with tales of the King's infidelities, and urges her to rebel:

[The King's] boundless pleasure buggers all he meets
As linkboys, fiddlers, frigs in open streets,
Forgets your joy; one cunt alone doth cloy.
A man, a maid should uncontrolled enjoy.
Like him, run on with pleasure, build your throne,
Fuck, frig, spend, riot, and the world's your own.

Rochester pays off old scores and has great fun in naming the cast. Lady Castlemaine is the nymphomaniac Fuckadilla; the Earl of

Mulgrave, his old enemy, is Pockinello; Louis XIV, who snubbed him, is Tarsehole the King of Gomorrah. But the full force of his mocking satire is directed at the King. When Clitoris says she wants to replace the Queen in the King's bed he replies:

> Bolloximian: But of ambition, Clitoris, you sue,
> Speak ill of her that I may fuck with you ...
> Pine, drag Clitoris to the bugg'ring hole;
> There on a couch lay the base traitress down.
> Fetch all the dogs and monkeys in the town,
> Force 'em to act each with vig'rous fire;
> Let 'em her cunt, her arse, her eyes quite tire.
> Then drowned in sperm, let the wild wretch expire.

Johnson sees in *Sodom* deep misogyny, expressed in the tones of an Old Testament prophet. Rochester's experiences of sexual illnesses had certainly soured him, and led to extremes of nauseated obscenity that even he was not to repeat:

> Their ulcered cunts, by being so abused
> And having so much fuck therein infused,
> And then not cleansed till they begin to stink,
> May well be styled love's nasty common sink.

However disordered his mind at this time, Rochester knew he was playing with fire. His attack on the King and his new mistress, de Kéroualle, was unforgivable. He took care to see that only people he could trust saw it.

In March 1673 Lady Rochester was in London for medical treatment. Like her husband she seems to have been treated by the Leather Lane pox specialists. One Godfrey Thacker wrote in a letter: 'his poor lady is now not only under the doctor's hands; but under the suspicion, of all that know them, to have been injured by him.'

Later that year Rochester wrote a satire that led indirectly to a new rupture with the King, and put their relationship on a more guarded and even antagonistic footing. The Italian Mary of Modena had come to England to marry James, Duke of York. In Rochester's 'Signor Dildo' the basis of the satire is the supposed excitement aroused among women of the court by the introduction of Italian dildoes. The verses caused much amusement, and eventually the King heard about them. He asked Rochester for a copy, and the Earl, who may have been drunk, handed him instead a satire on the King himself.

> Peace is his aim, his gentleness is such,
> And love he loves, for he loves fucking much.
> Nor are his high desires above his strength:
> His sceptre and his prick are of a length;
> And she may sway the one who plays with th'other. . .
> To Carwell [Kéroualle] the most dear of all his dears
> The best relief of his declining years,
> Oft he bewails his fortune, and her fate:
> To love so well, and be beloved so late.
> For though in her he settles well his tarse
> Yet his dull, graceless ballocks hang an arse.
> This you'd believe, had I but time to tell ye
> The pains it costs to poor, laborious Nelly
> Whilst she employs hands, fingers, mouth and thighs
> Ere she can raise the member she enjoys.
> All Monarchs I hate, and the thrones they sit on
> From the Hector of France to the Culley of Britain.

This time Rochester's banishment lasted about seven weeks. During it he assumed another of his disguises, posing as one of the merchant class and taking a house in the City of London so he could keep abreast of events at court. Hamilton in the *Memoirs of the Comte de Gramont* says he went to parties given by merchants and bankers and railed against 'the vices of a licentious court'. This made him popular, but the 'heaviness of their entertainments' bored him. Anyway, he was soon back in royal favour. On 27

February he was appointed Ranger of Woodstock Park, having once again survived a serious rift with the King. Lady Rochester, seemingly cured of the pox, at least for the moment, was nearing delivery of their third child. And Rochester was conducting an affair with the love of his life, an affair that would give him joy and pain.

## The cruelty of love

Elizabeth Barry had much to be grateful to Rochester for. He transformed her from a failure into one of the greatest actresses of the age. She had made a disastrous stage debut in 1674 at the age of 16. She was no beauty and had no discernible talent. Edward Cole wrote in his *History of the English Stage* that her acting was so bad 'several persons of wit and quality being at the play and observing how she performed positively gave their opinion she would never be capable of any part of acting'. But Rochester saw something in her the others had missed. He also fell in love.

He laid a wager with a friend that he could make a real actress of her. It wasn't the first time he had attempted such a transformation: Sarah Cooke, the lover who had spied on Temple and Howard as she lay in the bath, never amounted to anything even with Rochester's help. A satirist of the 1680s wrote after a performance by Sarah: 'Mistaken Drab, back to thy mother's stall'.

The Earl took Barry into the country and taught her, in the words of the actor-manager Thomas Betterton, 'to enter into the meaning of every sentiment; he taught her not only the proper cadence or sounding of the voice, but to seize also the passions, and adapt her whole behaviour to the situations of the characters'. He made her rehearse a part up to 30 times on a stage, 12 of them in full dress. For six long months Rochester laboured to transform this unpromising material, to such effect that once back on the London stage she became, and remained, a star.

Betterton described her return to the stage as 'incomparable'. Her first triumph was as Isabella in *Mustapha* by Rochester's friend and protégé Thomas Otway. Rochester had brought the King and the Duchess of York to see her. However, if on stage Mrs Barry was an ornament to her profession, off it she did little to improve its reputation. She was described as 'the finest woman in the world upon the stage, and the ugliest woman off on't'. Her hardhearted-ness was notorious. The satirists were particularly bitter:

> But slattern Betty Barry next appears
> Whom every fop upon the stage admires
> At thirty eight a very hopeful whore,
> The only one o' th' trade that's not profuse,
> (A policy was taught her by the Jews)
> Tho' still the highest bidder will she choose.

She was a trollop, available to anyone with the money, coldly mer-cenary. The satirist Tom Brown wrote of her: 'Should you lie with her all night, she would not know you next morning, unless you had another five pounds at her service.' She could no more be faithful than could Rochester.

Barry was dissolute, bad-tempered and violent. She and her fel-low cast member Betty Boutel quarrelled over a scarf just as Lee's play *The Rival Queens* was about to begin. As she uttered the line: 'Die, sorceress, die and all my wrongs die with thee!' Mrs Barry stabbed Mrs Boutel with such force that her blunted stage dagger penetrated Mrs Boutel's stays and pierced the flesh beneath to a depth of a quarter of an inch. The fact that Boutel had been Barry's predecessor in Rochester's bed may have added force to the thrust.

The affair between Barry and Rochester probably began in 1674, and ended in 1678. More than 30 letters between the couple survive, charting the course of the affair from the full exuberance of passion and love through doubt and suspicion to full realisation of her unfaithfulness. It has to be remembered that, bad though he was, she would sleep with any man for £5. In December 1677 she had their child. Rochester was sick in the country, and two months earlier had written to Harry Savile describing himself as being 'almost blind, utterly lame, and scarce within the reasonable hopes of ever seeing London again'. Savile told him that Barry was hard up, but Rochester was being pursued by creditors, and couldn't send her money. His salary as Gentleman of the Bedchamber was as usual unpaid. In March 1672 the arrears amounted to the large sum of £3,375 (more than £300,000 today). At that time the King's mistresses Barbara Villiers and Louise de Kéroualle were being paid £45,000 between them by the state. He wrote to Barry:

> Madam, Your safe delivery has delivered me too from fears for your sake, which were, I'll promise you, as burthensome to me as your great-belly could be to you. Everything has fallen out to my wish, for you are out of danger, and the child is of the soft sex I love. Shortly, my hopes are to see you, and in a little while after to look on you with all your beauty about you.

Then he found out that she was being unfaithful. He wrote, says Goldsworthy in *The Satyr*, that she was making the memories of their love so painful that he might as well hate her: 'I can never forget how very happy I have been, but the love that gives you the torment of repentance on your side, and me the trouble of perceiving it on the other, is equally unjust and cruel to us both, and ought to die.' On another occasion he wrote: "Tis impossible for me to curse you, but give me leave to pity myself, which is more than you will ever do for me.'

Barry was not a good mother, and given her ambitions to be the leader of her profession of actress it is hard to see how she could have been. Rochester took the child away from her, sending her a letter that is both tender and cruel:

> Madam, I am far from delighting in the grief I have given you by taking away the child; and you, who made it so absolutely necessary for me to do so, must take that excuse from me for all the ill nature of it. On the other side pray be assured I love Betty so well that you need not apprehend any neglect from those I employ, and I hope very shortly to restore her to you a finer girl than ever. In the mean time you would do well to think of the advice I gave you, for so lit-

tle show soever my prudence makes in my own affairs, in yours it will prove very successful if you please to follow it. And since discretion is the thing alone you are like to want, pray study to get it.

This cruelty, perhaps an example of the misogyny brought on by his attacks of the pox, should be balanced against his most tender love letters to her. Towards the end of 1677, almost overwhelmed with pain, he wrote:

Madam, This is the first service my hand has done me since my being a cripple, and I would not employ it in a lie so soon; therefore, pray believe me sincerely when I assure you that you are very dear to me; and as long as I live, I will be kind to you. P.S. This is all my hand would write, but my heart thinks a great deal more.

However, the child was never returned to Barry, whose reputation as both a great tragic actress and as 'a scandalous ... mercenary whore' grew. In his will Rochester left an annuity of £40 to the child, Elizabeth Clarke. She died in 1691 at the age of 14 and was buried at Acton. After a long and successful career Barry retired to the country at Acton when she was in her fifties. She died in 1713, possibly from the bite of a rabid pet dog, and was buried beside her daughter. The playwright Colley Cibber wrote in his obituary:

Mrs Barry, in Characters of Greatness, had a Presence of elevated Dignity, the Mien and Motion superb and gracefully Majestick; her Voice full, clear and strong, so that no Violence of Passion could be too much for her: and when Distress or Tenderness possess'd her, she subsided into the most affecting Melody and Softness. In the Art of exciting Pity she had a Power beyond all the Actresses I have yet seen, or what your imagination can conceive.

During the 1670s Rochester was under pressure on several fronts. Unpopular at court and embroiled in a bruising conflict with Barry, he became involved in an increasingly splenetic literary quarrel with the poet and playwright John Dryden. Rochester had helped him get the poet laureateship, and Dryden was grateful. However, he regarded Rochester as merely an amateur poet, and the two took to sniping at each other in print. Then in December 1679 three thugs beat Dryden up near Will's coffee house off Covent Garden, injuring him badly. There were several suspects, including the King's mistress Louise, Duchess of Portsmouth. The historian Narcissus Luttrell reported: "Tis thought to be done by order of the Duchess of Portsmouth, she being abused in a late libel called *Essay Upon Satire*, of which Mr Dryden is suspected to be the author.' Rochester, however, was also suspected. But Goldsworthy suggests in *The Satyr* that the most likely culprit was Philip Herbert, Earl of Pembroke, Louise's brother-in-law. He was a drunken brute: in January 1677 he killed a man in a duel at Long's notorious tavern in the Haymarket. He had 'played foul' in the duel, and spent a month in the Tower of London.*

But before the incident involving Dryden, Rochester's drunken recklessness and increasing contempt for the King got him into his worst scrape yet.

## Dost thou stand there to fuck time?

Four things ruled Rochester's life: his poetic gift, sex, syphilis and drink. As he grew older his moral anarchy became if anything more pronounced. Relations with the King reached a new low in June 1675 with the 'sundial affair'. Rochester had been drinking in the King's apartments together with his friend Buckhurst and some other young rakes. In the Privy Garden they came upon the dial, in fact an elaborate device for measuring celestial motions. The King was deeply interested in astronomy, and the dial gave him particular pleasure. It had been designed by a Jesuit priest, Father Francis Hall, who published a book describing how it worked. In the

---

* The following April in the same tavern Herbert killed Nathaniel Coney 'with a blow of his fist'. He was tried by his peers, found not guilty of murder but guilty of manslaughter, and discharged when he claimed 'the benefit of the statute'. Three years later he was convicted of murdering a man at Turnham Green. The King pardoned him; but he was dead within two years from drink and syphilis.

book, *Explication of the Dial*, there was a picture of the device; Johnson in *A Profane Wit* describes it as 'a fountain of glass spheres, or a giant candelabrum with tiered, branching arms ending in crystal globes'. Although there was a guard the drunken young men smashed it to pieces. It has been suggested that the dial looked rather phallic, and Rochester's words were variously reported as 'Dost thou stand there to fuck time?' and 'Kings and kingdoms tumble down, and so shalt thou.' It could be, and probably was, seen as a political act – the dial bore glass portraits of King Charles, Queen Catherine, the Duke of York, the Queen Mother and the King's cousin Prince Rupert. When Rochester sobered up the full horror of what he had done struck him, and as usual he went off to skulk in the country and await the King's punishment.

Charles reacted by leaving London in a fury for Plymouth. Accompanied by Harry Savile he set out on a cruise in his yacht *Greyhound* and disappeared. There was consternation – at the Admiralty, Pepys feared that the King had been lost at sea and his French mistress de Kéroualle was distraught. Then after ten days Charles landed on the Isle of Wight.

He seems to have cooled down fairly quickly, but later that summer Rochester learned he had a dangerous enemy at court. The Earl, who had been thrown by his horse and knocked unconscious, was still bedridden when a letter from Savile told him that de Kéroualle had 'more than ordinary indignation against him'. It seems two courtiers had repeated to her some of Rochester's candid satires against her. In vain he begged Savile to plead his case with the Duchess. Savile had to tell him that she was not to be placated, and the King did not want Rochester on bedchamber duty. Rochester's self-serving reply shows a streak of self-pity:

> She has ne'er accused me of any crime but of being cunning; and I told her somebody had been cunninger than I to persuade her so. I can as well support the hatred of the whole world as anybody, not being generally fond of it. Those whom I have obliged may use me with ingratitude and not afflict me much; but to be injured by those who have obliged me, and to whose service I am ever bound, is such

a curse as I can only wish on them who wrong me with the Duchess.

This air of injured innocence is just another disguise, for Rochester had written *Sodom*, in which she is portrayed as Clitoris.

By the beginning of 1676 Rochester had cause enough for self-pity. His sickness was so bad that rumours of his death circulated in London, and in February a letter to Savile says he has received 'the unhappy news of my own death and burial'. The antiquary Anthony Wood wrote in his journal: 'About 18 Apr., Earl of Rochester, died at London at 28 or thereabouts.' His eyesight was worse, he had pains in his joints and he was passing blood in his urine. Johnson suggests in *A Profane Wit* that the blood was caused by gonorrhoea, and the growing blindness and pain in his joints were caused by advanced syphilis. Doctors couldn't help: 'My pissing of blood Doctor Wetherly says is nothing. My eyes are almost out but he says will not do me much harm, in short he makes me eat flesh and drink diet-drink . . . '

Like many another sufferer, Rochester turned to books of 'physic', an area of knowledge that would be helpful later in the year when he adopted his most fantastic disguise of all. Meanwhile, in spite of his afflictions, he got into trouble again, and this time it involved death and disgrace.

In April 1676 Harry Savile, who had been to the races at Newmarket with the King, called at Woodstock on the way back to bring Rochester the good news that Charles was willing to receive him at court again. With two other men they got drunk in celebration. A year later Rochester reminded Savile how they had danced naked round a fountain:

Be pleased to call to mind the year 1676, when two large fat nudities led the coranto round Rosamund's fair fountain while the poor violated nymph wept to behold the strange decay of manly parts . . . P[rick] 'tis confessed you showed but little of, but for a[rse] and b[uttocks] (a filthier representation, God wot!) you exposed more of that nastiness in your two folio volumes than we altogether in our six quartos.

The euphoria continued. The King offered further evidence of his restored favour by giving Rochester a present of £300 and allowing him to build in the Privy Garden. In June, with time on his hands, the Earl went to Epsom for the races with Etherege and some other profligates. On the 17th, they and George Bridges and a Captain Downs met some musicians who refused to play for them. They tossed the musicians in a blanket, and a constable who became involved was beaten. He escaped and called the armed Watch. Etherege was sober enough to placate them with a 'submissive oration', and the Watch went away.

Rochester then drew his sword on the constable, who called for help. At this point Downs seized the constable to prevent Rochester stabbing him. The men of the Watch ran back, misread the situation and attacked Downs, one of them hitting him on the head with a pole. Downs picked up a stick to defend himself but a Watchman stabbed him in the side with a pike. With Downs lying fatally wounded, Rochester and the others fled. Andrew Marvell wrote in a letter: 'They told me Lord Rochester with Etherege, Bridges and Downs had in a debauch at Epsom caused the constable to defend himself. Rochester is said to have first engaged and first fled and abjectly hid himself when the rest were exposed . . . '

While the others passed off the episode as just another lordly scrape, Rochester was guilt stricken. His poem 'To the Post Boy' is a scream of self-disgust:

> Rochester: Son of a whore god damn you can you tell
> A peerless peer the readiest way to Hell?
> I've outswilled Bacchus, sworn of my own make
> Oaths would fright furies and make Pluto Quake.
> I've swived more whores more ways than Sodom's walls
> Ere knew, or the College of Rome's cardinals . . .
> Witness heroic scars, look here nere go
> Cerecloths [shrouds] and ulcers from top to toe.
> Frighted at my own mischiefs I have fled
> And bravely left my life's defender dead.
> Broke houses to break chastity and dyed

That floor with murder that my lust denied.
Pox on it why do I speak of these poor things?
I have blasphemed my God and libelled Kings;
The readiest way to Hell come quick –
Boy: Ne'er stir
The readiest way my Lord's by Rochester.

When Downs died the young profligates faced the possibility of trial for murder, and most of the blame was placed on Rochester. He doesn't seem to have been officially accused, but according to Johnson the King ostracised him, and he went into hiding. When his various homes were searched he was not found. The stage was set for the last and strangest of his disguises.

## Dr Bendo, the quack doctor

Rochester's many illnesses and his reading in the medical classics had given him a superficial knowledge of medicine. His own body was a medical text of a kind, covered as he was with ulcers and aching with the effects of the late stage of syphilis. By now he must have known his fate, and his state of mind doubtless contributed to the surreal adventure he now began.

Rochester assumed a new persona, Dr Alexander Bendo, 'famous Italian pathologist', and set up in business at Tower Hill. He went about in a false beard and oriental clothing, and advertised his services in a handbill:

To All Gentlemen, Ladies &, whether of City, Town or Country: Alexander Bendo wisheth all Health and Prosperity. Whereas this famous metropolis of England has ever been infested with a numerous company of those whose arrogant confidence has enabled them to impose upon the people either premeditated cheats, or, at best, the dull and empty mistakes of their self-deluded imaginations in physic, chymical and Galenic, in astrology, physiognomy, palmistry, mathematics, alchemy and even Government itself – the last of which I will not propose to discourse of since it in no ways belongs to my vocation as the rest do, which, thanks to my God I find much more safe, equally honest and therefore more profitable.

There are two accounts of the Bendo episode, one by Hamilton in the *Memoirs of the Comte de Gramont*, the other by one of the participants, Thomas Alcock. He had been a servant of the Rochester family for about 15 years, possibly as the Earl's secretary. Seven years after Rochester's death, Alcock wrote his more authentic account as a New Year's amusement for Rochester's oldest daughter, Anne Wilmot Baynton. The result, *The Famous Pathologist, or The Noble Mountebank*, might suggest to a modern mind some deep cleavage in Rochester's personality.

Rochester set up a kind of chemical factory for making medicines, where he appeared dressed in fantastical clothes:

an old overgreen gown which he religiously wore in memory of Rabelais his master, put on at the reception of his Doctor's degree at Montpelier, lined through with exotic furs of diverse colours, an antique cap, a great reverend beard and a magnificent false medal set round with glittering pearls, rubies and diamonds, hung about his neck in a massy goldlike chain ... which the King of Cyprus had given him for doing a signal cure upon his darling daughter, the Princess Aloephangina, who was painted in a banner and hung up at his elbow ...

He hoodwinked his customers by speaking to his helpers 'in a language which neither he nor they understood one word of'. He sold cures and

made predictions, casting nativities, interpreting of dreams, solving of omens, responses to horary questions, illustrations of signs and tokens, judgments upon moles, wens, warts and natural marks, according to their several kinds, and accidental positions in various parts of the body.

He took his patients into his laboratory to see his assistants at work preparing his 'cures'. These consisted of rubbish he found in the streets, although he claimed they were 'all Indies'. In fact they were 'ashes, soot, lime, chalk, clay, old wall, soap ... anything that came to hand'. Alcock describes the scene in the laboratory:

> Some stirring an old boiling kettle, of soot and urine, tinged with a little asafedita ... some grinding oils, with a stone upon marble, till they sweat again; while the drops from face and nose made ye medicine the bigger and consequently more beneficial; other labouring at the pestle and mortar, and all of them dressed like the witches in *Macbeth* ... We of the fraternity kept a perpetual jangling to one another ... in a jargon of damned unintelligible gibberish all the while, and indeed we judged it not convenient in our circumstances to do anything in plain English but laugh. And all this to amuse the gentle spectators ... that they might see, we took pains for what we had, and consequently were no cheats ...

He charged for his potions, but gave advice free. Alcock says he 'reaped a rich harvest of good gold and silver'. And as always with Rochester, there was a sexual dimension.

> Dr Bendo, among other practices, made judgments upon moles, wens, warts and natural marks ... And if the modest lady had any such about her where without blushing she could not well declare them; why the religious Doctor Bendo would not, for all the world, so much as desire to see it ... she was to leave a token with the doctor and appoint an hour when his wife was to bring it, as a credential that she came on that errand, upon which she was immediately to be admitted into the bedchamber, to view and report the matter.

The wife was of course Rochester himself in a new disguise. Did he get a thrill out of this transvestism? The 'Post Boy' poem suggests a stage of syphilis that probably included impotence. He had indeed 'swived more whores more ways than Sodom's walls/Ere knew, or the College of Rome's cardinals'.

As suddenly as he had appeared, Dr Bendo vanished. Rochester had become bored with his medical pranks, and the King even more bored without him. News of his zany activities reached Whitehall, and Charles recalled him to court. According to Alcock, the Earl 'pretended the quickest voyage from France that ever man did, which was the talk and admiration of the whole town, for those that saw his ostracism cancelled this night at Whitehall did the very next see him there in splendour dancing in a ball, in as great favour as ever'.

Alcock had enjoyed the strange interlude: 'But ah, fading joys! The pleasures we had so long fed on were now become meat for our masters, and the hungry court could no longer sustain her drooping spirits without the intellectual viands we had hitherto feasted on ...'

The court was agog to hear Rochester's account, the King included, but he also had other matters on his mind. Towards the end of the year Charles finally broke with Rochester's 'Cousin Barbara' Castlemaine, sending her and her 'sluttish' daughter Lady Sussex to France, having become tired of the gossip about 'their common nymphomania'. Inevitably some of the old careless gaiety of the court was fading.

## The gates of death

The shades were closing around Rochester, despite his surprising ability to bounce back from bouts of painful illness. In March 1678 he feared he was 'at the gates of death'. Gilbert Burnet, who would be with him two years later during much of his long death agony, described the 'sickness which brought [him] so near death before I knew him, when his spirits were so low and spent, that he could not move nor stir, and he did not think to live an hour ... He had in that sickness great remorses for his past life ... general and dark horrors ... '

Again he recovered. His friend Harry Savile, himself a sufferer from syphilis, wrote to him on 2 June saying there had been 'some scurvy alarums' about Rochester's health. Savile's illness had forced

him on to 'dry mutton and diet drink'. Nevertheless he was planning to marry an heiress. Nell Gwynn wrote in a letter that the
bride 'won't have too hard a time on't if he holds up his thumb'.

In July 1678 Savile wrote to Rochester from a pox doctor's in
Leather Lane, where he had been enduring 'a long tedious course
of physic which has entertained me ever since December last'. He
maintains the bantering tone the two fellow sufferers used when
writing about their syphilis, but cannot hide the pain. He might
have 'turned Turk' rather than suffer the effects of 'that mass of
mercury that has gone down my throat in seven months'. (Savile
died in 1687 at the age of 45, having suffered from syphilis for at
least ten years.)

He sent news of an old mistress of Rochester's, Jane Roberts,
who was a fellow patient and in an even worse condition.[*] To
Rochester, Savile's description of the ordeal she underwent from
the treatment for syphilis must have been particularly poignant. It
would, said Savile, 'make a damned soul fall alaughing at his lesser
pain. It is so far beyond description or belief that till she tells you
herself, I will not spoil her story by making it worse, or by making
your hair stand on end – and hinder anything else from doing so
for a month after so tragical a relation.' She died soon afterwards,
begging Bishop Burnet, who attended her, to warn the King
against the evils of the dissolute life. Burnet did so, by letter; the
King, who was furious, burned it.

The news of Jane Roberts's illness had the strange effect of
inspiring Rochester to another satire, full of gallows humour. He
imagines the 'vile enchanters' Doctors Barton and Ginman – presumably the pox doctors – leading forth their patients 'in chains of
quicksilver [mercury] to the loathsome banks of a dead lake of
diet-drink'.

---

[*]  Charles II liked sexually experienced women, and Rochester assumed the agreeable duty of seducing virgins and initiating them in techniques that would please
the King. Jane Roberts, the daughter of a clergyman, was one of the women he
passed on to Charles. When the King eventually discarded her she became a
whore.

Thus would I lead the mournful tale along, till the gentle reader
bathed with the tribute of his eyes the names of such unfortunate
lovers – and this, I take it, would be a most excellent way of celebrating the memories of my most pocky friends, companions and
mistresses.

This mood is all the more surprising given his own dire straits:

I am in a damned relapse brought by a fever, the stone and some ten
diseases more which have deprived me of the power of crawling,
which I happily enjoyed some days ago. And now I fear I must fall,
that it may be fulfilled which was long ago written for our instruction in a good old ballad,

> But he who lives not wise and sober
> Falls with the leaf still in October.

About which time, in all probability, there may be a period added
to the ridiculous being of
Your humble servant, Rochester.

His race was almost run. In mid-May he felt strong enough to
undertake a journey to his distant estates in Somerset. The journey
proved too much. Burnet described his final breakdown: 'This heat
and violent motion did so inflame an ulcer, that was in his bladder,
that it raised a very great pain in those parts: yet he with much difficulty came home by coach to the lodge at Woodstock Park.'
    Rochester was placed in a great oak bed. His wife and mother
hurried to the lodge, until recently out of bounds to all but profligates of both sexes. His mother took down obscene pictures from
the walls, the family doctor was called and saw that Rochester was
dying. The burst ulcer, says Johnson in *A Profane Wit*, was dis-
charging 'large amounts of purulent matter'. The King sent one of
his own physicians, who agreed that the only thing they could do
was give Rochester laudanum. Burnet, who was there until near
the end, wrote of Rochester's last days in his very popular *Some*

*Passages in the Life and Death of John Earl of Rochester.* On 19 June Rochester, in terror for his soul, wrote a 'Remonstrance', witnessed by his mother and all the servants, including the pig-boy:

> For the benefit of all those whom I have drawn into sin by my example and encouragement, I leave to the world this my last Declaration ... that from the bottom of my soul I detest and abhor the whole course of my wicked life ... and the greatest testimony of my charity to such is, to warn 'em in the name of God, and as they regard the welfare of their immortal souls, no more to deny his being ... no more to make a mock of sin, or contemn the pure and excellent religion of my ever blessed redeemer, through whose merits alone, I one of the greatest of sinners, do yet hope for mercy and forgiveness. Amen.

There followed a long series of conversations that ended, claimed Burnet, in the unbeliever's conversion. He reported that Rochester vowed to be 'strictly just and true; to be chaste and temperate, to forbear swearing and irreligious discourse, to worship and pray to his maker'. This is at odds with Rochester's translation of some verses of Seneca in February 1680:

> Dead we become the lumber of the world,
> And to that mass of matter shall be swept
> Where things destroyed with things unborn are kept.
> Devouring time swallows us whole;
> Impartial death confounds body and soul.
> For Hell and the foul fiend that rules
> God's everlasting fiery jails
> (Devised by rogues, dreaded by fools).
> With his grim, grisly dog that keeps the door,
> Are senseless stories, idle tales,
> Dreams, whimsies and no more.

Burnet visited him but was not there when he died at the end of July 1680, at the age of 33. He was buried in the family vault of

Spelsbury church. The only inscription is Anthony Wood's ambiguous elegy: 'In this vault also lies buried John Earl of Rochester. This John made a great noise in the world for his noted and professed atheism, his lampoons and other frivolous stuff; and a great noise after his death for his penitent departure.'

His wife and only son died the following year, and were buried in the vault. Rochester had asked his mother to burn his papers, including his memoirs. She did, an act of vandalism for which, as a wit said, 'Her soul is now burning in heaven.'

# Buckingham and the Merry Gang

THE MOST DAZZLING FIGURE AT CHARLES II'S court was George Villiers, Duke of Buckingham. He could not equal Rochester's wit, and he was a lesser writer – although a good one – while he had a European reputation as a depraved and extravagant rake. Yet his presence and panache won from Louis XIV the tribute that he was the only true English gentleman that he had ever met.

Burnet, who strongly disapproved of Buckingham, nevertheless wrote of his noble presence, adding: 'He was a man of ... a most lovely wit, wholly turned to mirth and pleasure ... ' He won the unwilling admiration of his enemy, the great Chancellor Clarendon: 'His quality and condescension, the pleasantness of his humour and conversation, the extravagance and sharpness of his wit, unrestrained by any modesty or religion, drew persons of all affections and inclination to like his company ... ' And the Puritan cleric Dean Lockier told Pope that he 'was reckoned the most accomplished man of the age in riding, dancing, and fencing. When he came into the presence chamber, it was impossible for you not to follow him with your eye, he moved so gracefully.' The politician and memoirist Sir John Reresby described him in his *Memoirs* as the finest gentleman he had ever seen.

He was good-looking, charming and witty. He was also dangerous. Bishop Burnet said he had 'no principles of religion, virtue or friendship'. His gift for mimicry and clowning made him a kind of court jester, but his commonplace book reveals a man of intellect and deep feeling.

His father George, the first Duke, had been a favourite of James I and Charles I. He was assassinated at Portsmouth in 1628 by John Felton, an army officer who had failed to get promotion and blamed the Duke. King Charles I adopted young George – he was just a year old when his father was murdered – and he was brought up with the Prince of Wales, with whom after he became King he was to have a complicated and sometimes difficult relationship.

After the Civil War broke out George and his younger brother Francis joined King Charles I at Oxford and were present when the Royalist commander Prince Rupert stormed Lichfield in April 1643. George was 15 and his brother a year younger. Alarmed that the boys might be seriously hurt, their relatives sent them abroad to finish their education.

In Paris Buckingham was reunited with the Prince of Wales. According to Burnet, writing many years afterwards, Buckingham 'having already got into all the vices and impieties of the age' deliberately corrupted the Prince. This is nonsense: Charles was never going to be a self-righteous prig like his father. By this time the Prince and his friend were 17 and 19, and they sowed wild oats like normal young men. The problem, says Chapman in *Great Villiers*, is that they went on sowing them 'till long past middle life'.

In the summer of 1648 King Charles I was a prisoner of the Parliamentary forces. The Villiers brothers, who had returned to England, joined forces with Henry Rich, Lord Holland, a brave but unreliable Royalist, in a hopeless attempt to turn the tide of war back in the King's favour. Holland collected a force of 600 men, with Buckingham as General of the Horse. Near Surbiton Common, Parliamentary forces caught up with them and they scattered and fled. Buckingham and Holland cut their way out, but there was no time to warn Francis Villiers. After his horse was killed he was surrounded by a company of Roundheads who hoped to take him prisoner. With his back against an oak tree he refused to surrender and fought against hopeless odds of six to one. His doomed stand became the stuff of Cavalier legend. Strong and fit, the 19-year-old aristocrat fought until one of the Roundheads climbed into the tree behind him and knocked off his helmet. He staggered forward and his six attackers closed in.

Inevitably it was later said that the house of Buckingham would have been spared much infamy if George Villiers had fallen with his brother. Instead he escaped, narrowly. At St Neots the Roundheads took Lord Holland, then were told that Buckingham and some others were still in a house where they had spent the night. As they surrounded the house Buckingham and his men charged them on horseback. He killed the captain of the Roundheads with his sword, and as the man's body crashed to the cobbles burst through to freedom. He escaped to join the Prince of Wales abroad. He was free but ruined – Parliament seized his estates. Lord Holland was executed.

On 30 January 1649, Buckingham's twenty-first birthday, Charles I was executed outside the Banqueting Hall in Whitehall. In the following March Parliament decreed that 'Charles Stuart [who was to succeed his father as Charles II] James Duke of York [his brother] and the Duke of Buckingham' were 'banished as enemies and traitors, to die without mercy wherever they shall be found within the limits of this nation'. Charles continued the struggle, with Buckingham playing an ambiguous role. The Duke spent much time at the French court, where he dazzled the courtiers. There were rumours of a liaison with the Queen. Charles made him a Gentleman of the Bedchamber and a privy councillor.

He and Buckingham returned to England and after an unsuccessful campaign in August 1651 they faced a stronger force under Cromwell at Worcester. Charles led a brave charge with Buckingham which achieved a momentary success, then their army was utterly routed. The two men went on the run, hiding in woods and cottages before Charles made his way to safety on the Continent. Buckingham went into hiding in London, with a price on his head, and it is to this period that E. Beresford Chancellor, in *The Lives of the Rakes*, attributes the story of his romantic involvement with, of all people, Bridget Cromwell, daughter of the Lord Protector himself.

Bridget was the wife of Henry Ireton, the regicide and close political adviser to Cromwell. She herself was said to be a stout republican. Buckingham had disguised himself as a Jack Pudding, or clown, and went about trying to gather intelligence while giving public performances in which he danced and sang and bandied witticisms with the crowd. Several ladies of quality fell for the handsome jester and his nights, if not his days, were spent in comfort.

Chancellor tells us that among the many 'fair ladies' who saw him and were attracted was Bridget Cromwell. 'But notwithstanding the ultra-puritanical attitude she assumed she was by no means... indifferent to grace and good looks in the other sex ... ' She invited him to visit her that night, and Buckingham, fearful but hoping to glean useful intelligence, agreed. She welcomed him with unmistakable ardour, and Buckingham eventually had to excuse himself by saying 'that he was a Jew, and by the Judaic law forbidden to have carnal connection with a Christian woman. Horror and amazement seized the lady cheated out of her pleasure and, one supposes, something like incredulity that one who was accustomed to play wild antics in public should develop a conscience at the very threshold of delight'. She made him promise to return the following night, and when Buckingham turned up he found she had summoned a Jewish rabbi, to discover if Buckingham really was a Jew. The Duke asked for time to consider the rabbi's arguments, saying he would return. Instead he left England, having first written to Bridget revealing that the man she had hoped to bed was an outlaw and her husband's and father's enemy. It is difficult now to know what to make of this farrago. Perhaps its importance lies in the fact that it was believed at the time.

In later years Charles was fond of recalling his adventures, and courtiers would exchange long-suffering glances when he began one of his Worcester anecdotes. Buckingham had no such fond memories of his experiences. He bore various grudges against the King, claiming that if he had been given command of the army he might have saved the day, and indiscreetly impugning the King's courage. He had also made a very dangerous enemy in the King's moralising chancellor and adviser, the Earl of Clarendon. Fortunately for him, the King soon grew tired of Clarendon's incessant lectures.

Parliament had conferred Buckingham's estates on their popular commander-in-chief, Thomas Fairfax. In 1657 Buckingham slipped into England to court and marry Fairfax's ugly daughter Mary, apparently by these actions deserting the Royalist cause and suggesting he thought it was hopeless. He was not a penniless suitor – Fairfax had never accepted that Parliament had the right to seize Buckingham's assets, and had never profited by them. Although the Fairfaxes, particularly Mary, were enchanted by the handsome Cavalier, many thought him utterly cynical. They were probably right. He wrote in his commonplace book: 'Wives we choose for our posterity, mistresses for ourselves ... Marriage is the greatest solitude, for it makes two but one and prohibits us from all others.'

In spite of his apparent disloyalty, Buckingham was soon plotting for Charles's return. He and Fairfax gathered an army to join General Monck, who was marching south. When Charles landed at Dover in May 1660 Buckingham was there to greet him, but the King received his old friend with marked coldness. Charles, Monck, and the Dukes of York and Gloucester left by coach, while Buckingham was in the outside boot seat, having jumped in before anyone could stop him. Yet by the time the party left Rochester for London the following day he was somehow back in favour. He had shown, to the dismay of his enemies, that in personal contact with the King he could work a kind of magic.

Buckingham had known extreme changes of fortune, and the first half of his life was full of adventure, danger, courage and gallantry. The second half was full of moral confusion, duplicity and foolishness. In a sense he never really grew up. In 1660 he suddenly acquired political power and an income of £20,000 a year (more than £2,000,000 today), a fortune he managed to squander by sheer persistence. Brian Fairfax, the great general's cousin, who loved and admired Buckingham, tried to give a balanced picture in his *Life of George Villiers*:

> The world has been severe in censuring his foibles, but not so just in noting his good qualities. For his person, he was the glory of the age and any court wherever he came. Of the most graceful and charming mien and behaviour; a strong, tall and active body, all of which gave a lustre to the ornaments of his mind; of an admirable wit and excellent judgment; and had all other qualities of a gentleman. He was courteous and affable to all; of a compassionate nature: ready to forgive and forget injuries ... but when he was provoked by the malice of some and ingratitude of others, he might show that a good-natured man might have an ill-natured muse ...
>
> The faults objected against him were that he loved women and spent his estate. His estate was his own. He had often lost it for the King, and might now be allowed to enjoy it himself ... His amours were too notorious to be concealed, and too scandalous to be justified, by saying he was bred in the latitude of foreign climates, and now lived in a vicious age and court; where his accusers of this crime were as guilty as himself. He lay under so ill a name for this, that whenever he was shut up in his chamber, as he loved to be ... or in his laboratory ... over the fumes of charcoal, it was said to be with women ...

Brian Fairfax does not mention a strong impulse to self-destruction. Time and again Buckingham's unstable temperament led him to inflict biting insults for the sake of a laugh, to try the King's patience with his jokes, to push their long friendship to breaking point and then to ask forgiveness. It says much for Charles's good nature that he almost always forgave, if not forgot.

And although Fairfax pleads that Buckingham's reputation as a womaniser was unfair, there is little doubt that he could match Rochester in heartless seduction. Chancellor quotes Burnet's story of their joint venture in debauching the wives of country gentlemen. They rented an inn on the Newmarket Road, where men with pretty wives or daughters were plied with drink until they collapsed, and the women 'sufficiently warmed to make as little resistance as would be agreeable to their inclinations'.

Chancellor says Charles was due to visit the races at Newmarket, and the two men, who were in disgrace at court at the time, thought they would be able to win back the King's favour by telling him of their adventures. First they decided to close their campaign with one further seduction. Nearby lived an old miser with a 'very pretty young wife':

> The old man was exceedingly jealous of his charming spouse, and kept her carefully under the surveillance of himself or of an elderly maiden sister who lived with him. He was one of the few whom Rochester and Buckingham never could prevail upon to accept of their hospitality – at least in company with his wife. As, however, he liked good cheer (when it cost him nothing) as well as most, it was arranged by the two reprobates that Buckingham should invite him to the inn what time Rochester, disguised as a woman, should go to his house and do his best to deceive the dragon (otherwise the maiden sister) who guarded it, and thus gain admittance to the young wife.

Rochester went to the house, drugged the maiden aunt, seduced the young wife and persuaded her to steal all the miser's money. He took her back to the inn and after enjoying her again handed her over to Buckingham, who also seduced her. When they tired of her they kicked her out, telling her to go to London 'to follow the only trade for which she was now fitted'. The miser returned to his house to find his wife and his money gone, and hanged himself. We are assured the courtiers laughed heartily when Rochester and Buckingham told this tale.

This is one of the darkest stories in the history of the English rakes. We could more easily believe it of Colonel Francis Charteris, subject of a later chapter, than of these two exquisites, men of feeling and literary distinction. But Burnet was a serious historian and so we must accept it.

Any politically ambitious man at Charles's court inevitably found that the quickest and best way to get his attention was through his mistresses. Buckingham was a cousin of Charles's gross and vicious but lovely mistress Barbara Castlemaine, née Villiers. They were natural allies against Clarendon, and for a long time they remained friends. Clarendon was an easy target for Buckingham, and Lady Castlemaine hated the old statesman. His long hectoring lectures to the King about almost everything he liked – his louche young friends the Wits, his penchant for tennis, swimming, yachting, indecent women, his disregard of affairs of state, were becoming unbearable. But for the moment the King thought the old man was too useful to be discarded entirely, and he was evasive when Buckingham suggested getting rid of him. In the bedchamber the other gentlemen were amazed at the reckless familiarity employed by Buckingham in his attacks. 'There goes your schoolmaster,' he said when Clarendon left the room. The King would answer with a shrug or a smile. He was playing a deep game.

Buckingham had other things on his mind. He was setting up a large glass-works at Lambeth, the first of its kind in England.[*] And in 1666 he had to leave the question of Clarendon unresolved when he headed north to organise defences against the Dutch. There he was joined by Lady Shrewsbury, and his life, already disorderly, descended into reckless chaos.

## Lady Shrewsbury's sharp-headed kisses

Anna Maria, Countess of Shrewsbury, was a troublemaker, the kind of woman who drives men mad with lust, frustration, anger, hatred or any combination she could contrive. 'Though nobody', says Hamilton, 'could brag that he alone had been kindly entertained by her, equally there was no one who could contend that his suit had been ill received.' Men died for her – her husband was slain in

---

[*]    The Venetian ambassador complained that the hitherto dominant Venetian glass trade had been ruined by the success of the Duke's factories.

an unequal duel with Buckingham, and in another duel over her between two of her lovers, Colonel Thomas Howard and Henry Jermyn, the latter's second was killed, although the two principals survived. Other lovers included Harry Killigrew, Rochester's friend, and Buckingham's cousin Lord Arran. The Comte de Gramont told Hamilton: 'I would take my oath she might have a man killed for her every day and she would only hold up her head the higher on account of it ... There are three or four gentlemen who wear each of them a yard of her tresses by way of bracelet, and nobody cares a pin.'

Sir Peter Lely depicted Lady Shrewsbury as one of his fleshy, sleepy-eyed goddesses, an imperious beauty. Buckingham wrote in his commonplace book: 'Such a woman was made to punish man, and the Devil to punish such a woman ... Sharp-headed kisses that go to wound desire ... Joy would have killed me, but that I could not die upon the lips of my life ... '

Shrewsbury was a Catholic who made her confessions to Buckingham to wound him. He feared she would surrender herself to her confessors: 'I should be afraid that she should not deny the secrets of her body to whom she discovers the secrets of her soul ... Upon the condition of absolving a woman from a thousand old sins 'tis easy to persuade her to commit a new one ... ' She clearly drove him frantic during the first months of their affair: between October 1666 and the following July he was involved in brawls and challenges with five different people, and was three times sent to the Tower. Chapman in *Great Villiers* says 'he changed into a bully and a fire-eater; his restlessness, his excitability turned into a raging fever that drove him from one excess to another.'

Lady Shrewsbury arrived at York with a party that included her husband and 'a great retinue'. Buckingham took a house for them and entertained them 'at vast expense'. Sir John Reresby, who had recently married one of the Countess's ladies, sent his bride away because he felt the Duke's house party was 'no good school for a young wife'. He was right – during the visit Lady Shrewsbury's husband seems to have caught his wife in some compromising situation with Buckingham, and there was 'a great quarrel of jealousy concerning the Duke'. After they had all gone back to London, Buckingham, whose duties kept him at York, got into a drunken quarrel and was challenged. Fortunately, the next morning when he and his opponent turned up with their seconds neither could remember what the quarrel was about, so the fight was abandoned.

As soon as he arrived back in London Buckingham renewed hostilities with Clarendon. He could not attack him directly so instead he quarrelled with Clarendon's ally, the Irish peer Lord Ormonde, by introducing a Bill against the importation of cheap Irish beef. According to Clarendon, during the course of the debate Buckingham 'assumed a liberty of speaking where and what he would, in a dialect unusual and ungrave, his similes and other expressions giving the occasion of much mirth and laughter ... and [said] ... that whoever was against the Bill had either an Irish intellect or an Irish understanding.'

Afterwards Ormonde's furious eldest son, Lord Ossory, challenged Buckingham. It was agreed they should meet within the hour at Chelsea Fields, but before hostilities could begin they were both arrested on the orders of the King. Ossory was sent to the Tower and Buckingham was ordered to apologise to the House. A few days later the elderly Marquess of Dorchester, another ally of Clarendon and Ormonde, jostled Buckingham as they took their places for a conference in the Painted Chamber in the Palace of Westminster. Buckingham pushed Dorchester's elbow aside and asked him in a loud voice if he were uneasy. 'Yes,' replied Dorchester, 'you would not dare do this if we were anywhere else.' 'Yes I would,' said Buckingham, 'I am a better man than you.' 'You lie,' exclaimed Dorchester. The ridiculous confrontation ended with them both being sent briefly to the Tower.

Within days Buckingham assaulted the Marquess of Worcester, grabbing him by the nose at a committee meeting and 'pulling him about'. He was sent back to the Tower, but was soon released. He quarrelled with the war hero Prince Rupert, Charles II's cousin, over the stabling of their horses. After Rupert pulled Buckingham off his horse and challenged him 'in the public street', the King himself had to intervene to end hostilities by pacifying his irate cousin.

One night Buckingham was sitting with Lady Shrewsbury in a box at the theatre when the troublemaker Harry Killigrew, one of her recent lovers and probably still jealous, began making faces at Buckingham and abusing him.[*] At first Buckingham merely told him to behave himself, but when Killigrew struck him on the head with the flat of his sword he jumped from his box and chased him across the theatre, beating him until he cried for mercy.

Killigrew apologised and left for France. He had in any case been banished by the King for spreading rumours about Lady Castlemaine, to the effect that she had revealed her lascivious tendencies at a very early age. But Killigrew had also been telling tales about Lady Shrewsbury, who had thrown him over in favour of Buckingham, and he was probably lucky to escape from the affair with his life. He was ambushed by some bullies and, says Goldsworthy in *The Satyr*, 'his travelling chair was run through by three sword-thrusts, one of which pierced his arm'. Buckingham denied being involved. We get some idea of what the King thought from a letter he wrote to his sister the Duchesse d'Orléans at the French court:

> For Harry Killigrew, you may see him as you please, and though I cannot commend my Lady Shrewsbury's conduct in many things, yet Mr Killigrew's carriage towards her had been worse than I will repeat; and for his démêlé with My Lord Buckingham, he ought not to brag of it, for it was in all sorts most abominable. I am glad the poor wretch has got a means of subsistence, but have one caution

---

[*] Hamilton in the *Memoirs of the Comte de Gramont* says that when he was Shrewsbury's lover, Killigrew used to boast at length about her 'most secret charms and beauties, which more than half the court were as well acquainted with as he was'. Buckingham, who had not yet tried her, was 'assaulted by endless descriptions of Lady Shrewsbury's merits [and] resolved at last to look into the facts himself'. Thus began what Hamilton called one of the longest affairs in England. Killigrew was furious and jealous. 'He directed all his eloquence against her ladyship. He attacked every inch of her with the most bitter invective. He drew a frightful picture of her conduct; and turned into faults all the charms he used to extol.'

of him, that you believe not one word of what he says of us here for he is a most notorious liar and does not want wit to set forth his stories pleasantly enough.

In March 1667 Charles suffered a considerable blow to his ego when the young beauty Frances Stuart, for whom he had been lusting since she became a maid of honour to Queen Catherine at the age of 14, eloped to marry the drunken Duke of Richmond. Charles had been courting her for five years, and he was bitterly upset. He wrote to his sister: 'You may think me ill-natured, but if you consider how hard a thing 'tis to swallow an injury done by a person I had so much tenderness for, you will be in some degree understanding the resentment I use towards her.'

Frances, a distant cousin, had encouraged Charles in public but in private always refused him the final proof of his success. Nevertheless he had always believed she would give in eventually. He told her he hoped to find her one day 'ugly and willing', but she thwarted him in both.

The arrival of Frances Stuart at court in 1662 had been a blow to Lady Castlemaine. The King began to behave like a love-sick adolescent, even writing verses about the young girl. He became so distracted that the Merry Gang formed a Committee for the Getting of Mistress Stuart for the King. It was obvious to all that the King had fallen violently in love with her, so to show she did not fear the young beauty Castlemaine took her into her bed and gave parties for her. At one of these she went through a mock marriage with Frances. Pepys recalled that Castlemaine, who was acting the role of bridegroom, 'rose, and the King came and took her place'. He was not, however, allowed to play the full part of bridegroom.

Anthony Hamilton said of Frances, who had spent some time at the French court, that it would be difficult to imagine 'less brain with more beauty'. He added: 'She was graceful, an accomplished dancer and spoke French better than her native tongue; besides she was polished, and possessed that air of fashion which is always so much run after, and which it is so hard to acquire, except it has been learned in France from very early youth.' At the King's request she posed for the engraver Philippe Roettier and her image as Britannia long adorned the British coinage. Charles particularly admired Frances' legs, which he publicly declared to be the most beautiful in the world. The new French ambassador called on her and, finding her with Charles, begged to see her legs, which she bared to the knees. As Chapman relates in *Great Villiers*, the ambassador 'sank, in silent adoration, on his own'.

In February 1664 Buckingham and the committee who planned to assuage the King's hopeless lust gave a party at which they hoped to get Frances drunk and into bed with Charles, but Castlemaine warned the Queen, who turned up at three o'clock in the morning and took her husband home. Buckingham, however, continued to use his formidable charm on the enigmatic Frances. He was hatching a plan to get Charles to divorce his barren wife and marry the young girl. To this end he advised Frances 'not to marry, except for some great fortune'. What the silly girl made of this can be seen by her eventual choice of husband. In the meantime she was so childish that only simple games and jokes held her attention. She liked playing blind man's buff, music, gossip and mimicry, but above all she liked building castles of cards. Buckingham could sing, write and play music – Pepys thought his music 'the best in the world' – he was an expert and very funny mimic and, of all things, a peerless builder of card castles.

The English court was the hub of a nation, not yet great in international terms but beginning to hum with the ideas and energy that would make her, in the next century, formidable. Yet every night some of the most powerful men at that court would gather by candlelight to entertain this young woman. Candles would be lit in her apartments and some courtiers would play cards, but at the biggest table of all Frances, bejewelled and lovely, surrounded by courtiers including Buckingham, built card castles. Sometimes she would invite young architects to compete with her, but no one could surpass Buckingham, who built higher than anyone. The architects, and even the expert Frances, would be reduced to handing him the cards and watching.

Then Buckingham would sing his own songs in French, English and Italian. There would be some dancing, and then he would do his imitations. Nobody was safe, but a favourite butt was Clarendon, whom Buckingham showed in all his pomposity. He would imitate one of the Chancellor's tedious moral diatribes, and march about carrying a shovel in imitation of Clarendon's mace. He made himself indispensable, and according to Hamilton, if he was not present when one of Frances's parties began she would send 'all over the town' for him.

Once when Buckingham was out of favour one of his rivals, the Earl of Arlington, thought he would try to replace him in Frances' esteem. He began to address her in a learned way, with 'worldly maxims and historical analogies', when to his utter chagrin she began to giggle at him and then to laugh uncontrollably. She had seen Buckingham mimicking the Earl, and she could not help herself. The baffled Earl retreated with another reason to hate Buckingham.

While the King was desperate to get Frances into bed, Lady Castlemaine was desperate to get rid of her. And Frances herself, perhaps surprisingly, wanted to escape. The King had become so importunate she feared she could not keep him at bay much longer, and she said she would marry any man with £1,500 a year. When the twice-widowed Duke of Richmond, a fourth cousin of the King, showed interest she intimated that she was willing. The Duke, who was 27, was an alcoholic and deeply in debt, so she must have been truly desperate.

Lady Castlemaine saw her chance. One evening Frances told the King she felt unwell and wanted to be alone. After he left her apartments the Duke of Richmond entered them. The King went to Lady Castlemaine, who had set the whole thing up. When a messenger gave her a secret sign, she told the King that Frances, far from being unwell, was probably in bed with the Duke. The King returned to Frances's apartments and found this was indeed the case. He was furious. On 3 April 1667 Frances married the Duke of Richmond in secret, and the King announced that he would never see her again, in effect banning her from court.

Buckingham told him that Clarendon was behind his betrayal by Frances Stuart, and remembering all those tiresome lectures about his pleasures, the King was half inclined to believe him. It seemed an opportunity to finally unseat the Chancellor, but at this moment Lady Castlemaine, angry at Buckingham's friendship with Frances, persuaded the King to send him away from court. Buckingham retired to Owthorpe, his Northamptonshire estate, with his wife and Lady Shrewsbury. There he played his violin, wrote songs and dabbled in chemistry.

Back in London, Clarendon contemplated this temporary set-back for his enemy. He was baffled by Buckingham's continued popularity with people from all levels of society. 'It cannot be imagined how great an interest [following] he had in both Houses of Parliament ... He found a respect and concurrence from them of different tempers and talents, and had an incredible opinion with the people.' The haughty statesman could not accept that the great Duke's instincts were genuinely democratic. The common folk liked his friendly manners and were amused by tales of his jokes at the expense of unpopular men like Clarendon himself. Buckingham supported freedom of conscience for noncon-formists such as Levellers, Presbyterians and Anabaptists. There were even fears at court that he would place himself at the head of the religious dissenters, and form a republic.

Buckingham had befriended the former Leveller Major John Wildman, whom he described as the finest statesman in England. Wildman, a lawyer and successful businessman, eventually became Postmaster-General under William III although he remained a republican. He was an enemy to despotism through fifty years, and remained a good friend to Buckingham through all his troubles.

Another Leveller friend, however, betrayed Buckingham. This man, one Braythwaite, was employed by the Duke as his steward. When the King remonstrated with him for hiring such a reprobate, Buckingham insisted that not only was he loyal but he was a remarkable man, whom the King should meet. Charles agreed, and they met at a supper party. Charles seemed interested in Braythwaite's knowledge of popular opinion.

When Buckingham left London Braythwaite sought a private audience with Charles. He accused Buckingham of high treason, saying the Duke had used astrology to forecast the King's death. A warrant was issued for Buckingham's arrest. He fled, whereupon a proclamation was issued forbidding anyone to shelter him from justice. Eventually Buckingham gave himself up, having first sent a message to the Lieutenant of the Tower that he would come to him when he had dined at an inn. He showed himself on the balcony to cheering crowds who had come to applaud the hated Chancellor's enemy, and then surrendered.

The King, who was already missing Buckingham's sparkling company, 'was very impatient to be rid of the business' and wanted him freed immediately, but Clarendon insisted on an investigation. But Buckingham was more than a match for the hostile panel of statesmen who questioned him, and was able to prove that the handwriting on the astrological chart was not his. The King was disgusted with the whole episode. He had quarrelled with Castlemaine, who supported Buckingham, over the affair. She subjected him to one of her semi-hysterical screeching rages. 'You are a fool!' she screamed. 'And if you were not a fool you would not suffer your business to be carried on by fools – and cause your best subjects and those best able to serve you to be imprisoned.' The King called her an interfering whore and jade. He was not a fool, and her days of power were numbered.

But Clarendon's days of power were already over. Within weeks he had his last audience with the King. As he limped away across the Privy Garden one August morning in 1667, tears pouring down his face, Lady Castlemaine, no early riser, ran into her aviary in her dressing gown to see his downfall. Being a Catholic, she crossed herself, believing, says Pepys, that she now had no rival in all the world. Clarendon looked up and saw her. 'Oh, Madam, is it you?' he asked. Reminding her that one day she too would grow old, he passed out of her life for ever.

That night the King told Buckingham that he would grant him anything he wanted. But the Duke asked for nothing, not even the destruction of Clarendon; that was something he would see to himself. He had the great Chancellor stripped of all his offices, and began the process of impeachment. Clarendon fled abroad, never to return. In exile he was to write his classic account of the Civil War and his own times.

Clarendon's fall left Buckingham as the King's principal minister. His enemies, including the King's brother the Duke of York, were for the moment unable to hurt him. At 40 years of age his intellectual powers dazzled the court Wits, that group of young men who included Rochester. He was bound to impress young Rochester, who was tasting the life of hedonistic irreverence to the full for the first time. However, the caprice and instability of the Wits mirrored Buckingham's own, and Lady Shrewsbury added volatility to the mix. At the moment of his greatest triumph the shadows were gathering around Buckingham.

In September 1667 Lady Shrewsbury went to stay in a convent in France. The reason soon became clear – her husband had issued a challenge to Buckingham. Quite why the normally complaisant Earl suddenly decided to take on the Duke, an expert duellist, is not clear. Nor is it clear why it ended as it did.

The King got to know of Shrewsbury's challenge and tried to stop the fight, but the Duke of Albemarle, who was to keep a close guard on Buckingham, misunderstood his instructions. On 21 January 1668 Buckingham and Shrewsbury met in a close at Barn Elms. With Shrewsbury were his seconds, Bernard Howard and Sir John Talbot, while a Mr Jenkins and Sir Robert Holmes acted for the Duke. Most duels at the time were purely gestural, ending when the panting participants decided honour had been served and before any serious damage was done. On this occasion, however, the six began a kind of general mêlée, and after a few minutes Jenkins was in serious difficulties trying to fight off Howard. Buckingham tried to help, but Howard 'ran furiously' upon Jenkins and stabbed him fatally.

Holmes then wounded Talbot in the arm, after which both stopped fighting. This left just Buckingham and Shrewsbury to fight it out. Buckingham had been slightly wounded – not seriously, but perhaps enough to shake him. He ran Shrewsbury through, his sword entering his adversary's right breast and coming out at the shoulder.

A doctor said that although Shrewsbury was gravely hurt he was likely to live. The Earl applied for a pardon for 'accidentally' causing Jenkins's death and for 'all assaults and batteries' on Buckingham and Holmes. This was granted, and at the same time Buckingham was pardoned for the attack on Shrewsbury. But on 16 March Lord Shrewsbury died, and there was an outcry.

It has been pointed out that public shock and disgust would have been even greater if Buckingham had refused the challenge. One reason for the widespread disapproval was the rumour, long believed and repeated by historians as late as the 1930s, that Lady Shrewsbury had been present at the duel, dressed as a page, had held her lover's horse and had slept with him that night, while he still wore a shirt spattered with her husband's blood. In fact she remained in France. It is not difficult, though, to see her hidden hand behind the whole affair: she surely could have stopped it if she had tried.

On Lady Shrewsbury's return to England, Buckingham took her to live with him in the family home, Wallingford House. When his wife protested that it was not for her and 'that other' to live together, he replied: 'Why Madam, I did think so, and have therefore ordered your coach to be ready to carry you to your father's.'

To Buckingham's annoyance Lady Shrewsbury put on a show of mourning for her dead husband. He wrote in his commonplace book: 'She weeps and beats herself; aye, she had need strike the rock to get water out of it.' And as she burst into tears he burst into verse:

> Disciplined tears which still in ambush lay
> Expecting but the word to march away

Men had not stopped dying for Lady Shrewsbury. Harry Killigrew returned from exile in France claiming that he had slept with her and any man could have her for the asking. One day as he left his house at Turnham Green he was attacked and left for dead with nine wounds by a gang of thugs; his servant was killed. Lady Shrewsbury watched, sitting nearby in a coach and six.

Buckingham was forced to defend her before the King, his brother the Duke of York and other gentlemen. 'They did not mean to hurt but to beat him,' he explained, 'and he did run first at them with his sword.' Both he and his mistress escaped unpunished from these scandals.

But Buckingham was always in danger of overplaying his hand. His absurd suggestion of kidnapping the Queen and sending her off to the plantations, to be kept in comfort but seen in London no more, so that the King could get a divorce, did not amuse Charles. Nor did the Duke's plan to raise revenue by pillaging the Church. And despite his huge fortune Buckingham was living far beyond his means. Of his income of £19,600 (around £2,000,000 today) a year, he had to spend more than £15,000 in wages, taxes and interest. When Charles gave him some pensions to ease his money troubles he characteristically began making plans to entertain 60 French noblemen who visited England in May 1671. He also began building the magnificent house at Cliveden for Lady Shrewsbury. Long before it was finished, their love had died.

In January 1674 Buckingham's enemies combined against him and he was dismissed from his great offices. He had appeared before the Commons to answer criticisms of his administration, and blamed those in authority over him. Clearly referring to the King and the Duke of York, he said: 'I can hunt the hare with a pack of hounds, but not with a brace of lobsters.' This extraordinary and peculiar image was remembered long after other witticisms of the Stuart court were forgotten. This time Charles could not forgive him.

Anna Shrewsbury too clearly had no further use for him. They parted, almost certainly at her wish. Two years later she married a Mr Rodney Bridges, and was again received at court. 'Alone, hated by all and hating all the rest', as Burnet described him, Buckingham went from woman to woman, not women of his own class but actresses or whores. He wrote in his commonplace book under the heading 'Fickleness': 'One mistress is too much, so that it is to be feared he will come to love none ... to love but one is the monastic life of love, and may justly be expected of sloth.'

His cynical attitude to these contacts is also recorded. 'I thought we had loved one another', he remarks of one hired lover, 'but I see we are both rivals in the love of my money. I promise you, you shall not exceed me in that passion.' He says of another: 'She goes purring up and down like a stroked cat ... Her beauty is like a mountebank's medicine, the price of it falls every day ...Wenches are like fruits, only dear at their first coming in. Their price falls apace afterwards.'

Yet when his love for Anna Shrewsbury was at its high tide he had written:

<blockquote>
What a dull fool was I<br>
To think so gross a lie<br>
As that I ever was in love before.<br>
I have, perhaps, known one or two<br>
With whom I was content to be<br>
At that, which they call 'Keeping company'.<br>
But, after all that they could do,<br>
I still could be with more.<br>
Their absence never made me shed a tear;<br>
And I can truly swear,<br>
That till my eyes first gazed on you,<br>
I ne'er beheld the thing I could adore.
</blockquote>

With his disreputable new companions he let himself go, in appearance and habits. Nell Gwynn, his friend to the last, tried to get him to smarten himself up. Through a mutual friend she pleaded with him 'to buy new shoes, that he might not dirty her rooms, and a new periwig that she might not smell him stink two storeys high when he knocks at the outward door'. Henry Savile said that Buckingham was 'out at heels and stunk most grievously'.

The truth was that he was spending more and more time with whores and toss-pots. The once most splendid and wealthy gentleman in England was becoming a broken-down country squire. He was weighed down with debt, it was believed his

CAROLVS II . *Magnæ Britanniæ, Franciæ et Hiberniæ* REX.
Regalis Societatis FUNDATOR et Patronus.

Merry monarch: Charles II was 'addicted to sexual indulgence'. We know the names of thirteen of his mistresses, but there were many one-night stands with actresses and whores and so innumerable royal bastards, five of whom were created dukes.

Above: The female rake: Lady Castlemaine, Charles II's greedy mistress. Her many lovers included the warrior Duke of Marlborough and the rope-dancer Jacob Hall, a man of magnificent physique capable of amazing sexual contortions.

Left: Pretty witty Nell: Charles II's long-time mistress Nell Gwynn, the little Cockney whose drolleries beguiled the king's tedious hours at court. She was the most faithful and least political of his mistresses.

The Catholic whore: Louise de Kéroualle, Charles II's French mistress, was rap-acious and haughty and widely disliked. She would threaten suicide to get her way with the king. Rochester satirised her as Clithoris in *Sodom*.

Below: Wicked wit: the dazzling and doomed Earl of Rochester. His short life was a chaos of drink, sex and brawls. Some of his verse was so obscene that for many years it was not published. He also wrote touching lyrics.

The peerless duke: George Villiers, Duke of Buckingham, was described by Louis XIV as the only true English gentleman he had met. Buckingham had wit, charm and matchless grace – but was known for squalid debauches with his friend Rochester.

Below: Rape-master: the amazing Francis Charteris in the dock, on trial for the rape of his servant Anne Bond. His career of infamy was without parallel even among rakes.

COLONEL FRANCISCO.

The trap: the procuress and bawd Mother Needham picks up a young girl fresh from the country in Plate 1 of Hogarth's *A Harlot's Progress*. Watching from the doorway is the notorious Colonel Charteris, one of her best customers.

Below: Hell-raiser: Sir Francis Dashwood, founder and presiding spirit of the Hell-Fire Club. Horace Walpole said of his sex drive that he had 'the staying power of a stallion and the impetuosity of a bull'.

*His Grace Philip Duke of Wharton*

King of clubs: Philip, Earl of Wharton, who presided over an early version of the Hell-Fire Club. His life of dissipation and support for lost causes was a template for later hell-raisers, including the Whig leader Charles James Fox.

That Devil Wilkes: The most important member of the Hell-Fire Club politically was John Wilkes, darling of the mob and champion of liberty. His love of libertinism was probably stronger, and he enthusiastically joined in the sexual cavortings.

Below: Sex and Satanism: The Earl of Sandwich, one of the most debauched members of the Hell-Fire Club. He was described as 'mischievous as a monkey and lecherous as a goat'. He was also an important statesman with a passion for hard work, and patron of the arts.

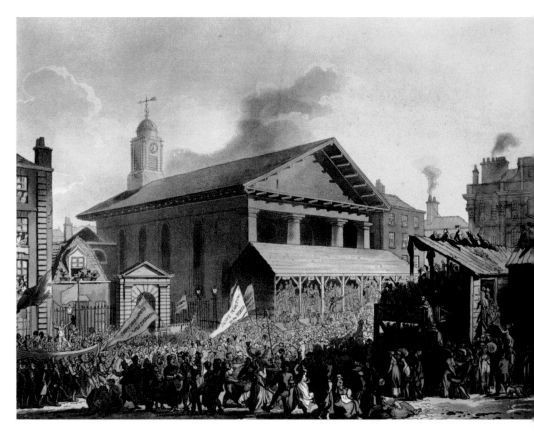

Garden of delights: an election meeting in Covent Garden in the eighteenth century. The throng of perambulating harlotry was so dense that the magistrate Sir John Fielding speculated that all the whores in the country gathered there.

income had shrunk to £6,000 a year and according to Chapman in *Great Villiers*, he had to borrow from his trustees for current expenses. Yet he continued to loom large in the complicated and dangerous politics of the time, was in and out of the Tower and in and out of Charles's favour.

The King could not do without his company for long, as Buckingham retained his wit and charm, but the Duke of York was a formidable enemy. After Charles died in 1685, Buckingham had no future at court. He attended the Duke's coronation as James II, wearing his Garter robes and carrying a coronet in the coronation procession. He walked alone, preceded by eight duchesses, including his wife, his cousin Barbara Castlemaine and Frances Stuart, and followed by Clarencieux and Norroy Kings-of-Arms, the Lord President of the Council, the Lord Privy Seal and a number of other high dignitaries. A drawing of the procession shows one of the duchesses, tall enough to be Frances or Barbara, looking back at him over her shoulder, as though he was already fading into the past.

He later had a private interview with James, and the King claimed that this noted atheist and republican had taken the sacrament with him 'after the Roman'. James was capable of putting all differences, even hatred, aside if he thought there was a chance of a conversion to Catholicism. And Buckingham was equally capable of letting the King make himself ridiculous.

Buckingham retired to Yorkshire, offering the King a farewell gift. James had expressed a wish to buy some of his deer, and through a friend the Duke replied: 'I cannot bring down my mind low enough to think of selling red deer, but if you believe his Majesty would take it kindly of me, I will present him with ten brace of the best that I have.'

Though most of his great estates were gone, he still had his father-in-law's riverside house in York and Helmsley Castle, once one of the mightiest strongholds in the country but now a great ruin with just a few intact rooms. In these the Duke made his home, passing his days hunting or in the laboratory he set up at the castle, where he tried to turn dross into gold. At night, whatever regrets he had were turned into another kind of gold, in his commonplace book: 'Methinks thy body is not a prison, but rather a tavern or bawdy house to thy soul.'

On 14 April 1687 his horse dropped dead beneath him during a hard day's hunting. The Duke then helped to dig out a fox. Afterwards, hot and exhausted, he sank down on the wet grass where he waited several hours for his groom to arrive with a fresh mount. Soon he was too ill to make it back to Helmsley, and was taken to one of his tenants' houses at the little town of Kirkby Moorside. It was clear to everyone, although not to Buckingham himself, that he was dying. His cousin Lord Arran, called to the bedside, tried to get Buckingham to see a clergyman. He suggested a Jesuit priest, thinking perhaps that Buckingham shared the royal religion, and the Duke angrily refused. He also refused to see a Presbyterian: 'those fellows always made me sick, with their whine and cant.' Eventually, exhausted, he agreed to see the local parson. When the cleric asked him what his religion was he gasped: 'It is an insignificant question.' He added: 'I have been a shame and disgrace to all religions – but if you can do me any good, do.' He died later that day.

Later, on 21 June, after a magnificent funeral paid for by James II, the Duke's body was laid in the family vault at Westminster Abbey, next to the father he had never known, his brother, and his bastard infant son by Anna Shrewsbury. There was no monument or effigy, but he had in effect written one in the commonplace book:

Fortune filled him too full, and he run over.

# Part 2

## Charteris, the

## Rape-Master General

# *Prelude*

IN MARCH 1712 FIVE 'PEERS AND PERSONS of quality' were involved in a scuffle in a tavern in the Strand. When, during the incident, the landlady was killed, 'The gentlemen laughed and ordered that she should be added to their bill.' This was just one manifestation of a sudden eruption of upper-class thuggery that afflicted the capital by night for several months. The streets of central London were suddenly full of such bullies, attacking inno-cent men and women in the streets, raping, slitting noses, cutting off ears and rolling people downhill in barrels. Swift referred to them as 'a race of rakes', while in *A History of Crime in England* the writer L. O. Pike described the antics of 'the roisterers who made night hideous in the eighteenth century. The "Mohocks", the "Nickers", the "Tumblers", the "Dancing Masters" and the various bully-captains . . . If they met an unprotected woman, they showed they had no sense of decency; if they met a man who was unarmed or weaker than themselves they assaulted and, perhaps, killed him.'

The Sweaters would surround a victim and prick his buttocks with swords as he tried to flee. The Bold Bucks specialised in rape; if they could not find victims in the streets they would enter houses and drag out screaming women, having first drunk so much that, in the words of Christopher Hibbert's *The Roots of Evil*, 'they were quite beyond the possibility of attending to any notions of reason or humanity'. Other groups called themselves the Scowrers, the Hectors and the Muns. The playwright Thomas

Shadwell portrayed the gangs in *The Scowrers*. The play makes fun of the Scowrers, suggesting that they at least were just high-spirited rowdies. They drank swingeingly at night and were plaguey qualmish the following morning. They boasted of the brave old days:

> Puh, this is nothing, why I knew the Hectors, and before them the Muns and the Tityre Tu's, they were brave fellows indeed: In those days a man could not go from the Rose Tavern [in Covent Garden] to the Piazza once, but he must venture his life twice.
>
> Bluster: If ever there was such a scowring in High Holborn since 'twas built, may I never taste Nants-Brandy more at midnight!
>
> Dingboy: The Nation will ring of us; such Exploits! such achievements! Not a window left in all the Inns of Chancery!
>
> Whachum: Then how we scowred the Market people, over-threw the butterwomen, defeated the Pippin-Merchants, wiped out the Milk-Scores, pulled off the Door-Knockers, Daubed the gilt Signs!
>
> Dingboy: But a pox on't, we were most confoundedly beaten by the Hellish Constable and his posse of Scoundrel Dogs.

The last and worst of these rakish gangs were the Mohocks. In 1710 four North American Iroquois chiefs visited London, among them the 'emperor' of the Mohawks, or Mohocks. Soon Richard Steele was reporting in the *Spectator* that 'a nocturnal fraternity with the title of the Mohock Club' were making trouble. They were led by an emperor of their own, a man with a Turkish crescent tattooed on his forehead. They would drink in a tavern and then surge out into the streets to stab and gouge out eyes. They would overturn coaches on to dungheaps, or force the Watch, the police, to retreat in pitched battles. In March 1712 Jonathan Swift wrote in one of the letters later published as the *Journal to Stella* that they had threatened him. 'Our Mohocks go on still, and cut people's faces every night, but they shan't cut mine.' John Gay wrote in his poem 'Trivia':

> Now is the time that rakes their revels keep;
> Kindlers of riot, enemies of sleep ...
> Who has not heard the Scowerer's midnight fame?
> Who has not trembled at the Mohock's name?
> Was there a watchman took his hourly rounds
> Safe from their blows, or new-invented wounds?
> I pass their desperate deeds, and mischiefs done
> Where from Snow Hill black steepy torrents run;
> How matrons hoop'd within the hogshead's womb
> Were tumbled furious then, the rolling tomb
> O'er the stones thunders, bounds from side to side ...

On 8 April 1712 the *Spectator* published a manifesto purporting to be from the Mohock emperor himself. He said, tongue in cheek, that their aim was to cleanse the streets of people of 'loose and dissolute lives'. Interestingly, in view of what was to come, the emperor named 'the Devil Tavern' as their headquarters. In June 1712 twenty Mohocks attacked a watchman named John Bouch in Essex Street, threatening to nail him up in his guard box and trundle him away. According to the subsequent trial at the Old Bailey, he arrested three of the ringleaders and drove the rest off with his sword. The prisoners were fined three shillings and fourpence apiece.

For whatever reason, this was the end of the Mohocks, who simply disappeared. Their emperor was believed to have married a wealthy woman and settled down. After that the friskier members of the upper classes formed themselves into clubs, out of which evolved the blasphemous hell-fire clubs.

But curbing the excesses of rich and powerful men, at a time when the upper classes both made the laws and frequently flouted them, proved almost impossible. This can be seen in the aftermath of the incident in which a landlady was killed in the Strand. Queen Anne had attempted to bring the 'peers and men of quality' involved in her murder to justice. She ordered an inquiry and the High Constable who had released the five from custody was sacked.

At a subsequent trial the five men were all acquitted. The Queen then offered a reward of £100 for information about people causing 'great and unusual riots and barbarities', but the outrages continued. Just as King Charles forgave his high-spirited young courtiers time and again for what amounted to criminal behaviour, there was still in the early eighteenth century an unwritten code that allowed upper-class young men considerable freedom to sow wild oats. And the very wealthy could bribe their way out of almost any scrape.

Moreover, women servants were regarded as legitimate objects of sexual exploitation for their masters, a *droit de seigneur*. As Roy Porter and Leslie Hall explain in *The Facts of Life*, 'Maidservants were fair game for male advances: rakes were not the worse thought of so long as they made arrangements for any resulting bastards.' It is against this background of upper-class rowdyism and relative impunity that we should see the career of our next rake, the extraordinary Francis Charteris.

# Colonel Charteris:

## Every Human Vice

COLONEL FRANCIS CHARTERIS, RAPIST, murderer, gambling cheat, usurer and fraudster, enjoyed if not a kind of impunity, then a remarkable knack of avoiding the full consequences of his actions. Yet Charteris was an almost unique figure, hated by the common people for abusing their daughters, and despised by the moral majority of the upper classes who felt that he was giving them a bad name. He was demonised in a flood of pamphlets, some of them blatantly political, such as the ironical *The History of Colonel Francis Ch–rtr–s: The Birth, Parentage, Education, Rise, Progress, and most memorable Exploits of that Great Man, down to his present Catastrophe in Newgate*. In it he was depicted as slandered by 'a pack of Scribblers, who write themselves into a Dinner at any Cost, without regard to Truth or even Common Decency'. This, says Jenny Uglow in *Hogarth*, was partly a reference to attacks on his friend Sir Robert Walpole, the Whig Prime Minister. Charteris's crimes were many and spectacular. A wealthy man with an enormous appetite for sex, on which he spent as little as possible, Charteris was sly, insinuating, greedy, cunning and utterly heartless. His sex drive, a kind a satyriasis, seems to have given him little peace.

He made a fortune from South Sea stock and from cheating at

cards and usury, and had great estates in Lancashire and Scotland. He boasted of seducing more than a hundred women, although rape would be more accurate in many cases. The pamphlet *Some Authentic Memoirs of the Life of Colonel C——s, Rape-Master of Great Britain* (1730) says he sent out servants to find 'none but such as were strong, lusty and fresh Country Wenches, of the first size, their B–tt–cks as hard as Cheshire Cheeses, that could make a Dint in a Wooden Chair, and work like a parish Engine at a Conflagration.' He owned brothels, and turned his house into one. He was accused of rape, using loaded dice, fraud, bearing false witness, denying his bastard children and, not least, being an associate of Walpole. He used his army rank, although he had been cashiered. His aristocratic connections got him out of several scrapes, as when he drew his sword on a constable in St James's Park, and when he raped a young virgin in the Scotch Ale-House in Pall Mall. He had to pay maintenance for the bastard child born to the girl. He was tried for rape at least twice, and sentenced to death once. According to Burford in *Royal St James's*, a Scots woman giving evidence against him said: 'This is the huge raw beast that ... got me with Bairn ... I know him by his nastie Legg for he has wrapt it round my Arse mony a guid time!'

He was reputed to have been the first lover of the noted courtesan Sally Salisbury, when she was little more than a child. Charteris is shown in Plate 1 of Hogarth's print series *A Harlot's Progress*. A sweet young country girl newly arrived in town is propositioned by a bawd, easily recognised by contemporaries as the notorious Mother Needham. At the time Hogarth made the print, about 1730, he described her as 'the handsome old Procuress ... well-dressed in silk and simpering beneath the patches on her face'. The colonel lurks in a nearby doorway watching the progress of this negotiation with his cringing servant Jack Gourlay, who acted as one of his panders.

Charteris was born in Edinburgh in about 1660 into a family of gentry with aristocratic connections. Nothing is known of his education. He is next heard of in Marlborough's army in Flanders, which he left under a cloud. There was an unlikely story that he stole meat from a butcher's at Bruges. His father then bought him a commission in a regiment of foot guards, but the officers refused to serve with him, and he returned to Edinburgh. His father tried again to get rid of his 'wicked Frank' by buying him a second commission when another regiment was raised in Scotland, and Charteris seems to have been abroad at the time of the Peace of Ryswick in 1697. He returned an accomplished gambler, the foundation, along with usury, of his vast fortune. 'Being a most expert gambler, and of a disposition uncommonly avaricious, he made his knowledge of gambling subservient to his love of money; and while the army was in winter quarters he stripped many of the officers of all their property by his skill at cards and dice,' says *The Newgate Calendar*, a record of criminal trials. 'He was, however, as knavish as dexterous; for when he had defrauded a brother officer of his money, he would lend him a sum at the moderate interest of an hundred per cent, and take an assignment of his commission as a security for the payment of the debt.' (Commissions were frequently bought and sold for high prices.)

Two noble young officers, John, Duke of Argyll and John, Earl of Stair, alarmed by the way Charteris was fleecing their friends, complained to their commanding officer. He reported to Marlborough, whose passion for women and money was almost as great as that of Charteris. Nevertheless the rogue officer was court-martialled, ordered to pay back his victims and stripped of his commission. His epaulettes were torn off and his sword broken in ritual humiliation. He does not seem to have been charged with another offence, which would also have merited a court martial. In August 1704 a newsletter printed the following item: 'One Charteris, an officer in the Horse Guards, is suspended by the Duke of Argyll, captain of the said troop, for having the impudence to place himself at the commander's table, and when he was turned out, to draw [his sword] upon the gentleman that was commanded to do it.'

Having been cashiered and forced to repay his victims, Charteris went to Malines, in Belgium. Short of money, one night he went into a field and hid his breeches. With his cloak carefully buttoned about him 'to hide the absence of his nether garments', he went to an inn. *The Newgate Calendar* says that he took a room for the night:

> Early in the morning he rang the bell violently, and, the landlord coming terrified into his room, he swore furiously that he had been robbed of his breeches, containing a diamond ring, a gold watch, and money to a considerable amount; and, having previously broken the window, he intimated that some person must have entered that way, and carried off his property; and he even insinuated that the landlord himself might have been the robber.
>
> It was in vain that the innkeeper solicited mercy in the most humiliating posture. Charteris threatened that he should be sent to Brussels, and suffer death, as an accessory to the felony. Terrified at the thought of approaching disgrace and danger, the landlord of the house sent for some friars of an adjacent convent, to whom he represented his calamitous situation, and they generously supplied him with a sum sufficient to reimburse Charteris for the loss he pretended to have sustained.

It is a measure of male tolerance at the time that not only was Charteris not ostracised, he was allowed to enlist again in the army, and soon had the rank of colonel in a cavalry regiment, in effect becoming an officer and a gentleman. His father died, leaving him a fortune, and he became laird of the family estates at Amisfield in Dumfries and Galloway. He married the daughter of Sir Alexander Swinton, afterwards Lord Mersington, a member of the College of Justice at Edinburgh. A contemporary said of her that she had 'scarce met with any other comfort since her marriage than that of universal commiseration'. They had a daughter, Janet, who married the Earl of Wemyss in 1720; their alliance was to pay off for Charteris when he later stood trial for the rape of a servant named Anne Bond.

One night after he was married he stayed at an inn in Lancaster where he fancied a beautiful young servant girl. At first she indignantly refused his gold, but she was eventually worn down by his experienced persistence and left his room a guinea richer. In the morning Charteris told the landlord that he had given the girl a guinea to change into silver for him, and she had not yet returned him the money. The girl was called, and had to produce the guinea. Charteris pocketed it, then told the landlord what had really happened. The girl was dismissed. The story got out and many people in Lancaster never forgot. Years later, when Charteris was a candidate for a parliamentary seat in the town, he found it almost impossible to find a room at any inn. He lost the election.

His skill at gambling was making him another fortune, although it was assisted by sharp practice. *The Newgate Calendar* tells how he once cheated the Duchess of Queensberry:

> The Duke of Queensberry was at this time commissioner to the Parliament of Scotland, which was assembled at Edinburgh, to deliberate on the proposed union with England. Charteris having been invited to a party at cards with the Duchess of Queensberry, he contrived that her Grace should be placed in such a manner, near a large glass, that he could see all her cards; and he won three thousand pounds [about £350,000 today] of her in consequence of this stratagem. One good, however, resulted from this circumstance: the Duke of Queensberry, incensed at the imposition, brought a bill into the House to prohibit gaming for above a certain sum; and this bill passed into a law.
>
> Our adventurer continued his depredations on the thoughtless till he had acquired considerable sums. When he had stripped young men of their ready cash at the gaming-tables, it was his practice, as before, to lend them money at an extravagant interest, for which he took their bonds to confess judgment, and the moment the bonds became due he failed not to take every legal advantage.
>
> By a continued rapacity of this kind he acquired several considerable estates in Scotland, and then removed to London, which, as it was the seat of greater dissipation, was a place better adapted to the exertion of his abilities.
>
> He now became a great lender of money on mortgages, always

receiving a large premium, by which at length he became so rich as to purchase several estates in England, particularly in the county of Lancaster.

In 1711 Charteris was found guilty of taking bribes from civilians to allow them to join the army briefly as a way of escaping prosecution for various offences. He was cashiered, arrested, taken to London and committed to custody of the Sergeant-at-Arms of the House of Commons. He had to kneel before the Bar of the House to receive a severe reprimand from the Speaker. The case generated a small literature. He was of course stripped of his command, for the last time. Queen Anne wrote to the Earl of Oxford in November 1711: 'I will take care Lord James Murray shall have Charteris's company in the Guards.' From then on Charteris had no right to style himself colonel.

Charteris later raped a miller's wife in Scotland at gunpoint, fled south and was found guilty in absentia. Some years afterwards, in 1721, finding it inconvenient to be unable to visit his Scottish estates, he petitioned King George I for a pardon. It was granted. *Fog's Weekly Journal* reported: 'We hear a certain Scotch Colonel is charged with a Rape, a misfortune he has been very liable to, but for which he has obtained a *Nolle Prosequi*. It is reported now that he brags that he will solicit for a Patent for ravishing whomever he pleases, in order to put a stop to vexatious suits which may interrupt him in his pleasures hereafter.' It is not clear that the pardon was for ravishing the miller's wife, and Charteris was so prolific a rapist it could well have been some other woman.

It is hard not to make Charteris seem like a comic-strip character of awfulness. If he had a saving virtue perhaps it was courage. He is said to have been in command of a royal regiment when the Jacobites took Preston in 1715, and to have taken part in the fighting. This may account for the King's pardon. However, according to another version of this story he offered his services to both sides before the battle, and was turned down by both because of his reputation. After the rebellion had been suppressed he claimed that 30 of his horses had been stolen by the Jacobites.

He is said to have been compensated with horses captured from the enemy.

Charteris became the lover of Sally Salisbury (1690–1724), the most famous courtesan of early eighteenth-century London, when she was barely into her teens. Sally was the first working-class 'Toast of the Town', or celebrity whore. She was wild, witty, beautiful, foul-mouthed and irresistible. By the age of 14 she had been seduced, poxed, cured, and, with the help of the famous bawd Mother Wisebourne, re-virginised. An early friend was the actress Elizabeth Barry, Rochester's protégée, who dropped Sally because of her rough manners and unpredictable temper.

Her wit and panache nevertheless made Sally a great favourite. At a grand society ball the hostess commented on the splendour of her jewels. As Walker relates in *Sally Salisbury*, the waspish whore replied:

'They had need be finer than yours, my Lady. You have but one Lord to keep you, and to buy you jewels, but I have at least half a score, of which number, Madam, your Ladyship's husband is not the most inconsiderable.'

'Nay, my Lady,' cried another guest. 'You had better let Mrs Salisbury alone, for she'll lay claim to all our husbands else, by and by.'

'Not much to yours, indeed, Madam,' replied Sally tartly. 'I tried him once and am resolved I'll never try him again; for I was forced to kick him out of bed, because his — is good for nothing at all.'

Charteris abandoned Sally in Bath – her wild madcap behaviour always made her too hot to handle – and she went back to work for Wisebourne, proprietor of a high-class brothel in Covent Garden. At some stage Charteris was again her lover, and she got him involved in a duel, in which he crippled a man. Although he had 'very frequent satisfaction of Sally, in a house of pleasure, for the damage sustained', Charteris felt that this pleasure was too dearly bought, and kicked Sally out for the last time.

Lady Mary Wortley Montagu[*] described in a letter the incident that led to Sally's death:

> The freshest news in Town is the fatal accident happened three Nights ago to a very pritty young Fellow, brother to Lord Finch, who was drinking with a dearly beloved Drab whom you may have heard of by the name of Sally Salisbury. In a jealous Pique she stabbed him to the Heart with a Knife. He fell down dead immediately but a surgeon being called and the Knife being drawn out of his Body, he opened his Eyes and his first Words were to ask her to be Friends with him, and he kissed her.

Finch, the son of the Countess of Winchilsea, forgave Sally, but his family insisted on prosecuting her. At the trial Sally claimed she had acted not from malice but from sudden passion, having discovered that Finch had given her sister a ticket to the opera. She suspected that he wanted to seduce her sister. Sally was found not guilty of attempted murder but guilty of assault and wounding. She was sentenced to a year in Newgate and fined £100. In spite of Finch's pleas she remained there, where she caught jail fever and wasted away. Here is how the Swiss commentator, César de Saussure, described her death:

> You will suppose her lovers abandoned her in her distress. They did

---

[*] Lady Mary Wortley Montagu (1689–1762), bluestocking, author, traveller and feminist, was the eldest daughter of the Duke of Kingston. Having rebelled against an arranged marriage and eloped with a Whig MP, she later wrote about her time in Turkey, where her husband was ambassador. She was renowned for her witty conversation and had a number of affairs. She introduced smallpox vaccination to England, although the disease had ruined her looks. Horace Walpole left a spiteful picture of her on a visit to Florence in September 1740:

Did I tell you Lady Mary Wortley is here? She laughs at My Lady Walpole, scolds My Lady Pomfret, and is laughed at by the whole town. Her dress, her avarice and her impudence must amaze any one that never heard her name. She wears a foul mob [cap] that does not cover her greasy black locks, that hang loose, never combed or curled ... Her face is swelled on one side with a [pox], partly covered with a plaister, and partly with white paint, which for cheapness she has bought so coarse, that you would not use it to wash a chimney ...

no such thing, but crowded into the prison, presenting her with every comfort and luxury possible. As soon as the wounded man – who, by the way, belongs to one of the best-known English families – was sufficiently recovered, he asked for her discharge, but Sally Salisbury died of brain fever, brought on by debauch, before she was able to leave the prison.

Sally was buried at St Andrew's, Holborn in February 1724. Her coffin was followed by four coaches, and six gentlemen bore it to the church. She was 32. John Cleland's *Fanny Hill* owes much to her life and legend, and she is another inspiration for Hogarth's print series *A Harlot's Progress*. It is not recorded whether Charteris was at her funeral.

After Charteris had been cashiered, reprimanded by Parliament and barred from all public employment he devoted himself wholly to his two passions, sex and money making. The South Sea Bubble, a financial crisis arising from corrupt mismanagement of the South Sea Company, had created a mania for stock market speculation.* In such an atmosphere Charteris flourished. He was known to be a heavy speculator in South Sea stock but unlike so many other speculators, he sold out some of his stock at the right time and kept the rest until the position stabilised.

---

\* The South Sea Bill, introduced in the Commons in April 1720, proposed that the company should take over a large part of the national debt in exchange for annual interest of 5 per cent and a monopoly of trade with the Pacific Islands and the West Indies. War with Spain meant there was almost no trade; nevertheless the stock was quoted at an inflated value. Large amounts of stock were given 'on credit' to MPs, ministers and members of the royal family. By the time the Bill became law in May the price had quadrupled, but the whole of the £2,000,000 raised in subscriptions had been handed over as bribes to politicians and brokers. There were no trading profits to provide dividends and by August the value of the stock was slipping inexorably.

Before the crash, however, £100 worth of stock reached £745, and some investors made large fortunes. The London bookseller Thomas Guy sold his huge holding in stages as the market rose; he made the immense fortune of £234,000, the largest of any speculator, using part of it to build Guy's Hospital. Not so lucky was the scientist Sir Isaac Newton, who sold £7,000 of stock in April and made a profit of 100 per cent. He went back into the stock and lost £20,000. 'I can calculate the motions of the heavenly bodies,' he is quoted as saying, 'but not the madness of people.'

Chancellor, in *The Lives of the Rakes*, says that Charteris also made money by seducing respectable women and then black-mailing them. He tells the story of 'a charming young widow who lived with her father and her own considerable family in Marylebone'. Charteris seduced her, took all her money and jewels and so terrified her that she went mad and died in an asylum.

For his most daring swindle Charteris chose as victim Francis Child, founder of one of the earliest banks in London and a future knight and Lord Mayor of London. In 1727 Charteris, who had an account at Child's bank in Fleet Street, wrote to him from Aix, where he had gone for his health, saying he intended to withdraw £5,000. When a stranger arrived at the bank bearing a bill for that amount, apparently from Charteris, Child paid out. Some time later Charteris arrived at the bank and asked to see his account. He demanded to know what had happened to the £5,000, claiming that he had changed his mind about withdrawing it. When Child told him about the mysterious stranger, Charteris said he knew nothing about him. Child had to pay up. To give some kind of credibility to his story – although everyone guessed the truth – he placed an item in the *Brussels Gazette* of 29 December 1727 saying:

> Colonel Charteris, who has been so fortunate in his time that he is said to have won Ten Thousand Sterling a year, was cured of the dropsy some months ago by a monk, and returned to England; but is come over again in search of one that lived with him whom he accuses of stealing a Bill of Exchange, to the amount of some thousands of pounds … which the Colonel knew nothing of till he went to the Bankers to receive his money, and found that the true bill had already been paid to some other person.

The anonymous author of the *Authentick Memoirs of the Life of Colonel Ch——s*, published in 1730 while Charteris was still alive, tells us about his house at Hornby in Lancashire. A kind of seraglio, it was kept by an elderly woman named Mary Clapham and supplied with likely girls by, among others, Jack Gourlay. Some were girls enticed to the house by the offer of jobs in domestic service. They were routinely raped, with the help of Gourlay and Clapham. However, things didn't always go Charteris's way. Chancellor tells us in *The Lives of the English Rakes* of one girl who had the courage to fight back, although he does not give her name or the date of the incident. It is not clear whether Charteris spotted the girl first, or was told about her by Gourlay. He decided to offer her a job as a maid-servant, a ploy which had worked successfully in the past. He heard that the girl was determined to work only as a lady's maid, so he disguised himself as a woman. He sent for the girl and when she called at his house, Hornby Lodge, Charteris was waiting in bed in the guise of 'a maiden lady of irreproachable character'. When they were alone 'Charteris flung off his disguise and springing from the bed made such unequivocal proposals as to leave no doubt of his intentions.' The girl screamed and put up such a fight that Charteris drew a pistol and threatened to shoot her. This somewhat B-movie scenario gains from being described in Chancellor's penny-dreadful style:

> At last, affecting to be overcome by fear, she agreed to comply with his desires if he would only put down the firearm and treat her kindly. Indeed she acted so well, or Charteris's passion got so much the better of his discretion, that he did as she suggested, and laying down the pistol came towards the young lady. In a moment however she eluded him, and seizing the pistol pointed it at him and swore she would kill him if she was not permitted to leave the house there and then. For once Charteris was hoist with his own petard and could do nothing but fume and swear – and agree. The girl thereupon rang the bell and when Gourlay, or whoever the man was who answered it, appeared, she swore she would shoot him unless he went before her downstairs and let her out. It is satisfactory to know that the girl escaped safe and sound from Hornby Lodge, leaving its master in a state of ungovernable fury and disappointed desire.

On another occasion he spotted an attractive servant girl at Epsom and engaged her as an upper servant for his London house in

George Street. Not long after she arrived Charteris raped her. When her father heard what had happened he rushed to London and applied to a magistrate for a warrant against Charteris. He was arrested and escaped a prison sentence only by paying large bribes, said by Chancellor to total £600.

Over the years, Charteris's attacks on unwilling young women cost him dear when husbands and fathers had the sense and courage to bring lawsuits against the great man. One of these cost him £800 in bribes to court officials. A cheaper escapade involved 'a tall and attractive young woman' (Chancellor, *The Lives of the Rakes*) whom he saw carrying a bundle of old clothes in a street near his London home. He stopped his carriage and told his servant to pretend he had some cast-off clothes to sell. The servant arranged to meet her at the Scotch Arms ale-house in Pall Mall. While he kept her talking in a private room there Charteris entered and attacked the girl. Her screams brought the landlord rushing in. He found the distressed woman with Charteris, sword drawn, standing over her. The furious fornicator had to pay her husband 20 guineas to get out of this scrape.

Others took their revenge in different ways. Charteris was told of a pretty but pious milliner who kept a shop in Westminster. He went to the shop, bought some small items and quoted some Bible texts to the girl. Eventually she agreed to accompany him to a Nonconformist assembly. Charteris whispered to the coachman the address of a brothel in Golden Square, and when he got her there the girl collapsed in a fit of hysterics and fainted. In reviving her with brandy he seduced her, and then spent the night with her. When he dismissed her the following morning, saying he had 'no further use for her', the girl replied, 'I can quite believe it,' and went demurely on her way. Some days later, as James Boswell said in his diaries about one of his own encounters, 'too, too obvious was Signor Gonorrhoea'.

Some of his victims were willing. Once when he was travelling from London to his Scottish estates he was taken ill at York, and a clergyman who had not heard of his fearsome reputation invited him to his home to recuperate. Within days one of the parson's

Charteris used his home in George Street to lure and rape young women looking for work as domestic servants.

daughters had become infatuated with Charteris, and hired a room in the city where they could be together. Some children playing in the house next door accidentally set fire to the building and Charteris and his young lover were forced to jump from the window on to mattresses spread on the street below. York was soon agog with the tale of the clergyman's errant daughter, and according to Chancellor, 'the young lady had forthwith to leave the district with a lost reputation'.

There are many other tales of Charteris being frustrated at the moment of consummation – by a dog which attacked him as its mistress was about to surrender, of a Mr Gardner, landlord of an inn at Chesterford who rescued one of his maid-servants and then turned Charteris out into the night with a long walk to the nearest shelter. There is certainly something suspicious about this plethora of stories without dates or names, and some must be different versions of the same incident. However, Charteris's most dangerous scrape of all is fully documented.

In 1730 Charteris was tried for the rape of a girl named Anne Bond, who had probably been recruited by Mother Needham as his servant. Needham (*c.*1660–1732) was one of a new generation of enterprising businesswomen who were transforming London's sex industry and would eventually make it one of the capital's most important commercial enterprises. Her main brothel was in Park Place, St James's, centre of high-class bawdry with royalty among its customers. She was a familiar figure, considered to be particularly predatory and cruel to her girls. She forced them to hire their clothes from her at exorbitant rates which meant they were always in debt. If they couldn't pay they were thrown into the debtors' prison.

For about 20 years Needham had procured Charteris the kind of strong fresh country wenches he liked. They once had a violent argument when he rejected a girl she took to his house in Bond Street, saying that the 17-year-old was 'too young for his rough usage'. Probably he didn't believe she was as young or fresh as Needham claimed.

Mother Needham fell into a passion, violently protesting that he was using her ill because she had been at great pains and expense ... should she be obliged to offer the girl elsewhere it would blow her market, since few gentlemen would choose what the colonel had rejected, and the girl might be on her hands for a long while or have to be disposed of to some player or even a barrister or else she had to make her into a hackney-harlot in a week.

The court was told that as soon as Anne Bond took up her post at his house in George Street, Hanover Square, he offered her money for sex. Although he virtually laid siege to her, she resisted. She had been told that she was working for a Mr Harvey, but heard a caller to the house ask for Colonel Charteris. Like many working-class girls she had heard of the great bogeyman, and she attempted to leave. Charteris told the servants to keep the doors locked. After almost a month, at seven one morning 'the Colonel rang a Bell and bid the Clerk of the Kitchen call the Lancashire Bitch into the Dining Room.' Charteris locked the door, threw her on to the couch, gagged her with his nightcap and raped her. When she threatened to tell her friends he horsewhipped her and took away her clothes and money. Anne told the story to a gentlewoman friend and Charteris was tried for rape at the Old Bailey.

Charteris's rich and aristocratic friends and relatives, including two Knights of the Garter, packed into the court and heard him sentenced to death for rape. But he was in Newgate less than a month before receiving a royal pardon, negotiated by his son-in-law Lord Wemyss, who bribed Lord Advocate Duncan Forbes of Culloden and promised him an annuity of £300 for life (about £36,000 today). It was widely believed that a large sum of money was also paid to Robert Walpole, the chief minister of state.

In addition, Charteris had to settle a large annuity on Anne Bond, while she was reported to have received £800 for signing a petition calling for his reprieve. One paper claimed that she was planning to get married, and that she and her husband were going to open a tavern called the Colonel Charteris's Head.

In all the affair may have cost Charteris £15,000 (about

£1,800,000 today), almost as painful to a miser like him as the noose itself. On 4 September 1730 the *Weekly News* carried this announcement:

> A few days since, Colonel Charteris sold off his South Sea stock and paid the following agreed-on sums by way of composition with the Sheriffs of London and High Bailiff of Westminster for the effects seized on his late attainder and conviction: viz., to Wm Morice, Esq., £5,000; to Mr Alderman Barber and Sir John Williams each £1,650 – total, £8,300.

The poet and playwright John Gay wrote to Jonathan Swift: 'Does not Charteris's misfortune grieve you? For that great man is like to save his life and lose some of his money. A very hard case!' The London mob were as indignant as Gay. Charteris was recognised in his coach as he drove through Chelsea with two women. He was dragged out and thrashed. He was 71, and after that we see only glimpses of his rapid decline. His medical adviser, a Dr Clarke, wrote to Duncan Forbes in February 1732:

> The terriblest patient I ever had in my life is your monster of a land-lord. I was obliged to go sixteen miles out of town to meet him on the road from Hornby, where they thought he would have expired. I lived two days in hell upon earth, and conveyed him with much difficulty on Wednesday last to Stoney Hill, dying exactly as he lived, but swearing little or not at all … He can neither sleep nor eat, and has no other complaint either of pain or of sickness, so that he seems to be dying of a decay of nature, his blood being exhausted … as for his own honesty, the only sign he has shown of it was one day when he thought he was going off he ordered with a great roar that all his just debts should be paid.

Meanwhile, in March 1731 Needham had been arrested – possibly for her role in introducing Anne Bond to Charteris – by the magistrate Sir John Gonson, a well-known scourge of prostitutes and procuresses. She was sentenced to the pillory and, according to a contemporary newspaper, was 'so severely pelted by the Mob that her life was despaired of'. She died soon afterwards, probably from her injuries.

Charteris himself died at his property in Stoney Hill, near Edinburgh, at the end of February 1732. When it became known that he was to be buried in the family vault at the Grey Friars' church in Edinburgh a mob gathered, and tried to seize the coffin. They were beaten off, but the coffin's descent into the grave was accompanied by a shower of dead dogs, cats and offal. He left a vast fortune, most of it to his grandson. People who helped him out of various scrapes were not forgotten: Sir Robert Walpole got his stable of horses, and the lawyer Duncan Forbes his mansion at Stoney Hill and £1,000.

An epitaph for this remarkable man, said at the time to be by Swift, appeared in the *Gentleman's Magazine* for April 1732:

Here continueth to rot
The Body of Francis Chartres,
Who, with an Inflexible Constancy, and
Inimitable Uniformity of Life,
Persisted,
In spite of Age and Infirmities,
In the Practice of every human Vice,
Excepting Prodigality and Hypocrisy:
His Insatiable Avarice exempting him
From the first,
His matchless Impudence from the second.
Nor was he more singular in the undeviating
Pravity of his Manners
Than successful in accumulating Wealth.
For, without Trade or Profession
Without Trust of Public Money,
And without bribe-worthy Service,
He acquired, or more properly created
A Ministerial Estate.
He was the only Person of his Time

Who could cheat without the Mask of Honesty,
Retain his primeval Meanness
When possessed of ten thousand a year.
And, having daily deserved the Gibbet for what
he did,
Was at last condemned to it for what
He could not do.
O indignant Reader!
Think not his Life useless to Mankind!
Providence connived at his execrable Designs
To give to after-Ages
A conspicuous proof and example
Of how small estimation is exorbitant Wealth
In the Sight of God,
By His bestowing it on the most unworthy of all Mortals.

It is interesting that this searing condemnation is all about money, and hardly mentions his other sins. Chancellor says in *The Lives of the Rakes* that 'nothing quite like him is to be found in history or fiction.'

When Charteris was tried for the rape of Anne Bond a print of him was published; it represents him standing at the bar of the Old Bailey, with his thumbs tied. Under the print was the ironic inscription:

Blood! – must a colonel, with a lord's estate
Be thus obnoxious to a scoundrel's fate?
Brought to the bar, and sentenc'd from the bench,
Only for ravishing a country wench?

Charteris's career in infamy was unique, but the next 30 years would see a great upwelling of rakishness, and what could be called its most notorious manifestation, the Hell-Fire Club of Sir Francis Dashwood at Medmenham.

# Part 3

# The Hell-Fire Clubs

# Prelude

ORGIES BY THE LIGHT OF FLICKERING TAPERS ... Great persons of state dressed as monks, drinking wine from the navels of virgins and sacrificing them to Venus on marble altars ... Satanic rituals which mocked the established religion ... A baboon being given the sacred host in an obscene mockery of the Mass ... Vigorous sex between masked men and women. These are just some of the ingredients of rumours that swept London in the 1750s, suggesting what many had long suspected – that a part at least of the aristocracy was utterly depraved. These 'monks' were believed to have fitted out an ancient rural abbey for their rituals and to be debauching local women, as well as their own wives, sisters and even daughters.

The rumours concerned the Hell-Fire Club established at Medmenham in Buckinghamshire by Sir Francis Dashwood, who lives on in romantic literature and Hollywood B-movies as the prototypical moustachio-twirling rake, his satanic laughter echoing through the ruins of an ancient abbey as he and his acolytes tossed off bumpers of port and deflowered virgins. The rumours were probably substantially true – although the women were certainly not virgins – but Dashwood was not the originator of the clubs where dissolute upper-class men gathered to concoct a heady mix of Satanism and sex. The first hell-fire clubs, mysterious in their origins, emerged in London in the 1720s. They were a sinister alternative to the gentlemen's clubs which were beginning to flourish in the St James's area and elsewhere.

The early eighteenth century was the age of clubs. The Whigs had the Kit Cat Club, the Tories the Board of Brothers and the Cocoa Tree. Membership of the Rump Steak was confined to those who had been publicly snubbed by George II. There were clubs for most tastes and weaknesses. Brook's and White's were for drinking and gambling, and the play was heavy. Dr Johnson presided over the Literary Club. But these early clubs were too civilised for some, for the untamed spirit of the Mohocks lived on. The members of the first hell-fire clubs were the natural successors of the disorderly gangs of upper-class youths who roared about London's midnight streets around the turn of the eighteenth century.

In 1720 rumours began to spread of blasphemous associations that mocked the official religion. There seem to have been three such clubs, with a total membership of about 40 'persons of quality' of both sexes. There was more than a hint of undergraduate naughtiness about their activities. News-sheets and pamphlets were filled with denunciations describing how the rakes who attended them ridiculed the third person of the Trinity, 'calling for a Holy-Ghost-Pie' at a tavern. The group which met in an apartment at Somerset House held orgies. But orgies were not all that uncommon among persons of quality: what the authorities were after was blasphemy. An anonymous pamphlet titled *The Hell-Fire-Club, kept by a Society of Blasphemers*, and published in 1721, contains the following verse:

> Among the worst, the very worst of men,
> Those men who of the Hell-Fire-Club will be
> Infernal Members, where in jollity
> Each man strives who in Sin shall most abound
> and fill his mouth with oaths of dreadful sound.

In 1720 it became common knowledge that Philip, Duke of Wharton, had been elected president of one of these hell-fire clubs. As far as the government was concerned this was the last straw. Wharton was a secret Jacobite, a turncoat who had been born at the heart of the Glorious Revolution. His life was a kind of template for the rakes who were to come. His father Thomas, first Marquess of Wharton, was one of the heroes of the revolution: he wrote its hit song 'Lilibulero', and boasted 'that he had sung King James out of three kingdoms', as Geoffrey Ashe recounts in his book *Do What You Will*. He brought up his brilliant son to be a pillar of the Whig establishment, subjecting him to intensive education in science, mathematics, metaphysics, languages and classical literature. But young Wharton had other ideas about how he would conduct his life, and at the age of 16 married Martha Holmes, the daughter of a mere major-general, with the aid of a Fleet parson.* The girl was said to be very comely and well educated, but the Marquess was furious. Gathering a posse and the Attorney-General he hunted the young couple down at midnight. He failed to get the marriage annulled but decided to part them by sending his son on the Grand Tour. Then he died, whether out of pique is not clear.

The young Wharton inherited the title and in spring 1716 set off for Europe, without his new wife but with seven footmen, a valet and a French Protestant teacher. Despite the latter he contacted Jacobite exiles in Paris, among them an Irishman named Gwynne who received him in an attic. Gwynne was startled when Wharton said he hoped the stairs didn't lead up to heaven, because if they did he would go down again, and he invited Gwynne to join him in hell. He flirted ambiguously with the Jacobites, accepting a knighthood of the Garter from the Old Pretender. When an English medical student was arrested for breaking windows at the British embassy he tried to persuade others to break some more.

Eventually he sat in the Irish House of Lords, supporting the

---

* Clergymen, real and bogus, performed marriages in and around the Fleet prison, claiming they were outside the jurisdiction of the Bishop of London. The ceremonies were cheap compared to conventional marriages, which were heavily taxed. They were also very popular – almost 3,000 were performed in the four months ending in February 1705. In 1753 a Marriage Act put an end to the practice by ruling that only church weddings were valid.

A Fleet Marriage. Clergymen, real and bogus, performed marriages in and around the Fleet Prison. The Duke of Wharton married his first wife in such a ceremony.

government. In 1718 a grateful King George I made him a duke, an astonishing honour for a non-royal minor, but if he hoped to bind Wharton to him he failed. Back in England Wharton denounced ministerial guilt over the South Sea Bubble, inducing Lord Stanhope to collapse with a cerebral haemorrhage on the floor of the House as he attempted to counter Wharton's accusations. By this time Wharton was already in trouble over money and drink. He had a tendency to brawl in public. He founded and largely wrote a newspaper, the *True Briton*, to castigate the government of Sir Robert Walpole. He avoided attacking ministers directly, instead inventing stories about politics abroad which readers knew were really commentaries on happenings in England. His central thesis was that the Glorious Revolution had been betrayed by corrupt Whig grandees, but Walpole's government was so entrenched he made little impression, and after eight months and 74 issues he gave up.

Just over two years earlier, in April 1721 George I had issued an Order in Council suppressing the hell-fire clubs. Wharton, clutching a Bible, made a speech in the Lords denying he was a patron of blasphemy. He went off to live at Twickenham, where he ran another rather permissive, but not blasphemous, club. His intrepid neighbour Lady Mary Wortley Montagu described it in a letter to her sister: 'Twenty very pretty fellows (the Duke of Wharton being president and chief director) have formed themselves into a committee of gallantry, who call themselves "Schemers" and meet regularly three times a week to consult on gallant schemes for the advancement of that branch of happiness.'

Lady Mary, clearly an enthusiast, adds that the renown of the Schemers 'ought to be spread wherever men can sigh, or women can wish ... 'Tis true they have the envy and the curses of the old and ugly of both sexes, and a general persecution from all old women; but this is no more than all reformations must expect in their beginning.'

The poet Alexander Pope, who was jealous of Wharton's success with Lady Mary (she had spurned his advances) and scornful of his wasted talent, left a venomous portrait of him:

Wharton, the scorn and wonder of our days,
Whose ruling passion was the lust of praise:
Born with whate'er could win it from the wise,
Women and fools must like him, or he dies ...
Thus with each gift of Nature and of Art,
And wanting nothing but an honest heart;
Grown all to all; from no one vice exempt;
And most contemptible to shun contempt;
His passion still to covet general praise;
His life, to forfeit it a thousand ways ...
A fool, with more of wit than half mankind;
Too rash for thought, for action too refined ...

The rest of Wharton's life was spent in the pursuit of lost causes. He dissipated his fortune and went to live on the Continent, where he became involved in Jacobite politics. He fell for an Irish maid of honour at the Spanish court, and married her after his wife died in 1726, becoming a Catholic to do so. The King of Spain gave him command, as colonel, of a regiment of Irish exiles.

His picaresque progress continued, as the following story shows. Back in France he met a young peer with a coach one night at St Germain and persuaded him to drive to Paris on 'important business'. There he hired a second coach, drove to the Opéra, hired six musicians, drove back to St Germain – it was now past midnight – and used the musicians to serenade some ladies in the palace. He then drove to Poissy with his peer and musicians where he serenaded an English gentleman who lived there. The gentleman invited them in to breakfast, but the musicians pointed out that they would be fined if they didn't get back to the Opéra in time for their normal duties. At this point Wharton explained to the peer that he hadn't any cash, and asked him to pay the musicians for their night's entertainment, as Ashe says 'promising to return the favour when opportunity served'. The rueful peer doubted if such an opportunity would ever arise, but nevertheless paid up.

Wharton died in May 1731 and was buried at Reus, near Tarragona. He was more important for what he foreshadowed than for any real achievements. But his memory lived on in rakish circles as an example of unrestrained sexual indulgence, mad spending and flouting of Protestant respectability. He was a role model to the great Whig leader and rake Charles James Fox and his club provided a template for the extraordinary brotherhood founded in the 1750s by Dashwood at Medmenham.

# The Mystery of Medmenham

AT THE HEART OF THE HISTORY OF THE ENGLISH RAKES is the Hell–Fire Club at Medmenham, and at the heart of the story of Medmenham is an intriguing mystery. What exactly went on in this ruined Cistercian abbey on the banks of the Thames six miles from West Wycombe? If the participants in the revels there were not exactly sworn to secrecy, they seem to have had a gentlemen's agreement never to reveal their secrets, and most of the original documents have been destroyed or have disappeared. So, over almost 250 years, speculation has built a towering legend about the obscene cavortings of some of the most important men in the land with women of high and low birth, of chromatic vice, orgies combined with Satanism and pagan rituals. The diplomat and author Sir Nathaniel Wraxall wrote in his *Historical Memoirs* that the rites practised at Medmenham 'were of a nature subversive of all decency'.

What made these lurid legends irresistible was the fact that those rumoured to be involved included at least one prime minister, a chancellor of the Exchequer, a First Lord of the Admiralty, various cabinet ministers, poets, England's greatest painter and an Oxford professor. When they tired of women of their own class they sent to London, where the great bawd of the age, Charlotte Hayes, had a ready supply of pretty young whores who would meet their needs. These stories made respectable people shudder. As we shall see, however, there is evidence both for the existence of the club and for the accuracy of some at least of the stories told about it at the time. None of the principal players refuted the stories or their part in them, even though some of them were important national figures who would have wanted to play down their roles. There are many clues to what the author Horace Walpole called 'The quintessence of their mysteries'.

The founder and presiding spirit of the club, Dashwood, is a puzzling and contradictory figure, for some time an almost hysterical anti-religious bigot who nevertheless later issued a revised version of the Prayer Book in collaboration with the American scientist and statesman Benjamin Franklin. He was a hopeless chancellor of the Exchequer but, according to Franklin, an efficient postmaster-general who 're-organised the postal services of England and provided something like a national postal service'. He was a cultivated patron of the arts and yet plunged enthusiastically into drunkenness and profligacy. He would say 'Taste the sweets of all things', and he had rakish tendencies to an exaggerated degree. According to Wraxall, 'he far exceeded in licentiousness of conduct anything exhibited since Charles the Second', while Horace Walpole said of his sex drive that he had 'the staying power of a stallion and the impetuosity of a bull'. A curious and almost wholly unreliable anonymous work, *The Fruit Shop*, published in 1765, called him 'a wight gifted with such frequent uprisings of the standard of humanity, as would do honour to any officer of the guards, young templar, lieutenant of the navy, or professed fortune-hunter of whatever denomination'.

Dashwood was superstitious and flirted with the black arts, and although he was said by some to have been briefly a Catholic convert he had a fixed contempt for Catholicism, which he expressed in childish mockery and blasphemy. This complicated mix helps to explain the widespread belief that his club was partly an excuse to work out his tortured fantasies of sex and religion. Dashwood was also amiable, gregarious, plain-spoken to a degree and more than a little childish. He had a real gift for friendship and leadership. Though no intellectual, he was quick and bright. His illegitimate daughter Rachel said of him that he was guided by 'a quick

perception more than by a sound judgment'. He 'generally preferred an epigram to an essay and a satirical poem to a discourse
on jurisprudence'.

Portraits show a jovial man with a large, round, happy face. He
has the uncomplicated look of a farmer or country clergyman.
Benjamin Franklin, a frequent visitor to Dashwood's family estate
at West Wycombe, wrote to his son in 1773: 'I am in this house as
much at my ease as if it were my own; and the gardens are a
paradise. But a pleasanter thing is the kind countenance, the
facetious and very intelligent conversation of Mine Host, who
having been for many years engaged in public affairs, seen all parts
of Europe, and kept the best company in the world, is himself the
best existing.'

Born in 1708, Dashwood was too young to have belonged to
the Duke of Wharton's original club. At 16 he inherited his father's
baronetcy and a great deal of money, and the general rakishness of
the times suited his inclinations. When he set out on the Grand
Tour in 1726 he was excitable and keen for all kinds of experience.
His tutor on the Grand Tour was a Catholic Jacobite. At Rome he
took Dashwood to the holiest shrines in the hope of converting
him, but Dashwood usually laughed at what he was shown. When
he saw penitents in the Sistine Chapel symbolically scourging
themselves with miniature whips he went back to his lodgings,
dressed in a long cloak and returned to the chapel with a real whip,
with which he laid about him, driving the terrified penitents out.
Horace Walpole, who tells the story in his *Memoirs of the Reign of
George III*, says they screamed '*Il diavolo! Il diavolo!*' as they fled.

According to his legend, after this episode he suffered some
kind of breakdown. One night he saw four green eyes glowing and
staring at him in the darkness outside his window, accompanied by
an unholy racket. His tutor heard his cries and found him cower-
ing in his room, convinced that he was being stalked by a four-
eyed devil. It was obvious to the tutor that it was two caterwauling
cats, and later he said so to a friend. Dashwood, who had meanwhile converted to Catholicism, heard about this and his old
antipathy to religion was renewed and strengthened.

Whatever we think of these stories, Dashwood seems to have had a bitter, mocking hatred of religion. Good judges thought that his judgment was so warped on this subject that he was half crazed. He was known to contemporaries as 'Mad Dashwood'.

Dashwood had a reputation as a rake long before he founded the Medmenham club. The *Town and Country Magazine*, assiduous chronicler of the folly of the upper classes, reported that he 'ingratiated himself with all the celebrated demi-reps and filles-de-joye upon the bon ton', another way of saying that he spent a lot of money on high-class prostitutes. He was said to have fornicated his way to Rome on the Grand Tour, and to have fornicated his way home, by way of St Petersburg – where he was rumoured to have slept with the Tsarina – and Turkey. He developed a fairly sophisticated taste for art, and back in London in 1732, living at 18 Hanover Square, he gathered round him like-minded art lovers to found the Society of Dilettanti. The 40 upper-class members met on the first Sunday of the month at the Bedford Head Tavern in Covent Garden. The serious business of the society was art and connoisseurship, although the members also represented the political opposition led by Frederick, Prince of Wales. One of the rules was that every member must have his picture painted. Dashwood chose to be represented as a Franciscan friar at his devotions. Around his tonsured head was a halo with the words 'San: Francisco di Wycombo' and he was gazing at a small replica of the Medici Venus.

Dashwood's politics were as erratic as his religious views. In Italy in 1739–40 he flirted with Jacobitism, corresponding with the Young Pretender and passing on news about events in England. The Catholicism of the Stuart circle deterred him from getting involved too deeply. He told his crony the Earl of Sandwich: 'I am at one with the gallant Prince. He has all the gifts of a true leader, and above all he is honest. But I detest most heartily the fripperies of Rome which emanate from his entourage . . . ' During a visit to Florence, Horace Walpole kept an eye on Dashwood on behalf of his father Robert's government.

Not the least remarkable thing about Dashwood was his ability to sustain a serious political career while being the most notorious rake in the country. In fact, for a while the Brotherhood was an important political power centre, its members holding some of the highest offices of state. Dashwood himself held high ministerial offices – he eventually became Chancellor of the Exchequer in 1762 despite confessing that he had no head for figures – and was admired by Franklin and George Bubb Dodington, a wealthy political power broker and one of the outer circle of friars. John Wilkes, whose contempt for the Brotherhood and their rites was ill concealed, although the sexual side appealed to him, liked and admired Dashwood. And even when the club itself was but a memory, Dashwood was regarded by the surviving members with warm affection. He was in many ways like Charles II, a kindly, gentle man with a passion for women and jollity, the ideal personality to found what was surely one of the most remarkable clubs in history.

## Do What You Will

It is not known when or where the Hell-Fire Club was founded, and its first meetings may have been in London. In 1748–52 Sir Francis had a road built to the village on his estate of West Wycombe. One of his many endearing traits was a care, unusual at the time, for the local peasantry. He championed commoners' rights, writing of his own lands: 'The parishioners will keep what they want, which is the wood, and Sir Francis Dashwood will not lose the privilege of hunting and shooting and his right of game as far as his manor extends.' He built the road to give local employment and relieve distress.

The chalk for the road was excavated from the ancient caves under West Wycombe Hill. Sir Francis directed his workmen to enlarge the caves by digging out a series of rooms, including a circular hall 60 feet high and 40 feet across, which are still there. The chamber, known as the Banqueting Hall, has four alcoves which may once have held statues. Benjamin Franklin referred to the caves vaguely in a letter, saying that the 'imagery' of West Wycombe is 'whimsical and puzzling ... below the earth as above it'. John

Hall Stevenson, a Dashwood disciple, wrote a poem with a note on the 'strange events which took place at West Wycombe Hill'. The poem contains the following lines, which may refer to the decorative scheme of the caves, to frescoes and statues now long gone:

> Where can I find a cave to muse
> Upon his lordship's envied glory,
> Which of the Nine dare to refuse
> To tell the strange and recent story?
> Mounting I saw the egregious lord
> O'er all impediments and bars;
> I saw him at Jove's council board
> And saw him stuck among the stars.

Some time in the early 1750s Dashwood rented Medmenham Abbey, six miles away from West Wycombe, from his friend Francis Duffield. A soldier and amateur painter, Duffield found the abbey rather inconvenient. A three-storey house, itself then partly derelict, had been built on the ruins, and Dashwood started turning the buildings into a suitable venue for the club. Workmen were brought in daily from London and taken back at night, so that the details of the conversion would remain a secret from the locals. They added a cloister and a mock ruined tower. The plain glass of the windows was replaced with stained glass. Under Dashwood's instructions they inscribed over a doorway in French Rabelais's slogan *Fay ce que voudras* – Do What You Will. While Rabelais had hedged his slogan with qualifications, Dashwood used it in the sense of 'anything goes'. The Gothic suggestiveness of the old abbey was enhanced with obscene statuary and phallic symbols. Horace Walpole, who visited it but was not directly involved in what went on there, left a helpful description:

> He [Dashwood] and some chosen friends had hired the ruins of Medmenham Abbey, near Marlow, and refitted it in conventual style. Thither at stated seasons they adjourned: had each their cell, a proper habit, a monastic name, and a refectory in common – besides

Medmenham Abbey, headquarters of the Hell-Fire Club. Sir Francis Dashwood and his disciples gathered there for their blasphemous rites.

a chapel, the decoration of which may well be supposed to have contained the quintessence of their mysteries, since it was impenetrable to any but the initiated. Whatever their doctrines were, their practice was rigorously pagan: Bacchus and Venus were the deities to whom they almost publicly sacrificed.

A small part of the abbey, perhaps only two rooms, was closed to all but the inner circle of Brothers, the group of 12 'apostles' who gathered round Sir Francis.* Of the other rooms, two of the most imposing were reached by a staircase hung with 'lurid pictures'. As Ashe describes in *Do What You Will*, 'The drawing room was decorated in Roman style and furnished with ornate sofas upholstered in green damask'. Next was the library, which consisted mainly of occult and pornographic works (Dashwood was interested in the occult) with false bindings which suggested they were religious works. On the walls were portraits of the members, their women friends and a series of portraits of English monarchs. That of Henry VIII was masked with a paper sticker as a reproof for dissolving the monasteries. Under the pictures ran a row of pegs for the Brothers' costumes, labelled with their pseudo-monkish names.

To the right of the main entrance was a refectory. Either here or in the drawing room were two statues of ancient gods of silence, their fingers to their lips. Behind the tower there were private cells with beds. A corridor led to a chapter room, with Latin mottoes around the walls. Outside on the lawn was an old chapel which had been redecorated with lewd frescos. Only the inner circle were admitted to the chapter room and the chapel while the secret rites were in progress. The rest of the abbey was surprisingly open to more or less casual visitors, such as Walpole.

We know the Brotherhood was meeting there in 1753, and possibly the previous year, before the building work was finished.

---

* The monks or friars were originally known variously as the Order of the Friars of St Francis of Wycombe, the Brotherhood of Saint Francis of Wycombe, the Monks of Medmenham, the Medmenham Friars and the Order of St Francis: the name Hell-Fire Club was not applied to it until long after the club had ceased to exist.

During their stay they were known by their monkish names. For example, Wilkes was known as John of Aylesbury, the constituency for which he was at one time MP.

The Brothers who gathered in this unique riverside clubhouse, usually on summer evenings, were wealthy friends and political contacts of Dashwood. Some were his country neighbours. The inner circle of 13 members was an elite who took part in the mysterious rites and could enter the forbidden rooms. Their leader was, of course, Dashwood. His 12 'disciples' have not all been identified, but they certainly included John Montagu, Earl of Sandwich, First Lord of the Admiralty; Paul Whitehead, a poet and pamphleteer and High Steward of the club; Dodington, Lord Melcombe Regis and MP; Thomas Potter, Paymaster General, Treasurer for Ireland and son of an archbishop of Canterbury; and Sir William Stanhope, son of Lord Chesterfield. Around them was a much larger group of lesser monks, including Wilkes, the poets Charles Churchill and Robert Lloyd, George Selwyn, MP and wit, and George, Earl of Orford. Finally, there was a large group of eminent visitors, including the painter William Hogarth, Franklin and Walpole, who almost certainly did not take part in any of the ceremonies. Other names tenuously linked to the club are William Douglas, Earl of March, a notorious rake (and the subject of a later chapter); the cross-dressing French diplomat Chevalier d'Eon; the novelist Laurence Sterne; the Hon. Jack Spencer, another rake; and John Hall Stevenson, poet and satirist, who would later form his own Hell-Fire Club at his castle in Yorkshire. Frederick, Prince of Wales, has been very speculatively identified as one of this group.

When we try to explore the rituals of the Brotherhood we come up against the locked doors of the chapel and the chapter room, and the tight lips of the inner circle, as obdurate as the stone gods of silence. Opportunities to establish the facts were missed in the early days. A local historian, Thomas Langley, interviewed the Medmenham housekeeper in her old age. Unhappily, he decided that what he learned should be 'buried in oblivion'. Early in the last century the minute book kept by the club's steward, Paul

Whitehead, was destroyed, as it was considered too obscene for publication.

An Irish writer named Charles Johnstone, who knew people on the fringes, gave a fictionalised account of the Brotherhood in a four-volume novel, *Chrysal*, published in 1760–5. Johnstone, a barrister who had to give up the law because of deafness, wrote part of it while a guest of Lord Mountedgcumbe, a naval officer. Mountedgcumbe had worked at the Admiralty with the Earl of Sandwich, had been a correspondent of Dashwood and was a close friend of Horace Walpole and George Selwyn. Johnstone seems to have picked up a good deal of gossip about the Medmenhamites, and the fact that the book was contemporary with the Brotherhood shows how early the conflation of fact and legend began.

Johnstone attacked Sir Francis Dashwood and his Brotherhood: 'You are astonished how such scenes of debauchery and excess could be supported, either by the fortunes of the entertainer or the constitutions of his guests.' Clearly the rumours he picked up were fairly specific:

> To prevent satiety or fatigues, these meetings were never protracted beyond a week at a time; nor held oftener than twice a year; by which frugality of pleasure they were always returned to with the keenness of novelty: And as for the expense of them, that was defrayed jointly by the whole community; (the superior contributing nothing more than any other member, except the first cost of building the convent, which he thought himself amply recompensed from, by the honour of having struck out the plan.)

A curious book published in 1779 gives further intriguing glimpses of the abbey. *Nocturnal Revels, Or, The History of King's Place and Other Modern Nunneries*, written by 'A Monk of the Order of St Francis', is a review of the contemporary London sex industry and its customers. It appears to be exceptionally well informed, particularly about the bawds and harlots of the capital. If the writer really was one of the Brotherhood, then it is a primary source and what it has to say must be taken seriously. It is largely from the *Revels* that we learn about the men and women parading in masks as they make their sexual choices, of women secluded there to have their bastards. 'The offspring of these connections are styled the Sons and Daughters of St Francis and appointed in due order officers and domestics in the Seminary, according to their different abilities, or by drawing lots.' Unfortunately for the credibility of the author, there appears to have been only one ancient servant at the Abbey, and the Brotherhood was not in existence long enough for any 'offspring' to grow old enough to fulfil that role. However, whoever the author was he clearly knew a good deal about the Brotherhood. He tells how Dashwood conceived the fraternity of the abbey:

> A certain nobleman who made the tour of Europe and ... made judicious observations, particularly [of] the different religious seminaries ... on his return to England he thought that a burlesque institution in the name of St Francis would mark the absurdity of such sequestered societies; and in lieu of the austerities and abstemiousness [of] their practices substituted convivial gaiety, unrestrained hilarity and social felicity.

The Brothers were free to amuse themselves 'without control or restraint'. The *Revels* gives women a more important role than some other accounts, saying they took part in the initiation ceremonies and became full members. They considered themselves 'as the lawful wives of the brethren during their stay within the monastic walls; every Monk being religiously scrupulous not to infringe upon the nuptial alliance of any other brother'. The *Revels* also claims that all the monks and their nuns took an oath of secrecy.

Letters between the friars are full of doubles entendres which make it all too clear what they got up to, although they are presumably an attempt at concealment. One friar, a man named John King, wrote to Dashwood on 3 September 1770 regretting that he could not attend a meeting: 'So in the mean time must pay all obedience to the Pillar* annexed the present standard of mirth to the Sisterhood, who are determined to exert their Spiritualities there, as [far as] their present condition are able, for I assure your lordship, their spirits are willing, but the Flesh is weak...'

Most important of all, the turbulent politician John Wilkes, who was associated with the Brotherhood but not a member of the inner circle, did not feel constrained by the code of secrecy and wrote about it in letters and elsewhere.

Using the scraps and clues available, a credible description of the Brotherhood's activities has been constructed. The most important ceremony seems to have been the initiation of a new member. Held after dark, it began with the tolling of a bell in the tower. The abbot and his 12 disciples performed their secret rites in the chapter room. Meanwhile the lesser friars gathered in the cloister. When the rites were finished, music from the chapel summoned them. They advanced two by two and their leader knocked three times on the door of the chapel. Sir Francis opened it and then retired behind the altar rail, where he and his 12 disciples stood facing the incoming procession. The light from wax tapers flickered on the obscene wall decorations.

The members elected an 'abbot of the day', and he had first choice of the women who had been invited. Again, there are clues to what happened when these arrived. Sir William Stanhope wrote to Dashwood in September 1758 saying he had some erotica for the library, adding that he hoped they would 'now and then occasion an extraordinary ejaculation to be sent up to heaven'. Stanhope also mentions 'that part of the Litany when I pray the Lord to strengthen them that do stand'. A baboon which had been sent from India took part in some of the ceremonies, dressed as chaplain. Dashwood apparently gave it the Eucharist, and this strengthened rumours of a satanic cult. This baboon was at the centre of the stories of blasphemous rites, as we shall see.

About the sexual orgies at Medmenham there is little dispute.

---

* Dashwood had erected a phallic edifice known as St Dunstan's Pillar as a guide to travellers near Lincoln.

The *Nocturnal Revels* states that each monk was allowed to bring 'a lady of a cheerful, lively disposition, to improve the general hilarity'. These women would arrive masked, unmasking only when they were sure there would be no embarrassing encounters with husbands or sons or people they knew. This suggests that they were gentlewomen. Ashe in *Do What You Will* states that guests in this class 'are said to have joined the Order and paired off with the Friars as "wives" during their stay'.

The evidence about the identities of the women who improved 'the general hilarity' is less certain. Some well-born women have been named as nuns of the Order, including Dashwood's friend Lady Mary Wortley Montagu. She was in her sixties when the club was founded, and so was probably at most only an honorary member. Although intrepid enough, it seems unlikely she ever visited the abbey during the rites. Two of Dashwood's mistresses, Elizabeth Roach and Agnes Perrault, and his half-sister Mary Walcot, are credibly believed to have been enthusiastic participants, as is Lady Betty Germain. Frances, Viscountess Fane, author of *Memoirs of a Lady of Quality*, has also been conjecturally linked to the club. John Hall Stevenson claimed that he had spotted Dashwood's step-mother Lady Mary Dashwood among the nuns, and in some verses entitled 'The Confessions of Sir F—— of Medmenham and of the Lady Mary, his Wife' (clearly a mistake: the name of his first wife was Frances) makes explicit reference to incest:

> Like a hotspur young cock, he began with his mother,
> Cheered three of his sisters, one after the other

One report says that local women were also invited to take part. The uncouth satirical poet Charles Churchill, himself a member of the Brotherhood, left the couplet:

> Whilst Womanhood in habit of a nun
> At Medmenham lies, by backwards monks undone.

This suggests some of the nuns were gentlewomen, or at least amateurs, as the highly experienced London professionals were hardly likely to be undone by anyone. Also mentioned in the literature is an apparatus known as the Idolum Tentiginis; Ashe in *Do What You Will* describes it as 'a sort of hobby-horse in the shape of a cock, with a phallus-beak turned backwards so that a woman bestriding it could stimulate herself while bouncing around'. Around the base of this object were inscribed in Greek the words 'Saviour of the World'. This same motto was engraved on phallic statues in the garden.

We know a good deal about those professionals, the London harlots who are said to have been involved. When the monks tired of the limited choice of relatives and neighbours, girls were either summoned from the brothels of London or were taken there by the monks. The arrival of coachloads or boatloads of pretty girls dressed in the height of metropolitan fashion in what was then a distinctly rural setting naturally caused gossip.

The delectable courtesan Fanny Murray has been plausibly suggested as one of the 'nuns'. She had been a mistress of the Earl of Sandwich, and the obscene *Essay on Woman*, which emanated from the Brotherhood, was dedicated to her.[*] And she once mentioned that she had 'waited on the Monks at Medmenham'.

Fanny was the chief 'Toast of the Town', as the most successful harlots were known, in the middle of the eighteenth century. She achieved fame exceptional even in that age of celebrity whores. A gallant who had drunk champagne from her slipper sent it to a noted chef to be turned into a dish on which he and his friends feasted. She was born in 1729 in Bath, where her father was a poor musician. According to the anonymous *Memoirs of the Celebrated Miss Fanny Murray*, published in 1759, she was orphaned at the age of 12, and became a flower-seller in the Rooms. Her first seducer when she was a very young teenager was the rake Jack Spencer,

---

[*] The scandal over the *Essay on Woman* made Fanny even more notorious. Pamphleteers produced 'Absolutely authenticated quotations from the Amours of Fanny Murray and her Monkish Friends of Mednam'. Gin cocktails were sold with names such as 'Gin and Fanny Sandwich', 'Fanny Murray's Nettle Juice' and 'Fanny Murray's Pick Me Up'.

favourite grandchild of the Duchess of Marlborough, who gave her 'a few tawdry gifts' before abandoning her. After several affairs – including one with Beau Nash, Bath's arbiter of taste, who was in his sixties – Fanny left for London. Her career took off when she appeared in Jack Harris's *List of Covent Garden Ladies*, a rough guide to the area's high-class whores. The well-known rake Richard Rigby said of her that she was 'followed by crowds of gallants … it would be a crime not to toast her at every meal'.

Another celebrity whore believed to have taken part was the lovely one-eyed Betty Wemys. She was known for getting very drunk in the Rose Tavern in Covent Garden, losing her glass eye and starting fights as she scrambled about looking for it on the floor. Lucy Cooper, reputed to have been one of Dashwood's mistresses, was another of the Medmenham girls. The victim of sexual and alcoholic exuberance uncommon even for her time and profession, she died in miserable poverty.

Other girls were supplied by the brothel-keeper Charlotte Hayes, who had a long career at the top of her profession, being born about 1725 and dying in 1813. In the early 1760s she was just beginning that ascent with her rakish partner, the Irish gambler and chancer Dennis O'Kelly, who would one day own the wonder horse Eclipse and part of the Duke of Chandos's old estate at Cannons. She entertained the future Prince Regent and one of his brothers at her mansion at Epsom. She and her girls would have been well known to some of the Brotherhood, who visited her brothels in King's Place, an enclave of elite bordellos in St James's.

It is likely that they told her when to have her coach ready to speed down to Medmenham. Lord Sandwich said of her, 'She keeps the Stock Exchange supplied with real, immaculate maidenheads.' Perhaps, but she was an expert re-virginiser of her girls, and said 'a maidenhead is as easily made as a pudding'.

Another bawd once believed to have supplied girls for the monks was Elizabeth Dennison, who kept a bordello near Drury Lane. Known as Hell-Fire Stanhope – Hell-Fire because of a liaison with Lord Wharton, and Stanhope because she had been a mistress of Philip Dormer Stanhope, Earl of Chesterfield – it was this nickname that probably caused her name to be linked to Medmenham.

So much for the companions in joyful lust provided for the Brothers. It is time to lift the veil on the men themselves.

## A triumvirate steeped in infamy

The most important member of the Brotherhood, politically and historically, was John Wilkes. Conspicuous for his political acumen and cynicism, his ugliness and wit, his love of libertinism (sincere) and liberty (apparently sincere), Wilkes was a politician, journalist and controversialist of rare flair and verve.[*] His coming together with Dashwood and the Earl of Sandwich was a climacteric in the history of English rakedom. These three veterans in debauchery interacted to fulfil the possibilities inherent in the failed career of the Duke of Wharton – Dashwood and Sandwich to explore the limits of sex and Satanism, Wilkes to press the limits of the Glorious Revolution further towards the real liberty of the individual.

To Wilkes Medmenham was very much a sideshow, almost a welcome distraction from his constitutional disputes with George III and his ministers. To the King he was 'that devil Wilkes', to the public the personification of the struggle of the freedom-loving Englishman against the state. The mob took to the streets with the cry, 'Wilkes and Liberty'. Yet one day, when he had become something of an Establishment figure himself, he would tell the King: 'I never was a Wilkite.'

Wilkes was born in October 1725, the son of a prosperous London distiller. He was a dazzling young scholar, and in 1744 went to the University of Leiden in Holland. A fellow pupil, reporting a conversation with a companion, recalled the impact his arrival made:

---

[*] Wilkes's gift for repartee on the hustings was rightly celebrated. 'Will you vote for me?' he asked at one election meeting. 'I'd sooner vote for the Devil,' shouted an opponent. 'But if your friend doesn't run, may I count on your support?'

When we came to John Wilkes, whose ugly countenance in early youth was very striking, I asked earnestly who he was; his answer was that he was the son of a London distiller or brewer, who wanted to be a fine gentleman and man of taste, which he could never be, for God and nature had been against him. I came to know Wilkes very well afterwards and found him to be a sprightly entertaining fellow, too much so for his years, as he was but 18 – for even then he showed something of the daring profligacy for which he was afterwards notorious ... He was fond of learning, and passionately desirous of being thought something extraordinary ...

In 1747 Wilkes married Mary Mead, an heiress ten years his senior. It was an arranged marriage, and it was unhappy. Wilkes later described it as 'a sacrifice to Plutius, not to Venus'. Mary Mead was a stout, dreary, devout woman, with no taste for or understanding of the glamorous metropolitan life her husband craved. He was lively, a brilliant conversationist: she had no conversation. Her mother was pious and garrulous and liked to speculate endlessly to the atheist Wilkes on theology. His beloved daughter Polly was born in 1750 and, says Ronald Fuller in *Hell-Fire Francis*, 'to her Wilkes gave all the affection he never pretended to offer to his wife'.* He found amusement elsewhere, in the company of Thomas Potter, who introduced him to the distractions of Bath and Tunbridge Wells. Potter wrote to him:

If you prefer young women and Whores to old Women and Wives... if Life and Spirit and Wit and Humour and Gaiety but above all if the heavenly inspired Passion called LUST has not deserted you and left you a Prey to Dullness and Imbecility, hasten to Town that you may take a Place in my Post Chaise for Bath next

---

* It is interesting that several of the club members married wealthy and compliant women. In 1745 Dashwood married a wealthy widow, Sarah, Lady Ellis, whom Walpole described as 'a poor, forlorn, Presbyterian prude'. Paul Whitehead, the High Steward and Secretary-Treasurer of the Brotherhood, married the ugly and half-witted Ann Dyer in 1735. He was amply compensated by her large fortune and treated her with patience and kindness, which must have been sorely tried. 'Mr Whitehead, there's a cow,' she would exclaim, plucking him by the sleeve.

Thursday morning whither I am hurrying from the ... loathsome Bawdy of the Nurses, the solemn and hideous Lullabies of my Mother in Law and the odious Yell of a young Female Yahoo that thrust herself into the World yesterday [Potter is referring to the birth of a daughter to his second wife].

Through Potter Wilkes got to know Dashwood and his circle. Dashwood, colonel of the Bucks Militia, chose Wilkes as his lieutenant-colonel, conferring on him a social distinction his birth did not merit. His new friends shocked his wife, and her mother found them a most unreceptive audience for her musings on Christian theology. In 1757, the same year he became Member of Parliament for Aylesbury – having shown his political wiliness in 1754 when he contested the parliamentary seat of Berwick by bribing a ship's captain, who was taking some of his opponent's supporters from London by sea, to land them in Norway – he separated formally from Mary.

Wilkes treated the Brotherhood as an elaborate practical joke. He did not share the superstitious mysticism of some of his fellow members, or their crazy obsessions. But he was highly sexed and fun-loving, and found the witty conversation, the gaiety, the drinking and particularly the women attractive.[*]

In a letter of October 1762 to the statesman Lord Temple, Wilkes says he has come from Medmenham Abbey, 'where the jovial monks of St Francis had kept me up till four in the morning'. Maddeningly, he does not say what they were doing until that hour. But there is little doubt that Wilkes played a full part in whatever was happening at the abbey. His name occurs more often than any other in the fragmentary cellar-book, which records what drinks the monks ordered. There are hints in another letter, from a Mr Hall of Berkeley Square to Wilkes in August 1761:

---

[*] Wilkes was an inveterate womaniser. He told James Boswell that when he was a student at Leiden he was 'always among women... My father gave me as much money as I pleased. Three or four whores; drunk every night. Sore head morning, then read. I'm capable to sit 30 hours over a table to study.'

Mr Hall presents his compliments to Mr Wilkes and is still under the scourge of an invincible cholic which has reduced him to such a state of contrition that he is obliged to live by rules entirely opposite to those of St Francis, whose shrine he venerates, but dare not approach under his present incapacity. He desires ye prayers of ye congregation and hopes their devotion may be attended with the choicest blessings of their patron, health, wealth and never failing vigour ...

Wilkes left a description of the abbey, mentioning the closed chapter room with its 'English Eleusinian Mysteries' and the figures of gods. He also gives us intriguing glimpses of the grounds, the backdrop, he suggests, for the more natural sexual activities: 'The garden, the grove, the orchard, the neighbouring woods, all spoke the loves and frailities of the younger monks, who seemed at least to have sinned naturally.'

But the satanic mumbo-jumbo began to pall and as his political aims diverged from those of the others he fell out spectacularly with his fellow monks. One of those whom commentators have associated with the Brotherhood, although probably only as an enthusiastic spectator, was the Earl of Bute, favourite of George III and lover of his mother Augusta. Bute was appointed Prime Minister in 1762. When it became clear that Wilkes could expect nothing in the way of office from the Bute ministry he went into opposition. In June 1762 he launched a newspaper, the *North Briton*, and published an attack on Bute which was a thinly disguised commentary on his affair with the King's mother. Her son was furious, but for the present Wilkes went unpunished. Wilkes's lively style gave the *North Briton* real punch. He was the first journalist to name names in full, and his attack on the Scot Bute and the many fellow-countrymen to whom he gave preference was overtly racist.

Wilkes readily admitted in private that he had nothing against Bute or the Scots. It was sheer opportunism: he was trying to force the government to give him a post. But the hapless Bute became a figure of fun. Because of his relationship with Augusta, mobs marched about waving boots – Bute was then pronounced 'Boot' – and petticoats. The Prime Minister was burned in effigy and Augusta was insulted at the theatre. Bute took to going about disguised, or accompanied by a bodyguard of bruisers. When he patched up a peace treaty to end the Seven Years War in 1763 hardly anyone thanked him. He said he hoped his role as peacemaker would be engraved on his tomb, moving someone to respond: 'The sooner the better.'

Bute now lost his nerve. He had been trying to resign for some time but the King wouldn't let him leave office. Nevertheless in April 1763 he went, saying that his continuance in office would cause further trouble for the King. Dashwood too resigned, and as Baron Le Despenser, the premier barony of England, a title revived for him, he gladly took his place in the Lords.

The third figure in the infamous triumvirate at the centre of the Hell-Fire Club story, John Montagu, fourth Earl of Sandwich, has been immortalised by the snack of that name, which was his invention. He was much better known at the time, however, as a politician and tireless lecher. It was said that the idea for the snack came to him during long sessions at the gaming table, where he was too involved to stop for a meal, but another and more likely version is that he would eat sandwiches during long days at the Admiralty. He certainly had a passion for hard work, coupled with a fury of enthusiasm for debauchery, an untameable lust that would have done credit to his great-grandfather John Wilmot, Earl of Rochester. He had certain rakish qualities other than his appetite for debauchery – wit and taste and a total disregard, amounting to contempt, for what other people thought of him. These were qualities he shared with Dashwood, who was drawn by Sandwich's detestation of religion. Sandwich was said to have staged a divine service in his village church at which he preached to a congregation of cats. It was the kind of parody of religion later believed to be a staple of the rites of the Friars of the Hell-Fire Club.

Sandwich succeeded to his own earldom in 1729 when he was barely 11. Lord Chesterfield said that he proceeded 'in one uniform, unblushing course of debauchery and dissipation' from his earliest youth. The anonymous *Life, Adventures, Intrigues and Amours of the Celebrated Jemmy Twitcher* asserted that 'no man ever carried the art of seduction to so enormous a height'. He shares with Thomas Potter the reputation of being the most depraved of all the Brotherhood. Horace Walpole, who had known him at Eton, and was never lost for a sneer, said there was 'an inveteracy, a darkness, a design and cunning in his character which stamp him as a very unamiable young man ... It is uncommon for a heart to be tainted so young.' Sandwich certainly had an unenviable reputation. He was 'as mischievous as a monkey and as lecherous as a goat'. Donald McCormick in *The Hell-Fire Club, The Story of the Amorous Knights of Wycombe* says that 'In his pursuit of Venus he fought a score of duels'.[*] He was 'universally hated', mean to his mistresses and treacherous to his friends.

Although many rakes dabbled in politics, Sandwich was almost unique among them in having a long career in government, much of the time as First Lord of the Admiralty. The *Dictionary of National Biography* blames him for the navy's unpreparedness at the time of the outbreak of the American War of Independence, saying he 'returned to his post at the Admiralty, 1771, and began to employ the vast patronage of the office as an engine for bribery and political jobbery, in consequence of which when war broke out, 1778, the navy was found inadequate and the naval storehouses empty'.

The contemporary picture of Sandwich is deeply unflattering. Recent historians have been kinder, pointing out that no man with a career lasting half a century in high politics, diplomacy and

---

[*] This so terrified his rivals that one of them, the diminutive peer Lord Mountford, is said to have hidden from him in a woman's petticoats. Mountford had called on the courtesan Kitty Fisher at her house in New Norfolk Street. He found Kitty dressed, patched and powdered ready for an evening at the opera. As he was a good customer she let him in, although she was waiting for her escort, Lord Sandwich, to arrive. As Mountford was about to leave he heard Sandwich's steps on the stairs and looked about for somewhere to hide. Kitty raised a corner of her huge hooped petticoat and told the tiny Mountford to slip inside. She chatted with Sandwich until it was time to leave, then went into an adjoining room, released Mountford and carried on to the opera.

war could be so negligible. N. A. M. Rodger, in *The Insatiable Earl* tries to redress the balance by pointing out that his 20 years at the Admiralty 'cover some of the most important administrative, social and political developments in the history of the Royal Navy, in all of which he was intimately involved, and in many of which he was the prime mover'. Sandwich certainly interacted with men of the greatest importance in different spheres. Rodger adds: 'The friend of Anson and Garrick, the opponent of Wilkes and Charles James Fox, the patron of Cook and the champion of Handel, Sandwich connected many diverse lives.' Indeed, he had more solid political achievements than any other member of the club, however exalted.

Sandwich was physically unattractive. He had a long, thin, lugubrious face, a tall ungainly figure which, according to Fuller in *Hell-Fire Francis*, 'loped clumsily, as if he had no proper control over his limbs'. Wags said he walked as though he was trying to go down both sides of the street at the same time. As Fuller adds, 'His Paris dancing-master made him swear a solemn oath never to reveal to a living soul who was responsible for teaching him deportment.' The satirist Charles Churchill wrote:

> Nature design'd him, in a rage,
> To be the Wharton of his age,
> But having given all the sin
> Forgot to put the virtues in

Churchill also said of Sandwich that his face was that of a man who had been half-hanged and cut down by mistake. Nevertheless he was a natural athlete and an enthusiastic and expert cricketer. He was also a tireless worker, hard-driving and efficient: he demanded that memoranda be kept to a single page, and was the originator of the oft-quoted response: 'Sir, your letter is before me, and will presently be behind.' It was said he kept mistresses ready to service him at the office, because he didn't want to waste time by leaving the building.

Besides his enthusiastic patronage of music and craze for

cricket he was passionately fond of theatre, opera, tennis, yachting, fishing and was a linguist, classicist and orientalist. Rodger describes him in *The Insatiable Earl* as: 'a bold traveller in his youth and later a patron of explorers, an amateur of history, astronomy and numismatics'. Sandwich's version of the Grand Tour showed his independence of mind. He chartered a ship, embarking on a voyage which lasted a year and took him to Italy, Corsica, Egypt, Sardinia, Sicily, Greece, Turkey and Cyprus, and home by way of Malta, Gibraltar, Lisbon, Spain and Minorca. The voyage gave him his love and knowledge of seafaring, and his deep interest in eastern eroticism.

When he returned to England in 1739 he went into politics. Family history – an ancestor had as High Admiral of the Fleet persuaded the navy to accept the Restoration – and love of the sea made the Admiralty a natural goal. He joined the faction of the Duke of Bedford, part of the Whig opposition to Walpole, and when Bedford joined the government in 1744 as First Lord of the Admiralty he took Sandwich as his colleague. Sandwich was 26.

High office and his reputation as a womaniser made for some easy conquests; among his papers are letters from women offering themselves to him. His half-hanged look was not a problem – in fact many women seem to have found him irresistible, if only by reputation. One, who claimed she craved nothing but 'the honour of your Lordship's closer acquaintance', said that though she was not promiscuous, she could not resist 'the galantest man of his country'. As George Martelli recounts in his book *Jemmy Twitcher*, she begged for a meeting 'any place, any day, any hour', and assured him that he would not be disappointed in her person. In a letter he made a defence of his philandering which would have served any errant politician from that day to this: 'I have never pretended to be free from indiscretion, and those who know me have been ... long accustomed to forgive my weaknesses, when they do not interfere with my conduct as a public man.'

Sandwich's habit of keeping mistresses – sometimes in his own home – and visiting brothels in the fashionable red-light district of St James's no doubt contributed to the break-up of his marriage. He had married the Hon. Dorothy Fane, the daughter of an Irish peer, in 1740. Twenty-seven years later she was declared insane. In 1751, when she was already showing signs of instability, he was dismissed from office by George II as a result of faction fighting in the government. With his career in limbo and his marriage under strain, he threw himself into the activities of the Hell-Fire Club.

The Medmenham circle was the background to one of the most spectacular of all fallings-out in English political history. Wilkes had continued to goad the administration, of which Sandwich was still a member. The two met socially and chaffed each other, as Ashe says in *Do What You Will*. But Sandwich disliked Wilkes, whom he probably regarded as an upstart. He had never forgotten Wilkes's riposte to his suggestion that he would either die on the gallows or of the pox. Wilkes had replied: 'That depends, my Lord, whether I embrace your mistress or your principles.'

With Dashwood and another member of their set, William Douglas, Earl of March, Sandwich plotted to bring down the upstart. Wilkes and Thomas Potter seem to have collaborated in writing the salacious *Essay on Woman*, a parody of Pope's *Essay on Man*.[*] While Pope begins:

> Awake, my St John! leave all meaner things
> To Low ambition, and the pride of kings.
> Let us (since life can little more supply
> Than just to look about us and to die)
> Expatiate free o'er this scene of Man;
> A mighty maze! but not without a plan.

---

[*] Traditionally Potter was regarded as the author, with Wilkes providing notes, but Peter D. G. Thomas in *John Wilkes, A Friend to Liberty* attributes the poem itself to Wilkes. I have compromised and suggested the whole project was a collaboration.

the Wilkes/Potter parody, dedicated provocatively to Sandwich's former mistress Fanny Murray, opens:

> Awake, my Fanny, leave all meaner things,
> This morn shall prove what rapture swiving [copulation] brings.
> Let us (since life can little more supply
> Than just a few good fucks, and then we die)
> Expatiate free o'er that lov'd scene of Man;
> A mighty maze! for mighty pricks to scan.

Perhaps the best lines are the parody of Pope's couplet

> Presumptuous Man! the reason wouldst thou find
> Why formed so weak, so little and so blind?

Wilkes and Potter change only one word, but it is a real flash of humour:

> Presumptuous Prick! the reason wouldst thou find
> Why formed so weak, so little and so blind?

Wilkes, who supplied amusing notes in the style of the pompous Bishop Warburton, a member of the House of Lords, attempted to have the poem printed privately for private circulation, and at least a 94-line section of the *Essay* was printed, along with some notes and three short poems probably by Wilkes. The printer, Michael Curry, ran off an extra copy of the *Essay* for himself, and it seems that friends of the government heard about it. Curry was offered bribes to hand it over, and threatened with prosecution. At first he resisted. Then, he later claimed, Wilkes accused him of betrayal: 'some expressions dropping from him which affected my private character', said Curry, he voluntarily handed over his copy to the Earl of March's chaplain, a sexual pervert named John Kidgell. This clergyman published a pamphlet denouncing the verses as 'volatile, saline Effluvia of the unchaste Imagination of a prurient Debauchee'. Then he tried to deny his part in the affair. It was too late. March handed over the material to the government. Wilkes's papers were seized, and Sandwich found another reason for perse-cuting him. It was a ribald lampoon on himself which, asserts Peter Thomas in *John Wilkes, A Friend to Liberty*, 'contrived to impugn his courage and morality in a single sentence'. This was a set of mock instructions to Sandwich, who was about to be appointed ambas-sador to Madrid: 'It is beneath your lordship to measure swords with the men, and we do most expressly restrain you to make all your thrusts at the women.'

In November 1763 Wilkes was accused in the Lords of libelling Bishop Warburton on the basis of the notes to the *Essay on Woman*. Sandwich read out the fragment of the *Essay* with obvious relish, pausing from time to time to comment on its indecencies and blas-phemies. The comic irony of the situation was not lost on his audi-ence. Here was a known member of the Order of St Francis, a man who was about to be expelled from another club, the Beefsteaks, for blasphemy, expressing shock at the *Essay*'s puerile couplets. Sir Francis Dashwood, now in the Lords as Baron Le Despenser, who had been at best a lukewarm member of the plot, remarked in a stage whisper that it was the first time he heard Satan preaching against sin. Others objected to the reading. A Lord Lyttelton, named by Ashe in *Do What You Will* as one of those associated with the monks, called out to Sandwich to stop, but other peers roared 'Go on!' Bishop Warburton denied being the author of the notes, and said the 'hardiest inhabitants of hell' could not listen to such blasphemies. The House decided that the material was 'a most scandalous, obscene and impious libel'. Potter's name was never mentioned, and the plotters allowed it to be assumed that Wilkes was the author, without saying so.

While Wilkes was under attack in the Lords over the *Essay* he was also in trouble in the Commons over the notorious edition no. 45 of the *North Briton* which the administration claimed was 'a false, scandalous and seditious libel, containing expressions of the most unexampled insolence and contumely towards His Majesty, the grossest aspersions upon both Houses of Parliament, and the most audacious defiance of authority of the whole legislature'. This arose from an article questioning the truth of parts of the King's address, written of course by ministers. At the same time Wilkes was challenged to a duel by another politician, Samuel Martin, who felt he had been maligned in Wilkes's paper. Wilkes may have been set up, for Martin had been practising his marksmanship. When they met in Hyde Park in November 1763 Wilkes was badly wounded in the stomach by Martin's second shot.

Wilkes went to Paris to recuperate and visit his daughter. While he was there he was expelled from the Commons, found guilty of publishing seditious and obscene libels and declared an outlaw. For the moment he remained in exile.

The public's verdict on Sandwich was severe. John Gay's *The Beggar's Opera* was playing at the time, and when the imprisoned highwayman Macheath spoke the line 'But that Jemmy Twitcher should peach I own surprises me', the audience laughed and cheered. From then on Sandwich bore the stigma of the nickname Jemmy Twitcher.

As if class hostility alone could not explain Sandwich's antipathy to Wilkes, a story was circulated involving the Medmenham baboon, which Wilkes was said to have dressed up to look like the Devil. Released from a cupboard, it jumped on to Sandwich's shoulders and by the time it had been driven off Sandwich was almost insensible with fear. This story as well as much else that is at least semi-legendary about the Brotherhood, derives from Charles Johnstone's novel, *Chrysal*.

The full title of the novel is *CHRYSAL: or, the Adventures of a Guinea. Wherein are exhibited Views of several striking Scenes, with Curious and interesting Anecdotes, of the most Noted Persons in every Rank of Life, whose Hands it passed through, in America, England, Holland, Germany and Portugal.* One of those through whose pocket the guinea passes is clearly Wilkes, although like the other members of the Brotherhood he is not named. 'Sandwich' wins the guinea in a wager on a race between two maggots. The following day Chrysal is taken by his new owner to 'a party of pleasure of the most extraordinary character' at a mock-monastery. There the Dash-

*The Mystery of Medmenham* 149

wood figure, called the Superior, provides wine and women, and the ritual includes devil worship.

The Superior leads 12 members of an inner circle. On a lower level is another circle of 12, which includes Sandwich and Wilkes. A vacancy has been caused by the death of a member of the inner circle and the two compete to fill it. Wearing white robes they kneel in the chapel and pray to Satan, watched by the Superior and the rest of the inner circle. Sandwich gets their vote, and they all sit down to dinner. But Wilkes has planned his revenge. He has hidden a baboon dressed as the devil inside a chest, and while Sandwich is calling on Satan to join them he pulls a cord and the baboon leaps out. Most of the monks flee, but the baboon jumps on Sandwich, and he begs for mercy, pleading that he is not so wicked as he pretends. Later Wilkes denies he is the culprit, claiming the baboon got in through a window. He is betrayed by servants who helped with the trick, and expelled.

While Wilkes, Dashwood and Sandwich were historically important figures, other members of the Brotherhood were by no means negligible. Wilkes was introduced to the club in 1758 by the wealthy and perverted Thomas Potter, who was for a time secretary to Frederick, Prince of Wales, and also Vice-Treasurer for Ireland. In the Commons he made scintillating and cynical speeches. Hogarth depicted him as the winning politician in *Chairing the Candidates*. The son of an archbishop of Canterbury, Potter inherited £100,000 from his father and 'proceeded to spend it on orgy upon orgy'. It was written of him:

> He drank with drunkards, lived with sinners,
> Herded with infidels for dinners.

He is said to have 'hounded his first wife to the grave', though unhappy marriages were common among the members of the Brotherhood. 'Rich, handsome and witty, Potter was also madly extravagant and famous for his sexual adventures', observes Ashe in *Do What You Will*. One of these was the seduction of Bishop

Warburton's wife. This would have an echo in the *Essay on Woman* affair. Potter had a passion for watching executions and was believed to be so close to necrophilia that he copulated in churchyards.

The satirical poet Charles Churchill was introduced to the Brotherhood by Wilkes in 1762. Churchill's enduring friendship with another member and poet, Robert Lloyd, forms a counterpoint to the destructive conflict between Sandwich and Wilkes. Hogarth caricatured Churchill as a beer-swilling bear, and Churchill was singularly frank about his own ugly ungainliness.

> His face was short, but broader than 'twas long,
> His Features tho' by Nature they were large,
> Contentment had contriv'd to overcharge ...
> O'er a brown Cassock, which had once been black,
> Which hung in tatters on his brawny back,
> A sight most strange, and awkward to behold ...

If he looked a little like a wild animal, he was also a fearsome and fearless critic, described by Fuller in *Hell-Fire Francis* as 'the best-feared satirist since Pope'. His short life was a frenzy of toil, poverty, fame and dissipation. He married a girl named Martha Scott in the Fleet prison and she made him miserable. Burdened with two unwanted children, he followed his father's wishes and became a clergyman although he had no vocation: he 'prayed and starved on forty pounds a year' at Rainham in Essex. He was not a success – it was said he eked out his stipend by selling cider to the villagers, and despite his literary talents his sermons were dull:

> Whilst, sacred dullness ever in my view,
> Sleep at my bidding crept from pew to pew.

In 1758 his father died and Churchill took his place as incumbent at St John's, Westminster. He taught English at Mrs Dennis's Boarding School for Girls, the 'Ladies' Eton', in Queen Square. He also renewed his friendship with his old Westminster schoolfellow, Robert Lloyd.

Churchill was an unhappy priest, and Lloyd an unhappy school-master at Westminster School. He wanted to be a poet, and wrote pleasant, facile but self-pitying verses:

> My rhymes, alas! will catch no fish,
> To swim in sauce upon my dish;
> And for these notes, however clear,
> Will the next Dolphin [a pub] give me beer?

While Churchill consumed his life in savage enjoyment of all that rakishness had to offer, Lloyd was prone to remorse:

> A Rake! Alas! how many wear
> The brow of mirth with heart of care!
> The desperate wretch reflection flies,
> And shuns the way where madness lies.

In 1761 Churchill wrote the immensely successful satire on contemporary actors, *The Rosciad*. He was able to pay back Lloyd's father, who had discharged the two young men's debts in the vain hope they would become respectable. He also had enough to buy a gold-laced hat and blue coat, white silk stockings and silver buckles. Although he had given up any pretence to being a clergy-man, the Dean of Westminster objected to the way he now strutted about town in his finery. Lloyd wrote:

> To Churchill the bard cries the Westminster Dean,
> Leather breeches, white stockings! Pray, what can you mean?

They became very scandalous. John Wilkes said in a letter to the Duke of Grafton that they were 'generally employed in celebrat-ing the mysteries of the god of love'. When John Armstrong was mildly critical of Churchill in his poem 'Day', Churchill riposted with 'Night', published in October 1761. Wilkes, to whom 'Day' had been dedicated, at once wrote to Churchill to dissociate himself from its criticisms, and a friendship began which ended only with Churchill's death. They were both courageous, hated cant and were full-blooded rakes. Churchill wrote to Wilkes: 'Though I will not get drunk with every Fool, I am above being thoroughly sober with an honest fellow like you.' Wilkes introduced him to the Medmenham rites in the summer of 1762 when he was 30, and the renegade priest shared his friend's healthy contempt for them. However, he enjoyed himself among the nuns, and from time to time had to retire from the fray to recover from a dose of the pox. In 1762–3 both he and his mistress had the disease, and he underwent the mercury cure.

Having introduced Lloyd to London's night life, Churchill now took him along to meet the Friars. When Wilkes launched his anti-Bute newspaper the *North Briton* in June 1762 he recruited Churchill and Lloyd to help him harry the ministry. Bute was rumoured to be a member of the Medmenhamites,[*] and the attacks by Wilkes and Churchill show the disarray the Brotherhood had fallen into. With his eye as ever on the main chance, Wilkes offered to desist if he were given the governorship of Canada – he would take his two acid-penned helpers with him, Churchill as chaplain, Lloyd as secretary. It is fascinating to speculate how the duo would have fared in the bracing atmosphere of the frontier. The deal was rejected, perhaps by minds with a keener sense of the ridiculous.

The poet Paul Whitehead, Dodington's assistant, was a member of the inner circle of disciples, and Dashwood's right-hand man. Known among members as Paul the Aged or Paul of Twickenham, he was regarded as the Brotherhood's moving spirit after Dashwood. A poet and political hack-writer, as the club's record keeper he knew all its secrets. He planned and probably supervised the Brotherhood's rites, saw to it that the abbey was well supplied with fine wine, and collected the subscriptions. His bitter atheism and

---

[*]  Horace Walpole states in his memoirs that Bute liked 'masquerading in becoming dresses'.

his sense of humour made him an apt crony for Dashwood – he once organised a parade of tramps, beggars 'and all the cripples in Holborn' to process through London in fancy dress travestying the annual Masonic march. In respectable old age, worn out by his exertions in the service of Satan and Venus, he complained in his 'Epistle to the Arch-Fiend' that he was being singled out for blame:

> Why on me alone should your vengeance thus fall?
> Why not Thomas, or Francis, as well as St Paul?
> On Aylesbury John why your anger not place
> Who, all must allow, is so brim-full of grace?

Dashwood treated Whitehead, who was the son of a tailor, with amused contempt, yet the steward was his most ardent follower, remaining faithful to the ideals of the Brotherhood after the club was disbanded. Though a reformed rake, living at Twickenham, he still refused to enter a church and was known for his sulphurous utterances, described by a neighbour as 'desultory, vociferous and profane' (Hawkins, *Life of Samuel Johnson*). His half-witted wife died in November 1768; as Fuller says in *Hell-Fire Francis*, Whitehead, who had come to feel for her 'a kind of protective fondness', was heartbroken. He died six years later, after destroying, page by page, all the evidence he had collected about the activities of the club. He left his heart to Dashwood, and £50 for a marble urn to hold it.[*]

---

[*] The heart, shrivelled to the size of a walnut, was one of the curiosities shown to visitors to the abbey after it became a tourist attraction. In September 1839 a visitor slipped it into his pocket and it vanished.

# The Fires Die Down

D URING THE SECOND HALF OF THE 1760S, John Wilkes had been contemplating a return to Britain and politics. He missed the excitement of stirring up controversy and being the centre of attention, and he had money troubles, not helped by his extravagant and tempestuous mistress, the 19-year-old Italian opera dancer Gertrude Corradini.* To stop the author-ities seizing it he had sold the Manor of Aylesbury, part of Mary Mead's estate, for the comfortable sum of £4,000 (around £370,000), but the friend to whom he had entrusted the trans-action had used the money to stave off his own bankruptcy. In early 1768, with debts piling up and another expensive mistress to maintain, he returned to London and fought an election in the City. He came last in the poll, but almost immediately contested another election in Middlesex, and was carried to the top of the poll on a wave of anti-government sentiment.

---

\* Corradini used to veil the picture of the Virgin Mary which hung above her bed when Wilkes visited, but was very lascivious. Wilkes recalled: 'She was a perfect Grecian figure, cast in the mould of the Florentine Venus, excepting that she was rather fuller and had flatter breasts. Extremely delicate in person, she continued constantly attentive to every circumstance which could give herself or a lover pleasure. She possessed the divine gift of lewdness, but nature had not given her strength adequate to the force of her desires.' When she became aware that Wilkes was broke she stripped his house of anything of value and disappeared. By then he had other sexual interests – his many conquests included Mademoiselle Charpillon, who had taken Casanova's money but rejected his advances when he was in London.

Wilkes's subsequent political career was extraordinary. In April he surrendered to the authorities and was held in the King's Bench prison, where his presence became a focus of popular discontent. During the so-called George's Field Massacre on 10 May, trigger-happy troops facing a pro-Wilkes mob opened fire, killing seven people including a woman orange-seller and a man on a passing hay cart. There were widespread riots in the city. At the Palace of Westminster politicians could hear the now familiar shouts of 'Wilkes and Liberty!'

Although his outlawry was reversed on a technicality, Wilkes remained in prison for two years on the libel charges. In 1769 he was again expelled from Parliament, but as a popular hero his re-election was a formality. Time and again he was expelled, and just as often the electors showed their contempt for the administration by returning him. Finally the Commons declared that the defeated candidate, Henry Luttrell, was the winner. Wilkes moved his campaign to the City of London. Bolstered by the Society of the Supporters of the Bill of Rights, which helped with his debts, he was elected Lord Mayor and in 1774 MP for Middlesex. He had finally made it. When the Gordon Rioters attacked the Bank of England in June 1780, one of its defenders was Alderman John Wilkes. The great champion of liberty and friend of the people later claimed he shot two of the mob which attacked this symbol of capitalism and oppression. Encountering an elderly woman in the street who called out 'Wilkes and Liberty', he rebuked her: 'Be quiet, you old fool. That's all over long ago.' The playwright Sheridan, himself something of a political gadfly, is believed to have been the author of a verse that mocked Wilkes:

> Johnny Wilkes, Johnny Wilkes,
> Thou greatest of bilks,
> How changed are the notes you now sing!
> Your famed Forty-Five
> Is Prerogative,
> And your blasphemy, 'God save the King'.

John Wilkes was among the defenders of the Bank of England
when the mob tried to storm it during the Gordon Riots.

It was true that Wilkes had changed his tune: it is his earlier achievements that win our admiration. Perhaps the most important of these was to champion and win the cause of freedom of the press to report parliamentary debates. The King and his administration had tried to suppress such reporting by legal action against the printers. Wilkes ran rings around them, organising the considerable powers and privileges of the City against the Commons. He humiliated the King's government and forced it to back down. Since 1771 and 1775, debates in the Commons and the Lords respectively have been reported, thanks to Wilkes.

He later lost the support of the radical mob, and although he had used them he had scant respect for them. Horace Walpole recalled a Wilkes speech in 1775 on the Middlesex Elections: 'Though he called the resolutions of the last Parliament a violation of Magna Carta, he said, in a whisper to Lord North [the Prime Minister] he was forced to say so to please the fellows who followed him.'

Sex was always a vital strand in Wilkes's life, some thought to the detriment of his other great love, politics. His amours, says Thomas in *John Wilkes*, would fill a book. He once said he loved all women except his wife, and he loved a good many of them at the same time. His affair with Mademoiselle Charpillon lasted a surprising four years, but she was too expensive and he ditched her in 1777. The following year at Bath he met Amelia Arnold, who was to be his mistress until his death. Aged 24, she was three years younger than his daughter Polly. When Amelia had a daughter Wilkes set the pair up in a house at Kensington Gore. While he visited frequently, by living elsewhere he preserved his freedom to pursue other women, including one Sally Barry.

It was this affair that caused a newspaper to mock the aged roué's fading powers: 'Alderman Wilkes is finishing his *Essay on Woman* in the neighbourhood of Soho; but it is a weak and miserable performance.' Thomas speculates that it was Barry Wilkes was hurrying to meet when a friend stopped him in St James's Street. 'Don't stop me,' said Wilkes. 'I have got an erection now. Did it go down I don't know when I shall have another.' He is reputed to have told his apothecary, shortly before his death: 'My sins of omission are daily increasing, my sins of emission daily diminishing.' He died in December 1797, aged 72. Nathaniel Wraxall, who knew him towards the end of his life, recalled:

> In private society, particularly at table, he was pre-eminently agreeable; abounding in anecdote; ever gay and convivial; converting his very defects of person, manner, or enunciation to purposes of merriment or of entertainment. If any man ever was pleasing who squinted, who had lost his teeth and lisped, Wilkes might be so esteemed. His powers of conversation survived his other bodily faculties. I have dined in company with him not long before his decease, when he was extenuated and enfeebled to a great degree; but his tongue retained all its former activity, and seemed to have outlived his other organs. Even in corporeal ruin, and obviously approaching the termination of his career, he formed the charm of the assembly.

Dashwood's club ceased to exist about the time the last volume of *Chrysal* was published, but it was not disbanded, it seems to have just fizzled out. Julie Peakman in *Lascivious Bodies* believes Wilkes had made it so notorious that Dashwood hurriedly stripped the abbey of any 'incriminating' evidence for fear of 'recriminations and possible scandal', but this seems unlikely – Dashwood was impervious to public scorn. Whatever the reason, when Walpole visited the abbey in 1763 he found some of the splendid furnishings had gone, and the place was neglected.

At that time the club wasn't quite finished. Fragments from the cellar-book show that the brethren were still meeting there in 1764, and a letter dated 11 August of that year from another member, John Tucker, to Dashwood states:

> My heart and inclination will be with your Lordship and your friends at Medmenham at the next Chapter, but I am cruelly detained here by the sickness of my mother ... if this should reach your Lordship at Medmenham I pray you will present my filial duty

to our Holy Father, and fraternal love and respect to the pious brotherhood, to whom I wish all possible joy, spirit and vigour.

Less than two years later, on 22 March 1766, he writes: 'I was last Sunday at Medmenham, and to my amazement found the Chapter Room stripped naked.'

Local legends long hung about the abbey, which became a tourist draw. The legends also mentioned the nearby caves, even suggesting that they were used by the monks for their rites long after the abbey was abandoned. By this date, however, most of the monks were old and likely to have found the chill damp of the caves unbearable. It is hard to see why the expensively equipped abbey should have been allowed to become dilapidated if they wanted to carry on. Like other parts of the puzzle, the caves can be fitted into the bigger picture only speculatively.

Time was taking its toll of the monks. Potter, borne down by his illnesses – he once described his gout, scurvy and palsy as 'a petty triumvirate' which 'shook him to atoms' – died unrepentant in June 1759. In November 1758 he had written to Lord Chatham:

> I know not what to say. I am supposed to be out of all present danger, yet for this week I have been allowed to put nothing in my mouth but Asses milk and buttermilk. Gout is banished from the number of my complaints, and the whole series of my disorders is attributed to bile violently acrimonious, constantly overflowing, and never properly secreting either through some natural deficit or some other obstructing concretions in the gall bladder. The latter seems probable as I now have constant pain in that region. I wish this idea may be well founded, for such a disorder is critical and must in a short space either yield or prevail . . .

George Bubb Dodington died before he could attend the last meeting of the Friars. 'Old, cold, withered and of intolerable entrails', he would snore in his great armchair after dinner, no longer waking up, as he once had, to fire off witty remarks in his husky bass and embarrass the ladies. He was grotesquely swollen with dropsy, and the burden of his enormous belly made him stumble as he walked. One day in July 1762 he tripped and fell down the kitchen stairs. As he lay dying he inserted a clause in his will, leaving £500 to Baron Le Despenser for 'building an arch, temple, column or additional room' to house his ashes. His Vanbrugh mansion at Eastbury Park near Blandford in Dorset, one of the largest in the country, he did not live to see completed. He left it to Lord Temple, who blew it up with gunpowder after vainly offering £200 a year to anyone who would consent to live in it.

Though the Medmenham meetings gradually petered out in the middle 1760s, Sir Francis continued occasionally to use the abbey for entertaining, and the cellar-book shows members were there in 1770. In 1771 an event of great interest at the time took place there, although whether it was directly connected to the Brotherhood is not clear. A jury of aristocratic matrons assembled to examine the genitals of the French transvestite and secret agent the Chevalier d'Eon de Beaumont. He had once been sent on a secret mission to Russia, where he disguised himself as a woman so effectively that the Empress was taken in. Although the Chevalier became a captain of dragoons and was a formidable swordsman, there remained some doubt about his gender, and he continued to dress as a woman during his stay in England. Bets amounting to £120,000 (more than £10 million today) were laid by London clubmen on whether he was a man or a woman. The panel of matrons could not make up their minds. After 'a most thorough investigation' they decided the issue was still 'doubtful'.[*]

In 1777 Duffield sold the abbey. Sir Francis's love of rites and show now found an outlet in his patronage of his local church, St Lawrence's, which he had been working on since 1760. It would be easy to accuse him of hypocrisy, but it was of a piece with his love of showmanship and spectacle. And the church itself was almost as dramatic a piece of stage-management as anything that happened at the abbey.

---

[*] When the Chevalier died in 1810 there was a post mortem, at which another rake associated with the Brotherhood, the Duke of Queensberry, was present, and it was finally established that he was a man.

As Ashe says in *Do What You Will*, 'By any standard of that time, the church was about as unecclesiastical as a church could well be.' A woman considered it 'as striking as a fine concert or ball room. 'Tis indeed an Egyptian hall, and certainly gives one not the least idea of a place sacred to religious worship', while Churchill wrote of St Lawrence as

> A temple built aloft in air
> That serves for show and not for prayer.

It was very odd, with armchairs and ornate pillars and a font that resembled a Rosicrucian lamp. The ceiling was decorated with a depiction of the Last Supper in which Judas was the dominant figure. The organ alone cost Dashwood £6,000. The church was on a hill, its 80-foot tower topped by a 20-foot golden ball which could be seen for miles around. Inside the ball was a chamber with benches round the sides, and Baron Le Despenser, as Sir Francis now was, would sit there singing songs and tippling with Wilkes and Churchill, against whom he does not seem to have borne a grudge. Wilkes wrote:

> Some churches have been built for devotion, others from parade of vanity. I believe this is the first church which has ever been built for a prospect ... built on the top of a hill for the convenient devotion of the town at the bottom of it ... I admire the silence and secrecy which reigns in that great globe, undisturbed but by his [Dashwood's] jolly songs very unfit for the profane ears of the world below.

He also referred to it as 'the best Globe Tavern I was ever in'.

The neighbours were shocked by the strange church, and rumours began to circulate about what went on in the golden globe. There were suggestions that the old Brotherhood was meeting there, but as Ashe says, 'They would have been cramped, and their favourite activity would have been very tricky indeed.'

In a sense, however, the church was used for reunions. When

Dodington died in 1762 Sir Francis complied with the request in his will and had him buried there in an open hexagonal structure, with columns and urns and arches. In 1769 Dodington was joined by the body of Sir Francis's wife Sarah. Whitehead's heart remained in an urn there until it was stolen.

Nor had Sir Francis lost his taste for bizarre ceremonies. In 1771 he opened the gardens of his home, West Wycombe House, to the public to mark the completion of a portico at the west end of the building, called the Temple of Bacchus, with a statue of the god inside. Once again, to the scandal of the neighbours, it was a pagan ceremony: a high priest led a procession of fauns and satyrs wearing skins and vine leaves across the grounds and into the portico. Eventually they embarked on a boat while cannon fired and the locals, won over by Sir Francis's hospitality, applauded.

There was an even more elaborate if more conventional ceremony for Whitehead's heart. In 1775 the urn was placed on a bier in West Wycombe House. A company of the Bucks Militia was drawn up on the lawn, their officers wearing crepe armlets. There was a band, and two music masters and seven choirboys. At a signal from Sir Francis on the terrace the procession circled the house three times, the band playing, the boys singing. Six grenadiers entered the house and carried out the bier with the urn, and the whole procession moved slowly to the gate and up the hill to the church. The church bells tolled and guns fired salutes. The procession circled the mausoleum three times and the urn was placed inside. The soldiers fired three volleys and marched off to 'a merry tune'. Sir Francis had certainly earned his lasting reputation for eccentricity.

Two years after Whitehead's funeral his collected poems were published, with a memoir by Commodore Edward Thompson. The commodore was also the well-informed author of the *Meretriciad*, a kind of verse gossip column on women of pleasure.[*]

---

[*] Thompson was a war hero and man of parts and his rough verse is amusing, if sometimes hard to follow. It would be interesting to know how he acquired his detailed knowledge of the demi-monde in a busy career which included editing an edition of the poet Andrew Marvell's works.

He dedicated the Whitehead volume to Dashwood, and the latter's acceptance infers approval of the contents. So Thompson's summing up can be taken as the official line on what went on, although as with everything concerning the Brotherhood it is indirect:

> Now all that can be drawn from the publication of these ceremonies is, that a set of worthy, jolly fellows, happy disciples of Venus and Bacchus, got occasionally together, to celebrate Woman in wine; and to give more zest to the festive meeting, they plucked every luxurious idea from the ancients and enriched their modern pleasures with the addition of classic luxury.

That could hardly be more ambiguous.

Sir Francis held office again, as a successful joint postmaster-general, and drafted a pro-American peace plan which, says Ashe in *Do What You Will*, 'Benjamin Franklin warmly approved'. They revised the Book of Common Prayer when Franklin visited West Wycombe in 1773. The result was not apparently much used in England, but found wide acceptance in America, where it was known as the Franklin Prayer Book. Their version of the Creed is interesting: 'I believe in God the Father Almighty, Maker of Heaven and Earth; And in Jesus Christ his Son, our Lord. I believe in the Holy Ghost; the Forgiveness of Sins; and the Life Everlasting. Amen.' Ashe comments that Saint Francis of Wycombe could do away with most of the Creed, but not with the forgiveness of sins.

In 1774 Dashwood's last mistress, a former actress named Mrs Barry – an echo of Rochester – had a daughter. In November 1781 several members of the Dashwood household saw Paul Whitehead's ghost beckoning in the grounds. Dashwood's sister Lady Austen reported seeing it to the poet Cowper. In December Dashwood died, and was buried in his church.

Although he and his friars cannot bear comparison with the Merry Gang of Charles II's court, they were mostly poets or versifiers, men of taste, wit and charm. They had maintained their

enthusiasm for about a dozen years, longer than most undergraduates sustain their desire to shock. They were escapists and rebels,
and perhaps harbingers of the Romantic movement in its Gothic
phase.

## Rebirth at Crazy Castle

After the Brotherhood's demise, embers of the Hell-Fire movement flickered into life across the British Isles. Wilkes had once
written to his friend John Hall Stevenson rebuking him for not
believing his account of proceedings at the abbey. Stevenson
replied:

> *Le Diable d'Ennuie* possessed me all at once and drove me as he did
> my Brethren ye swine down a precipice where I am now suffering
> among the Damned that are bathing in sulphur at Harrogate, for not
> believing that there was anything miraculous in the shrine of St
> Francis. Say a mass for me . . . Do give me a line with yr. absolution
> for my transgressions to St Francis, and a hint of the world to come.

Stevenson had inherited Skelton Castle, near Saltburn in Yorkshire,
and renamed it Crazy Castle. In *Do What You Will*, Ashe describes
him as a bitter anti-Catholic, a collector of pornography and a
hypochondriac who went to bed whenever the east wind blew in
the belief that he was dying. In his mad castle he set up a fraternity
on Medmenhamite lines, calling it the Demoniacals. Dashwood
was roped in as adviser. The only other person of note associated
with it was the novelist Laurence Sterne, author of *Tristram Shandy*,
who was vicar of Sutton-on-the-Forest in Yorkshire. He seems to
have been mainly interested in the castle library, but endorsed
Stevenson's schemes. The Demoniacals began by holding rituals
that entailed parody baptisms and assumed names, but soon degen-
erated into a drinking club whose members gambled and told
dirty stories.

There are hints of another hell-fire club in London about this
time in *The Fruit Shop*. It gives an account of a 'sect of philogynists'

– womanisers – who held orgies preceded by rituals. There is no way now of knowing if this 'sect' existed, but others in Ireland and France certainly did. A Dublin Hell-Fire Club had been revived after many years of inactivity, its leading light one Thomas 'Buck' Whaley. He was said to have set a man-trap which caught a farmer's daughter; he had her killed and smoked 'like a side of pork' and served up among his fellow members. Their regular toasts were 'The devil' and 'Damn us all'.

Students at Oxford and Cambridge seem to have formed hell-fire clubs early in the nineteenth century. In 1809 Lord Byron, who had just left Trinity College, Cambridge, held a meeting at his home, Newstead Abbey, to commemorate Medmenham, and drank burgundy from a human skull. And with this feeble gesture, the hell-fire spirit finally guttered and died.

# Part 4

# Old Q:

# The Rake of Piccadilly

$\mathcal{P}$ rel$\widehat{u}$ de

ABOUT THE MIDDLE OF THE EIGHTEENTH CENTURY, commercial sex was the most important industry in London. Its
income has been estimated at about £10 million (consid-
erably more than £1 billion today) a year, more than double that of
the nearest comparable industry, building. Much of its success was
due to a group of enterprising businesswomen, who first copied
and then surpassed the best that Paris had to offer in the way of
perfumed splendour. Their luxury brothels, concentrated in the St
James's area, attracted business magnates from the City, politicians
from Parliament nearby, upper-class members of the Pall Mall and
St James's Street clubs, and courtiers – including some of George
III's sons, the royal dukes, led by their brother the Prince of Wales.
To fleece this rich flock the bawds assembled the loveliest and most
fascinating girls of the town. Concentrated in the small area of St
James's, small enough to walk around even when drunk, was every-
thing the man of affairs cared about or needed: politics, good food,
gambling and sex. There never was a better time to be a rake.

And with the upper classes 'more permissive than in any subsequent generation until the twentieth century', as I. M. Davis says
in *The Harlot and the Statesman*, and with their pockets full of new
money from what was already probably the strongest economy in
the world, there never was a better time to be a celebrity whore.
A good part of this wave of money was supplied by William
Douglas, the aristocrat eventually known as Old Q.

The heart of London's sex industry was an insignificant alley called King's Place off Pall Mall, where almost all the houses were luxury brothels, charging prices only the wealthy could afford. The German traveller Baron J. W. von Archenholz described in *A Picture of England* (1789) what they got for their money:

> The Noted Houses situated in a little street in St James, called King's Place, in which great numbers of nuns are kept for People of Fashion, living under the direction of several rich Abbesses ... You may see them superbly clothed at public places, even those of the most expensive kind. Each of these Convents has a Carriage and liveried servants, since these ladies never deign to walk anywhere except in St James's Park.

The baron says that the prices in the King's Place nunneries were so exorbitant 'as to exclude the Mob entirely'. The most important of the King's Place brothel-keepers was Charlotte Hayes, who as well as supplying girls to the Hell-Fire Club at Medmenham was the leading organiser of late Georgian London's sexual night life.

Hayes had a genius for self-advertisement. Her masterstroke was a 'Tahitian Feast of Venus'. Captain Cook had recently discovered Tahiti, and he reported that the natives copulated in public. Hayes, seeking to counter the attractions of the Pantheon, a vast pleasure complex which opened in Oxford Street in 1772, invited her wealthiest clients to the feast, at which 'twelve beautiful spotless nymphs all virgins will act out the Feast of Venus as it is celebrated in Oteite' under her direction. Madame Hayes intended to 'play the part of Queen Oberea herself', and she hinted that some of the maidens would be as young as 11 years old. A contemporary report stated: 'Twenty-three Gentlemen of the highest Breeding, including five Members of Parliament' gathered in her drawing room to watch as 12 athletic young men faced the aforesaid 12 maidens. After the youths had presented the girls with strange dildo-shaped objects the couples copulated with 'passion and dexterity'. The audience watched this performance with growing excitement for some time and then joined in. Later they adjourned to supper. The cost of entry was astronomical.

Hayes had plenty of competition. Perhaps the most important was Sarah Prendergast, who had married into the Prendergast family of brothel-keepers and became one of the most successful and wealthy of all bawds. She was best known because of an absurd and amusing scandal involving one of her customers, the Earl of Harrington, known because of his sexual preferences as Lord Fumble. He and his wife were a notably lecherous pair, she for her lesbian affairs and for frequenting brothels and he referred to by the *Westminster Magazine* as 'a Person of the most exceptional immorality'. In 1773 the magazine spoke of him as having 'sacrificed all appearance of Decency … for the lowest amusements at the lowest Brothels … ' The *Town and Country Magazine* said he was 'as lecherous as a Monkey'.

He kept a harem in his mansion, 'which comprised a Negress in a feather'd Turban, a young girl in pseudo-classical dress, another [dressed] as a Country-wench, as well as a Mandolin-player … ' The *Town and Country Magazine* said of the Earl and his wife: 'His Lordship is an impotent Debauchee and his Lady a professional Messalina [the cruel and debauched wife of the Roman emperor Claudius] who has little cause to be jealous – she would rather be inclined to laughter at this liaison'. Lady Harrington, whose reputation was such that she was indeed known as the 'Stable Yard Messalina', had a weakness for both sexes. When her lesbian lover Elizabeth Ashe deserted her for a diplomat she was 'quite devastated … her character had been demolished by this desertion.'

The scandal which engulfed the Earl in 1778 was exceptional in an age of sexual scandal, and threatened to get out of hand. Like other brothel-keepers, Mrs Prendergast kept fewer than half a dozen resident whores, sending out for others when business was brisk. When the season was over and the customers went to popular spas or seaside resorts to take the cure, the bawds would close their brothels and follow, taking their choicest 'pieces' with them. One of Prendergast's best was Amelia Cozens, who later became a King's Place bawd herself, and another was a Jewish girl named

Nancy Ambrose. One night in November 1778 the peevish Earl, whose sex drive was low, found that none of Prendergast's girls appealed, so she sent out to the bawd Mother Butler of Westminster for fresh supplies. Mother Butler supplied her with Country Bet and Black Susan. That useful guide to eighteenth-century vice the *Nocturnal Revels* says that having ordered them to undress, the Earl 'began his manual operations, which were succeeded by theirs'. After an hour 'his Lordship fancied he had been highly gratified ... they thought they had earned their present with great labour and much difficulty to bring his Lordship to the zest of his amorous passion.' However, the earl paid them only three guineas, much less than they expected for their exertions.

When they returned to Mother Butler's she asked for her cut of 25 per cent. Bet refused and Butler seized her clothes. Bet called the police and Butler was charged with theft. Clearly she had not been paying the appropriate bribes – generous greasing of palms usually kept the bawds and brothels of St James's safe from prosecution. For, with the aid of a vindictive magistrate, Mrs Butler was charged with keeping a house of ill-fame and of ordering Bet 'to go in company with another woman of the lowest order to meet the Earl of Harrington at the house of Mrs Prendergast, who keeps a seraglio in King's Place'. Bet spread the damage further by accusing Mrs Butler's husband, a Sergeant Spencer Smith of the Grenadier Guards, of aiding his wife by transporting girls by coach to the King's Place brothels. Her deposition added that the Earl visited Mrs Prendergast's establishment on Sundays, Mondays, Wednesdays and Fridays and had two girls on each occasion.

This mix of sex, aristocracy and money appealed to the readers of popular publications such as the *Westminster Magazine*, the *Morning Post* and the *Morning Herald*. Harrington was enraged by the press coverage. According to Burford in *Royal St James*, he 'flew into a great passion, stuttering and swearing and ... waving his Cane and shouting: "Why! I'll not be able to show my Face at Court"' He demanded that Mrs Prendergast buy up all the copies of the papers she could find, and she sent six people out to do this. The posse went to clubs and coffee shops where papers were displayed for members and customers to read, and stole them. Prendergast paid Bet five guineas to drop the prosecution.

Although all parties were eventually mollified, Mrs Prendergast felt something special was needed to restore confidence in the discretion of aristocratic night spots. She sought subscriptions for a Grand Ball d'Amour at which 'the finest women in all Europe would appear *in puris naturalibus*'. This meant beautiful courtesans and equally beautiful aristocrat amateurs who enjoyed the same freedoms. Toasts of the Town included the Hon. Charlotte Spencer, whose minimum rate was £50 (about £4,200) a night; Gertrude Mahon, daughter of a minor aristocrat and known as the Bird of Paradise because of her liking for gaudy clothes; the rope dancer Isabella Wilkinson, who specialised in the diplomatic corps; the courtesan Harriet Powell, at one time mistress of Lord Melbourne; and Lady Henrietta Grosvenor – 'of moderate Beauty, no Understanding and excessive vanity' – who had been involved in a great divorce scandal involving the Duke of Cumberland.

The ball was a triumph, and Mrs Prendergast cleared a profit of more than £1,000. The naked beauties danced for hours while an orchestra played facing the wall so as not to embarrass them. Afterwards the masked dancers repaired to 'sophas, to realize those rites which had been celebrated only in theory. The fervency of the devotion, upon this occasion, could scarcely be paralleled; and it is somewhat extraordinary that Lord Grosvenor and Lord L——r enjoyed their own wives without knowing it; and strange to tell! pronounced their imaginary Lais's most excellent pieces.' The *Nocturnal Revels* claims that when they realised they had unwittingly given each other so much gratification the Grosvenors were reconciled. Lady L——r however gave her husband 'a Neapolitan complaint', not for the first time. It was 'a favour which she had received a few days before from a Foreign Minister, much esteemed among the ladies for his uncommon parts and amorous abilities'. After the orgy there was a banquet. When the carriages were called, Ladies Grosvenor and Lucan and the Bird of Paradise 'disclaimed their attendance-fee', donating the money to the servants. The ordinary whores who attended

# The Satyr and the Sadist

INTO THIS LOUCHE WORLD OF EASY MORALS and easy money came the strange figure of the future Earl of March, William Douglas, whose fabulous wealth would for years contribute substantially to the prosperity of the sex industry. However in 1746, when he first appeared at White's Club in St James's Street, he was probably aged 22 and far from wealthy. Unlike most of the other major figures at the club, who had been educated at Eton, he had gone to Winchester. This alone would have made him seem a provincial, but as he was also a Scot he was a complete outsider.

White's was founded in 1693 by an Italian named Francesco Bianco, originally as a chocolate house. By the time Douglas arrived Bianco had anglicised his name to White and the choco- late house had become the most fashionable and exclusive gentle-men's club in London. It was in fact two clubs, the Old Club and the Young Club, and members of the two regarded each other with the usual incomprehension of one generation for another. Douglas was introduced to the Young Club by George Selwyn, a member popular for his wit, his stoical bearing of large gambling losses and his warm and generous personality. Weak, languid, without guile and totally unambitious, he inspired the greatest affection: 'him I really loved', wrote Horace Walpole, another Old Etonian member, when Selwyn died in 1791.

The friendship between Selwyn and Douglas was a true attrac-tion of opposites. Selwyn's languor extended to sex. Although he accompanied his friends to the brothels of St James's and even to the Hell-Fire Club at Medmenham, he would spend the evening talking to the bewitching girls over supper or a drink, or to the bawds themselves, while his friends were engaged upstairs. He made it appear that it was all too much trouble, although it has been speculated that if he had ever accumulated enough energy his inclinations would have been for men. His new friend Douglas was in contrast the lecher of the age, a man with an almost inexhaustible sex drive.

There was a dark side to Selwyn's sexuality, from which Douglas was altogether free. Selwyn was a secret sadist, fascinated by acts of cruelty committed by others. Public executions were his favourite entertainments, and he sometimes attended them in female disguise. He became an authority on torture, liked to see the victim dispatched slowly, was disappointed if the executioner rushed the job and robbed him of the pleasure of contemplating the convulsed victim and his agonised face slowly blackening in the death struggle.[*]

Selwyn was also suspected of 'necrophiliac leanings'. He and Thomas Potter must have had a lot to discuss, although Selwyn was ashamed of his vice. On execution days he would declare that he had no intention of attending, and would sit drinking wine in White's. But he would become more and more agitated as the hour approached and his blood lust rose, and eventually he would jump to his feet and hurry away. When Lord Holland was on his deathbed Selwyn called to see him. Asked by a servant if he should show Selwyn in, his lordship replied: 'If I am alive I will be delighted to see him, and if I am dead, he would like to see me.'

There was one other blot on his record. He was sent down from Oxford for blasphemy, having cut his arm and let the blood drip

---

[*] Selwyn was said to have gone to Paris to see Robert Francois Damiens broken on the wheel for attempting to assassinate Louis XV. As he pressed forward, the executioner warned him not to approach too closely, but on being told how far Selwyn had travelled to be present, bade the crowd make way for him, saying: '*Faites place pour Monsieur; c'est un Anglais, et un amateur!*' (a connoisseur). After being tortured Damiens was tied to four horses and torn to pieces.

into a chalice, saying to his friends: 'Drink this in memory of me.'

Most examples of wit, repeated later in the wrong milieu and when the element of spontaneity is lacking, don't work, but some of Selwyn's still do. Told that a member of the club had gone to France to evade his creditors, including the money-lenders, Selwyn remarked that it was one Passover the Jews would not be celebrating. He attended the execution of the rebel Jacobite lords on Tower Hill, and saw how they dropped their handkerchiefs to signal to the executioner that they were ready for the fatal blow. When Selwyn next visited his dentist he dropped a silk handkerchief to show he was ready for an extraction. Chided for gawping as the Jacobite Lord Lovat's head was struck from his body, Selwyn said he would attend the undertaker's when it was sewn back on prior to burial. (He tried to buy the head of one of the executed lords.)

Selwyn's father was not rich, and the young man was addicted to gambling, for which he had neither the patience nor the cunning to be successful. Consequently he was sometimes a heavy loser, and had to be careful about money. A series of sinecures, including the posts of Clerk of the Irons and Surveyor of Meltings of the Mint, Registrar of the Court of Chancery in Barbados, Paymaster of Works and Surveyor-General of Works, helped keep him solvent. He was also an MP.

Perhaps one reason Selwyn admired Douglas was the latter's extraordinary skill and success as a gambler. One of the first things that struck Douglas about the gambling at White's was its mindlessness. The gamblers wagered large sums without reckoning the odds. Often they were drunk when they hazarded fortunes. Unlike Charteris, Douglas didn't have to cheat to win a steady stream of large bets. There was easy money to be made from men who would bet as they walked from the club to Mrs Comyn's brothel on the likelihood of getting a venereal disease there. One member even tried to manipulate the odds by betting that he would get the pox, then seeking out a diseased young harlot to make sure that he won his bet.

Death always seemed to offer good prospects for a wager: young members would gamble on how long various members of the Old Club would survive, or on how many MPs would make it to the end of the current parliamentary session. The club's entry book records some of these bets: 'Lord Montfort wagers Sir Jon Bland one hundred guineas that Mr Nash outlives Mr Cibber.' Both gamblers committed suicide before the issue could be decided. One day a man collapsed in the street outside and was carried into the club. Bets were taken on whether he would live or die. When a member suggested that a doctor should be called he was shouted down – this would be an unwarrantable interference with the odds.

Amid all this fevered gambling Douglas kept his head and his money, and made a lot more. He kept a betting book in which he recorded each wager, and always carried exactly £50 when he went gambling – this was the amount he was prepared to lose. If he did lose it he went home to bed. He was in effect a professional gambler. He appears much later under his own name in Thackeray's *The Virginians*: 'My Lord March has not one devil, but several devils. He loves gambling, he loves horse-racing, he loves betting, he loves drinking, he loves eating, he loves money, he loves women; and you have fallen into bad company, Mr Warrington, when you lighted upon his lordship. He will play you for every acre you have in Virginia.'

The one exception to this ruthlessness was George Selwyn. Douglas bankrolled him through all his folly, and risked large parts of his own capital to save him from bankruptcy, as the following letter from him shows:

When I came home last night, I found your letter on my table. So you have lost a thousand pounds which you have done twenty times in your lifetime, and won it again as often, and why should the same thing not happen again? I make no doubt that it will. I am sorry, however, that you have lost your money; it is unpleasant. In the meantime, what the devil signify the *le fable de Paris* or the nonsense of White's! You may be sure they will be glad you have lost your money; not because they dislike you, but because they like to laugh.

They shall certainly not have that pleasure from me ... As to your banker, I will call there tomorrow; make yourself easy about that, for I have three thousand pounds now at Coutts's. There will be no bankruptcy without we are both ruined at the same time.

At another time he refers to Selwyn as 'my best and only real friend'. In 1747 Douglas became Earl of March and Ruglen. He inherited Scottish estates, and was also paid a considerable sum in compensation when certain hereditary rights in Scotland were abolished. And he now brought off one of the betting coups of his career. He gambled that it was possible for a four-wheeled carriage to travel 19 miles in one hour. This was thought to be ridiculous – most coaches and post-chaises of the period lumbered along the bad roads at a few miles an hour. March examined the question with his usual care. He knew that a good light carriage drawn by four fast horses could reach speeds of ten miles an hour or more over good roads. But 19 miles an hour?

Those who took up March's challenge were not all the usual wealthy mugs of White's. The main wager, for 1,000 guineas, was with Theobald Taafe and Andrew Sprowle. Taafe was a notorious gambler, described by Walpole as 'a gamester, usurer, adventurer'. March shared the bet with the Earl of Eglinton, another Wykehamist, who also had an unsavoury reputation. There were many other bets, and a great deal of money would change hands.

The Long Acre area was the centre of coach building, and March approached a builder there named Wright with his plans. Coaches at the time were massive and strong, meant to resist the shock of hitting potholes. In consultation with March, Wright came up with a revolutionary design, dispensing with the carriage in which the passengers travelled and instead building two sets of wheels joined to a central bar. The driver rode on a tiny seat suspended on leather straps between the two rear wheels. Horses were trained with such severity to pull this stripped-down racer that seven died before March had the team of four that he wanted. Each of the horses would carry a rider on its back.

The date of the event was 29 August 1750, the venue Newmarket Heath. A large crowd gathered, and March told the jockeys to restrain the horses over the first few miles to encourage further betting. When the race against the clock began, however, the highly strung horses could not be restrained, and covered the first few miles at a speed of almost 26 miles an hour. All betting ceased, and Taafe and Sprowle knew they had lost. March's contraption covered the full 19 miles in 53 minutes and 27 seconds.

The expenses of developing the carriage and buying horses were so great that March made little money out of the event, but it confirmed his reputation as a gambling man. This reputation was tarnished a little when he was caught cheating. An Irish racehorse owner spotted March's jockey removing the lead weights placed in his saddle as part of the handicapping system, and challenged March to a duel. The Irishman turned up at the duelling ground accompanied by a servant who was carrying a heavy burden covered by a cloth. The Irishman removed this to reveal a coffin, with a brass plate bearing March's coat of arms and the date of his death – the day of the duel. March immediately apologised. He lost face for a time at White's, not for cheating – even gentlemen cheated – but for refusing to defend himself. With true patrician hauteur, he didn't care.

One of his wagers led to a court action. To begin with Douglas was not involved. Two young sportsmen, a Mr Pigot and a Mr Codrington, were chatting after racing finished for the day at Newmarket. They decided to have a wager on which of their fathers would die first. As Pigot senior was 70, and Codrington senior 50, they could not decide the odds and called on Lord Ossory to adjudicate. He decided that the wager should be 500 guineas to 1,600 – slightly more than three to one against the survival of the older man. Codrington junior didn't like the odds and backed out, only for Douglas to step in and accept the wager. In other words, he would lose 1,600 guineas if the younger man died first. Shortly after the men entered the wager in their betting books a messenger arrived at Newmarket to tell young Pigot that his father had collapsed and died that morning. Douglas commiserated with his rival – and then claimed his winnings.

The young man refused to pay, saying that his father had died before the wager was made and it was therefore void. The case was heard in the King's Bench before Lord Mansfield. He ruled in favour of Douglas, deciding that at the time the wager was agreed both men believed their 'runners' were still alive.

Pigot might have been better served by a more aggressive approach. William Douglas had already shown that he would back down if physically threatened. One night in a St James's Street gambling 'hell' an Irishman called 'Savage' Roche accused him of cheating and took him by the ears. 'See, gentlemen,' Roche is reported as saying, 'how I treat this contemptible little cock-sparrow. As a man he is too much beneath me, or I would treat him as a gentleman.' A challenge would have been the almost invariable response of a gentleman, but Douglas slunk away.

He was a lifelong lover of the turf, and saw unfold the career of the wonder horse Eclipse, owned by the bawd Charlotte Hayes's husband Colonel O'Kelly. Eclipse was never beaten, and punters became so tired of O'Kelly's forecast, 'Eclipse first and the rest nowhere', that it became impossible to find any rivals. Douglas knew better than to challenge this prodigy, but there were opportunities elsewhere. He was a fine horseman and sometimes rode his own mounts in races. Once one of his young jockeys reported that a betting syndicate had tried to bribe him to lose a race. Douglas told him to accept the bribe, and he himself went on accepting heavy bets on the result. On the day of the race Douglas appeared in the paddock wearing a long coat, and spoke to his jockey. At the last moment he announced that he would ride in the race himself, and took off the coat to reveal he was wearing the Douglas racing silks. He won, of course.

While his gambling coups, growing wealth and reputation as an astute investor would have earned Douglas a footnote in the history of his time, his womanising made him a legend. If, in *George IV, The Grand Entertainment*, Steven Parissien goes too far in saying that when he became Duke of Queensberry Douglas 'spent most of his money on prostitutes and champagne', he was nevertheless a most generous contributor to the sex industry over many years.

One of the bawds who supplied him with pretty young putative virgins was the celebrated Mother Windsor. When he was almost 60 the *Rambler* magazine carried a caricature of Windsor bargaining with him over three young whores – one of them only 15. Douglas says: 'They are very young. Will you warrant them?' Mrs Windsor replies: 'Warrant, my Lord! I am astonished at you ... They are chaste, virtuous girls ... One has almost got her maidenhead!' In the end he takes all three of them. He usually had at least one full-time mistress as well.

Douglas never married, but when he was younger he was linked to two society women. The first was Frances Pelham, daughter of Henry Pelham, at one time Chancellor of the Exchequer. By no means beautiful, she was effervescent, even fiery at times, good company but unstable. A friend quoted Pope in an attempt to describe her:

> Strange flights and stranger graces still she had,
> Was just not ugly, and was just not mad

Just how serious Douglas was is hard to know. White's betting book carries the entry for 4 June 1751: 'Lord March wagers Captain Richard Vernon, alias "Fox", alias "Jubilee Dicky", fifty guineas to twenty that Mr St Leger is married before him.'

Douglas kept the poor woman dangling, 'playing all the tricks of the male coquet' as the indefatigable diarist Lady Mary Coke wrote in her *Journals*. Mary was herself falling in love with Douglas, and had more than a passing interest in the outcome. As her frustration grew, Frances Pelham became more querulous. During one quarrel she told him it would be no good trying his luck elsewhere, as he had such an ugly wizened little face. As Henry Blyth relates in *Old Q, The Rake of Piccadilly*, Douglas replied that 'his face must be old, since it could remember hers for so long'. Frances left the room in tears.

When her father, who disliked Douglas, died in 1754 there seemed no further bar to marriage, but William hesitated. It gradually dawned on Frances that the young dancing girls he picked up at the opera meant more to him. Always unstable, she became an obsessive gambler. Mary Coke wrote in her *Journals*: 'I have seen her at that villainous faro table putting the guineas she had borrowed on a card, with the tears running down her face – the wreck of what had been high-minded and generous.'

The man who had broken her heart was small and slightly built, but wiry and durable. He was not handsome – his most prominent feature, exaggerated in the countless caricatures of him, was a large hooked nose between piercing dark eyes. He was dapper, carefully dressed and exquisitely polite, if rather distant. He had the rake's gift of making women he was interested in feel better about themselves. The next woman to get this treatment was Lady Mary Coke herself.

In 1756 the Earl of Drumlanrig, heir to the title of Duke of Queensberry, died of consumption. An even greater blow to the Queensberrys was the fact that William Douglas was the new heir. They didn't know him well but they knew his reputation.

The Duchess of Queensberry was the beautiful, remarkable and eccentric Kitty Hyde, a wit widely loved and admired among the intelligentsia. The poet Matthew Prior wrote of her in 'The Female Phaeton':

> Fondness prevailed, Mamma gave way;
> Kitty at Heart's Desire
> Obtained the Chariot for a Day
> And set the World on Fire.

She went on doing so. When John Gay followed up the success of *The Beggar's Opera* with a sequel, *Polly*, the Prime Minister, Sir Robert Walpole, used his influence with George II to have it banned. He had been deeply offended by the way he had been caricatured in the play. Kitty leapt to Gay's defence and was banned from court. She wrote to the King:

The Duchess of Queensberry is surprised and well pleased that the King has given so agreeable a command as to stay from the Court,

where she never came for diversion, but to bestow a great civility
upon the King and Queen; she hopes by such an unprecedented
Order as this, the King will see as few as He wishes at His Court,
particularly such as dare to think, or speak the Truth . . .

She bore Gay and her husband, who had been popular at court,
off to their country estate at Amesbury in Wiltshire. The King
tried to persuade the Duke to stay, but he went where Kitty
decreed, and he had to resign his post as Admiral of Scotland. Of
course it wasn't really exile from society; the Queensberrys had a
fine town mansion in Mayfair.

Later in life Kitty became more eccentric than ever, preferring
peasant dress to the expensive clothes worn by her social equals.
When George II died in 1760 she was welcomed back to court.

Not long afterwards she held a ball at her Mayfair house. Among
the guests was George Selwyn, who didn't care for dancing and
found the ballroom draughty and cold. He found a cosy little room
with a fire, closed the door and settled down to sleep. Kitty found
him, but instead of waking him she sent a carpenter to remove the
door from its hinges. Selwyn took the hint and went home.

After their two sons died and William Douglas became their
heir, the Queensberrys were anxious about the question of who
might succeed him. Stories of William's philandering continued to
reach them after they retired permanently to Amesbury, and they
feared he would never marry. When they heard rumours of a
romance between him and Lady Mary Coke they travelled to
London to see if they could arrange a match. Mary, William and a
few of their friends were invited to tea at Queensberry House.

William and Lady Mary had been lovers for some time, but it
was just another affair to him, and it would last only until he
became bored or found someone else. He resented the Queensberrys' interference and Lady Mary's complicity, and decided to
make them pay. When he arrived he nodded distantly to Mary and
gave all his attention to the elderly Lady Bute. Lady Mary's private
journals describe the afternoon in all its frigid awfulness. William
eventually bowed stiffly and withdrew.

If Lady Mary hoped for a reconciliation, she was soon disappointed by the news that Douglas had fallen for an Italian adventuress, the Contessa Rena. The Countess had been abandoned by the Count and had come to London to marry a wealthy Englishman, only to find after she arrived that he had married someone else. Douglas was introduced to her by a mutual friend at a ridotto in the Haymarket; they danced together so expertly that the floor was cleared for them, and Douglas began one of the most intense affairs of his life.

He continued to dally with women of his own class, including Lady Mary's friend, Lady Jane Stuart, and Lady Henrietta Stanhope. Horace Walpole heard a rumour that Douglas was about to marry Lady Anne Conway, and he wrote: 'I don't believe it. Parents and relations, if it is so, may lock all knives, ropes, laudanum and rivers, lest it should occasion a violent mortality among his fair admirers.' It is impossible to know whether Douglas was trifling with these young women, or sleeping with them. He was certainly sleeping around, as the Rena – the term used by Douglas and George Selwyn – found. Douglas however remarked that she had 'some indulgence for my follies', and she needed it. One of the first challenges to her hold on him was from the teenage singer Teresina Tondino, whom Douglas picked up at the opera. She is mentioned often in his correspondence with George Selwyn, and Douglas referred to her as though she was a child – she was little more. Presents were bought to keep her happy, and he fretted when she was ill or peevish. When the time came to part for good in the autumn of 1765 he seemed heartbroken. He wrote to Selwyn, who was to accompany her:

I am just preparing to conduct the poor little Tondino to Dover, and as I shall hardly be able to write to you there, I shall endeavour to say two or three words to you while she is getting ready. I am sure you will be good to her, for I know you love me; and I can desire nothing of you while I shall feel so sensibly as your notice to her.

She will tell you of all my intentions, and I shall write to you when I am more composed. My heart is so full that I can neither think, speak, nor write. How shall I be able to part with her, or bear to come back to this house, I do not know. The sound of her voice fills my eyes with fresh tears. My dear George, *J'ai le coeur si serré que je suis bon à present qu'a pleurer*. Farewell! I hear her coming, and this is perhaps the last time I shall see her here. Take all care you can of her . . .

Douglas was now 40, a good age at the time, and still sexually robust. He took on another young opera singer and dancer, Anna Zamperini, born in Venice in 1745. Having told Selwyn that he had taken a violent fancy to her, which was later 'a little abated', he asked him to explain the situation to the Rena: 'I love her vastly, but I like this little girl.'

His name continued to be linked to various society women, but also to a series of demi-mondaines and harlots. As well as being one of those in the outer circle of the Hell-Fire Club, he was a familiar figure in London's night life.* Most of the information about the latter role comes from the gossip columns of magazines and newspapers. For as long as his prodigious sex drive lasted, which was until he was almost in his eighties, Old Q, as he later came to be known, patronised the more fashionable brothels, including those kept by Mother Windsor and Sarah Dubery. His housekeeper, Maria Brown, also called Moreton, wrote in *Memoirs of the Life of the Duke of Queensberry* that he 'employed that skilful Procuress Mrs D— [Dubery] to procure his Sultanas . . . candidates were paraded for inspection . . . she seldom served him with a dish that he could not make at least one meal upon. If he approved, he rang a bell and Mrs D . . . had to school the Novitiate in her duties . . . '

One of the women he met in this way, Kitty Fredericks, 'the very Thaïs of London', seemed as likely as anyone else to become

---

* Although he was close to the Medmenhamites, Douglas's political career was brief and unsuccessful. As we have seen, he was involved in bringing down John Wilkes in the affair of the *Essay on Woman*. But he was dismissed as a Lord of the Bedchamber to George III after backing the Prince of Wales's struggle to secure a Regency Bill.

his wife. She had originally been one of Charlotte Hayes's girls, and that great bawd had used her renowned grooming skills to transform her 'from a shaggy tail'd uncomb'd unwash'd filly' into a delightful young woman, educated and well spoken, a good dancer with a knowledge of French. As was the way with such girls, before she was introduced to Douglas she had been the rounds, Charlotte having first sold her off 'at a good price' to the Earl of Uxbridge. Her next full-time lover after the Earl died in 1769 was Captain Richard Fitzpatrick, who was killed in the American War of Independence. Kitty had to leave her fine house in Pall Mall and return to the brothel, now being run by Catherine Matthews, who had taken over the Hayes establishment at No. 5 King's Place. Mrs Matthews became one of several panders employed by Douglas, and he acquired Kitty for £100 a year, 'a genteel house' and a carriage. For a while Douglas seemed to his friends to be as smitten as he had been by the Rena, and they expected him to marry her. However, in 1779, when he was in his middle fifties, they quarrelled and parted. Kitty became one of the best known and highest paid courtesans of the epoch, the darling of high society. For all his unconventionality, Douglas probably could not bring himself to marry so far out of his class.

In 1766 Douglas bought a plot of land in Piccadilly near the present Hyde Park Corner, then semi-rural. It was a bold move. The mansions of the super-rich were creeping westwards along Piccadilly, but they were still a little isolated and the area was plagued by highwaymen and footpads. Douglas spent two years building a mansion at No. 138, and in that time the centre of gravity of fashionable London moved steadily westwards, confirming his good judgment. Later he would be so closely identified with the area that he would be known as Old Q of Piccadilly, and it was at his mansion that he died.

About this time he suffered almost the only check to his social ambitions when he was blackballed for membership of the Old Club at White's. The explanation was that he spent so much time abroad in France that he was regarded as a foreigner. But the real reason was his unpopularity: he had made many enemies by his success at gambling, and his role in the *Essay on Woman* affair still rankled. For all his parvenu status, Wilkes was a more popular man.

In contrast, Charles James Fox had joined the Young Club in 1770 when he was barely 21, and then intimated that he would like to be admitted to the Old Club as well. Douglas warned him that it might take a lifetime, but just months later Fox was welcomed in. It was another sign to Douglas that he would never be accepted at the heart of the aristocracy, despite his great wealth.

Douglas had other preoccupations in the 1770s. Gambling was still a passion, and he formed a successful partnership with the jockey 'Hell-Fire Dick' Goodison, so named because of his scorching finishes. Racing was no longer the sport of amateur gentlemen. Professionals were now 'making a book' to handle bets, and the Jockey Club, controlled by Douglas along with other aristocrats including Grafton, Northumberland, Grosvenor, Devonshire and Clermont, was establishing the laws. Douglas was particularly keen to win the new Derby Stakes, first run at Epsom in May 1780. But he never succeeded, although he entered horses on seven occasions between 1781 and 1796.

His rivalry with the wild young Irishman Richard Barry, seventh Earl of Barrymore and friend of the Prince of Wales, was almost comical. None of Douglas's horses was ever 'placed' – that is, finished in the first three. Barrymore's horse was third at his first attempt, and he beat Douglas in other races. Known as 'Hellgate' because of his profligacy, particularly in gambling, he had extensive estates and an income of £20,000 (about £1,500,000) a year that for a while was sufficient for his extravagance. In the course of his brief racing career he is believed to have run through £300,000, which earned him Douglas's contempt. He further annoyed Douglas by buying a larger and grander mansion in Piccadilly than the one owned by Douglas. Barrymore was fond of acting, and even built a full-sized theatre at his country home at Wargrave in Berkshire.

But by the spring of 1792 Barrymore was in financial trouble. He had to sell his Piccadilly mansion and its contents, and it must have given Old Q great satisfaction to buy it. Creditors pressed in, obtaining court orders against the Earl. The Wargrave theatre, where the Prince of Wales had often been a guest, was pulled down and the materials sold. The props and costumes went to auction by Christie's. His stables, on which he lavished a fortune, were closed and the horses sold.*

In 1793 Barrymore's short and 'feverish existence' ended suddenly at the age of 24. While he was driving in a carriage a hunting gun propped against the side accidentally went off, shooting him in the eye. When his affairs were finally tidied up it was found that he was still solvent.

The third Duke of Queensberry died in October 1778, at the age of 80, and Douglas inherited one of the richest dukedoms in the country. Apart from the income, there were the properties: Queensberry House in Burlington Gardens, Mayfair, Amesbury and its 5,000 acres in Wiltshire, and Drumlanrig Castle in Dumfriesshire. He had been wealthy before – now he was fabulously rich.

But he had no use for any of these properties. He didn't like Scotland, Amesbury was too far from London and he preferred his Piccadilly mansion to Queensberry House. If he had to have a country place – and as duke he was expected to entertain somewhere outside the city – he wanted something nearer the capital. In 1780 he bought Cholmondeley House, overlooking the Thames at Richmond, not far from Horace Walpole's Strawberry Hill and only nine miles from Piccadilly. He filled the 1708 house with the fittings from Amesbury and renamed it Queensberry House. The London house of that name he sold to Lord Henry Paget.

Otherwise his life changed little. His aristocratic hauteur was greater than ever. The Earl of Carlisle wrote to George Selwyn: 'St James's Street seems entirely to belong to him, and he has an exclusive right to drive in it.' Because of the large letter Q displayed on the doors of his coach, he soon became popularly known as Old Q.

---

\* One horse, Chanticleer, was sold for 2,700 guineas to the Duke of York. When the Duke sold his stud shortly afterwards he received only 500 guineas for the horse.

# Mie-Mie and Bloaters:

## Old Q's Legacy

OLD Q'S ALMOST INNUMERABLE AFFAIRS and sexual encounters seem to have resulted in only one child. But her story is remarkable, not only because she was herself reviled as a traitor and gross libertine but because she married one of the most notorious rakes of the nineteenth century, an immensely wealthy intellectual and connoisseur, gambler, woman-iser and pervert of sulphurous reputation whose spite reached out beyond the grave to settle old scores.

On the evening of 25 August 1771 Douglas sat down in White's Club in St James's and wrote to George Selwyn:

> Last night Madame Fagniani was brought to bed of a girl. They wished it had been a boy; however *cette princesse héritera les biens de la famille*; so that they are all very happy. She is vastly so to have it all over, and to find herself quite well after having suffered a great deal, which I believe women always do on these occasions, but particu-larly with their first child.

The Marchesa Fagniani was Douglas's mistress, and the child was his. He nevertheless denied paternity, to society at large if not to Fagniani and Selwyn. However, the more Douglas denied paternity the more the idea of being a surrogate father appealed to Selwyn. He had always doted on children, and once he saw the child there was no going back. George Selwyn was in love.

Madame Fagniani did not want the encumbrance of a child. She was a colourful character with a certain past. In the winter of 1765 the novelist Laurence Sterne met her in Milan, and a charming romantic interlude ensued. The story of the encounter is told with all the parson's roguish wit in *A Sentimental Journey through France and Italy*: 'I was going one evening to Martini's concert at Milan and I was just entering the door of the hall, when the Marquisina di F ... was coming out in a sort of hurry – she was almost upon me before I saw her; so I gave a spring to one side to let her pass – she had done the same, and on the same side too: so we ran our heads together ... ' Sterne closes his amusing account of their meeting with the words: 'I will only add, that the connection which arose ... gave me more pleasure than any one I had the honour to make in Italy.'

Fagniani had been a fairly successful singer and dancer who married into the Milanese aristocracy. It was an open marriage – she and her husband both agreed that life was too short to stand on ceremony, as she had told Sterne when she seduced him. Among her lovers was Lord Pembroke, friend of Douglas and also of Casanova – a man with a libido the equal of theirs. Pembroke brought the Fagnianis to London and passed the Marchesa on to Douglas. At the time Douglas was 45, the Marchesa about half that age. Her husband the Marchese was introduced by Pembroke to the gambling hells of Mayfair where he lost most of his money. Douglas then paid his debts in return for more or less exclusive rights to his wife's body. The result, in view of the wide experience of all involved, was surprising. When Fagniani became pregnant and told Douglas he was the father he put the rumour about clubland, with a rare hint of a sense of humour, that the child was actually George Selwyn's. How they laughed at White's and Brooks's.

To start with, the Marchesa left the child, which had been christened Maria Emily, in Douglas's hands. He found the ideal protector for it in Selwyn, who gave the infant the appropriate nickname Mie-Mie. His friends were astonished to see the great wit, gambler and man-about-town fondling a child which was not even his own. Lord Thomond was shocked when passing Douglas's house in Piccadilly to see Selwyn sitting outside on the steps with the baby on his knee.

As the years passed, Selwyn began to think of the child as his own. It was a great wrench when he had to send her to a boarding school, Miss Terry's at Campden House, Kensington. He demanded regular reports on her progress, and worried about her like any loving parent. Douglas regarded the whole affair with detached amusement; the Marchesa, watching from abroad, realised that with two wealthy protectors the child was an asset, and she decided to cash in. She demanded its return. Selwyn countered by offering to endow the child with his fortune. The Marchesa replied that this was an insult, and demanded that Mie-Mie be restored to her immediately.

Fagniani, who had left the child with a stranger for six years without troubling herself about her welfare, was probably trying to put pressure on Douglas to renew their relationship as well as screwing money out of the two men. Selwyn appealed to Douglas to help him; that cool man of business, who now had mistresses younger than Fagniani and knew well the game she was playing, sympathised but said there was nothing he could do. Selwyn, plunged into morbid grief, then put his case before the Austrian ambassador, who promised to pass the facts on to the Austrian governor of Milan. Eventually Selwyn realised the child would have to go back to its mother. When he did send Mie-Mie away, it was in a specially fitted carriage which he bought for the purpose. He was inconsolable, and the well-intentioned attempts of friends to help could only make things worse. The Countess of Upper Ossory told him about the artist Sir Joshua Reynolds's niece, who was being bothered by an admirer. This man called at her home, and on being informed she was not there told the footman to tell her to take care, 'for he was determined to ravish her (pardon the word!) whenever he met her'. The Countess implored Selwyn to 'keep our little friend [Mie-Mie] at Paris while this mania lasts'.

After he had been separated for almost a year Selwyn could stand it no longer, as the Marchesa had no doubt anticipated. He raced across the Channel to meet her, paid her a sum of money and had the child restored to him. He may have again promised to make the child his sole heir. The salon hostess Madame du Deffand, who met him in Paris while he was waiting for the Marchesa to arrive, told Horace Walpole she took him to be quite mad. 'He neither eats nor sleeps for thinking of the child.'

Back in London Selwyn noticed that Mie-Mie had changed, and not for the better. She had become selfish and vain. What struck visitors to the Selwyn household even more forcefully was how like her real father the Duke of Queensberry Mie-Mie was becoming in appearance (Douglas had just succeeded to the title). While no great beauty, Mie-Mie was pretty and was developing a self-conscious allure. At last Queensberry began to take an interest in her.

When he was still fairly active Selwyn had often taken Mie-Mie visiting, and in 1782, when she was 11, he took her to see Louisa, Marchioness of Hertford, a stiff grande dame who was regarded as one of the mistresses of the Prince of Wales, although the relationship was almost certainly never consummated. There she met the Marchioness's grandson, an ugly little boy with red hair and prominent teeth. They disliked each other on sight, but would one day marry and become one of the most dissolute couples in an aristocracy noted for moral insouciance. The little boy would grow to be one of the most notorious of all rakes, with a reputation to rival Old Q's.

Mie-Mie, conscious that she would be a person of wealth and consequence, was fascinated by her wicked 'uncle', as she believed him to be. By the mid-1780s, when she was in her teens, she was already showing an interest in men, and the kind of man she liked was a younger version of her uncle, sexy and far from respectable. She also made no secret of her interest in money. She herself, tall and precociously well developed, had a charm of manner that attracted even those who were unaware that she would be a wealthy heiress. As Blyth notes in *Old Q*, 'She represented for them the best of two worlds, for to the height, colour and freshness of an English beauty she added that foreign touch of provocativeness which they found so intriguing.'

George Selwyn saw the warning signs. All too clearly it seemed to him that here was a female rake in the making, and he was in a constant agony of suspense when Old Q took her off to the opera or the theatre lest he should introduce the girl to a handsome young adventurer. Although only in his middle sixties, Selwyn was becoming old and infirm. Mie-Mie treated him off-handedly, occasionally charming him but usually ignoring his genuine health problems.

By January 1791 Selwyn was an old man. Almost 70, he was now afflicted by gout and dropsy. Horace Walpole wrote to a friend: 'I am on the point of losing, or have lost, my oldest acquaintance and friend, George Selwyn, who was yesterday at the extremity. These misfortunes, though they can be so but for a short time, are very sensible to the old; but him I really loved, not only for his infinite wit, but for a thousand good qualities.'

Selwyn died a few days later at his house in Cleveland Row. In his last hours he had friends read passages of the Bible to him. Unlike many of them, he had lived a blameless if useless life, its only real sadness that the child he loved returned him little affection. Most of his fortune went to her; the rest he left to Old Q, a man already wallowing in wealth. They had been friends from the day they met. A tribute to Selwyn written at the time included the lines:

'Twas social wit which never kindling strife,
Blazed in the small sweet courtesies of life;
Those little sapphires round the diamond shone,
Lending soft radiance to the richer stone.

The loss of his one true friend must have hit Douglas hard, but it was at this time that he embarked on a notable piece of vandalism that showed him at his most flinty-hearted. He sold to be felled for timber the magnificent woods on his Drumlanrig estate, which were regarded as one of the glories of Scotland. Two years earlier Robert Burns, who knew the area well, had excoriated Douglas:

> All hail! Drumlanrig's haughty Grace,
> Discarded remnant of a race
> Once godlike great in story;
> Thy forebears' virtues all contrasted,
> The very name of Douglas blasted,
> Thine that inverted glory!
>
> Hate, envy oft the Douglas bore;
> But thou has superadded more,
> And sunk them in contempt;
> Follies and crimes have stained the name,
> But, Queensberry, thine the virgin claim –
> From all that's good exempt.

Now, in 1791, he despaired. Nearing the end of his short life, he wrote 'On the Destruction of the Woods near Drumlanrig':

> 'Alas!' quoth I, 'What ruefu' chance
> Has twined ye o' your stately trees?
> Has laid your rocky bosom bare?
> Has stripped the cleeding o' your braes?
> Was it the bitter eastern blast
> That scatters blight in early spring?
> Or was't the wil'fire scorched their boughs,
> Or the canker-worm wi' secret sting?'
>
> 'Nae eastlin blast,' the sprite replied;
> 'It blew na here sae fierce and fell,
> And on my dry and halesome banks
> Nae canker-worms get leave to dwell:
> Man! cruel man!' the genius sigh'd

As through the cliffs he sank him down –
'The worm that gnawed my bonnie trees,
That reptile wears a ducal crown.'

William Wordsworth weighed in with a sonnet that began:

Degenerate Douglas! oh, the unworthy Lord!
Whom mere despite of heart could so far please,
And love of havoc (for with such disease
Fame taxes him) that he could send forth word
To level with the dust a noble horde
A brotherhood of venerable trees.

Douglas carried on regardless. The felling of the trees was stopped only a short time before his death, when another nobleman bought up what was left to preserve them. If Old Q ever saw the poems he probably laughed.

As though his real sexual achievements were not remarkable enough, Old Q's reputation had now become encrusted with legend. It was rumoured that in his long heyday he delighted in re-enacting the judgment of Paris, the goddesses being played by prostitutes and Paris by himself. It was also said that his sexual powers increased with advancing years, and he presided over tremendous orgies at his houses in Richmond and Piccadilly.

He was still enjoying a life of carefree hedonism, although on rare occasions his once superabundant sex drive let him down. In her memoirs Mrs Moreton, the housekeeper at his Piccadilly mansion, 'formerly President of His Grace's Harem', quotes a revealing little tale in which one of the young girls recruited for Queensberry's service by the procuress Mrs Dubery describes how she was picked up: 'I had been with a lady to buy a few yards of lace at a shop in Bond Street, when perceiving an elderly and motherly-looking woman looking steadfastly at me in the shop . . . we instantly fell into conversation.'

The girl, a most willing victim, abandoned her friend and went with Mrs Dubery to Old Q's Piccadilly mansion, where Mrs Moreton told her what was expected. The girl goes on:

It has been remarked, how justly I know not, that men who have the least ability to please our sex are the most gallant: there seems to be a peculiar variety in impotence that prompts a debilitated deb-auchee to give the public a high idea of his manly powers and feats of love.

Old Q, as he was then called, though not yet past that time of life which secludes a man from the fair sex, was nevertheless of a weak constitution; and certainly a smaller number of ladies might have suited him best, and gratified every dawn of passion he was so willing to fan ... An impotent pretender is, perhaps, of all things the most ridiculous and contemptible. A man may, by art, conceal most of his other faults and imperfections; but in this case, he is obliged to expose his poverty upon the pretence of his being rich; and the only apology for his crime is destroyed by his inability of committing it.

From the Sultan's renown at that time in the annals of gallantry, I had framed very high notions of his figure and strength; but I was not in the least displeased to find him otherwise, and there was nothing Herculean about him.

We supped together; and after this short tête-à-tête, retired to the bedroom. Here I could not help feeling the indelicacy of getting into bed before a man and a total stranger; for I had not got so far the better of my natural modesty, as not to be shocked at this impropriety before a nobleman of the first distinction, but I found this was a ceremony he ever insisted upon, and which I was accordingly obliged to submit to. Here I should choose to close the scene with a drawing of the curtains; but so chaste and moral a person as 'Lady Vane has told us, that her good man after striving an hour to obtain what neither he could take or she give, fell asleep': It may not here be thought too improper to own that the Piccadilly Sultan left me as good a maid as he found me; after making a violent fit of coughing his apology for a sudden retreat from the field of love.

What would the clubmen of St James's have made of this? The great lover's powers were failing.

After George Selwyn's death Mie-Mie went to live with his old friend, Lord Carlisle, one of the executors of his will, whose children would inherit Selwyn's fortune if she died. Gossips said she showed her regard for her dead guardian by often wearing his last gift to her, a superb diamond necklace once worn by Katharine Parr.

As soon as she heard of Selwyn's death Mie-Mie's mother, the Marchesa, wrote to Lord Carlisle saying she wanted to be reunited with her daughter. Her husband was still alive, but blind and mad from syphilis. This time the old woman received no financial sweetener – Mie-Mie and Lord Carlisle made it clear they wanted nothing to do with her.

When Mie-Mie reached the age of 24 in August 1792 she went to live with Old Q in Richmond. He rather admired her blatant fortune seeking, and was already looking for a noble and wealthy match for her, having long ago decided that she would inherit his great wealth to add to the modest fortune she had from Selwyn. In the meantime he needed to find her a female companion who would act as chaperone, and appointed a friend of his from Fontainebleau, the Duchesse de la Trémouille, who was a little older than Mie-Mie and whose mother was an intimate friend of the French Queen, Marie Antoinette. From Mie-Mie's point of view she was an admirable choice – she was plain, and no competition when it came to husband hunting.

There were obstacles to finding an aristocratic partner. Mie-Mie shared her father's strong sensuality – when she was 21 there had been rumours that she had given birth to an illegitimate child. Gouverneur Morris, the American minister to France, met her when he visited London in 1795, and recorded his impressions:

This Mdlle Faniani is an extraordinary person. She bears the name of the husband of her mother. George Selwyn, of famous memory, left her his fortune in the persuasion that she was his child, and the Duke of Queensberry looks upon her as the issue of his loins, treats her with the tenderness of a parent, and will, it is supposed, bequeath a great part of his fortune to her. Scandal, in the meantime, says she is already a mother by unknown aid. She has fine eyes and an intelligent countenance ... very impressive eyes.

Her figure was no longer so trim, and her prominent nose showed signs of turning down to meet her chin, like her father's. Still, she would be very rich.

After looking around among the sons of his titled and wealthy friends, Old Q's gaze came to rest on Francis Charles Seymour-Conway, Earl of Yarmouth and heir to the Marquess of Hertford. This was the red-haired boy Mie-Mie had first met when she was 11. His father had extensive estates in England and Ireland, and the son would one day inherit great wealth. On the other hand, he was six years younger than Mie-Mie and already a drinker and gambler, a noted libertine about whom 'there already hung the hint of perversion'. He was not attractive: as described by Blyth in *Old Q*, his hair was 'of a bright and forbidding red, his eyebrows were thick and bushy, and his eyes were small and bloodshot. But his most distinguishing feature was the pair of white buck-teeth which protruded from the centre of his upper jaw and which gleamed savagely when he smiled.'

The young couple were often seen together, and although Mie-Mie was not in love with Yarmouth her sexual impetuosity was such that she became his mistress – and was rumoured to be pregnant. It was common knowledge that the spendthrift Yarmouth found it difficult to live on his moderate allowance. Old Q made it clear to the young man that Mie-Mie's husband would find him a generous father-in-law.

With Old Q's encouragement, but without his father's knowledge, the couple married on 18 May 1798 at Southampton. The haughty Hertfords were scandalised and furious. Their son was barely 21 and just up from Oxford. The bride in this hole-in-the-corner, hushed-up affair was almost 27 'and fully looked her age'.

She also had a certain reputation. For all these reasons she was never accepted as one of the family.

Old Q gave them as a wedding present the house in Piccadilly that had once belonged to Lord Barrymore, the legendary 'Hellgate', and for a time they seemed happy enough there. On 2 February 1799 Mie-Mie reportedly gave birth to a girl. As this was only a little less than nine months after her marriage the rumours of pregnancy must have been unfounded. Or the date of birth may be suspect – the birth was not recorded at St George's, Hanover Square, the appropriate church for Piccadilly. Soon after the birth Lord Yarmouth left to resume his former habits, though Mie-Mie lured him back long enough to become pregnant again and give birth to a son in February 1800. With that she and her husband were free to pursue their separate lives. The Hertfords, who had no illusions about their son, were relieved that he had produced a legitimate heir, and Old Q was quietly pleased that the blood of the Douglases would run in the veins of the fourth Marquess of Hertford.

For his age the Earl had the formidable reputation of being the most thoroughgoing gambler and roué in England. Like Old Q, he was expert and successful at the gaming tables, sometimes winning £40,000 in a night (about £1,800,000). The wealthy and be-fuddled men who gathered round the tables of St James's gambled as recklessly as Regency clubmen and Yarmouth found easy pick-ings. He was also a successful investor on the Stock Exchange, with the advice of one of the most astute City magnates of the day, Abraham Goldsmid.

In 1802, when the Treaty of Amiens brought a respite in the war with France, Mie-Mie, tired of the Hertfords' sneers, went to Paris. Old Q was now 75, blind in one eye and no longer virile. As he kissed her goodbye he may have sensed he would never see her again.

Mie-Mie travelled to Paris with Yarmouth. Both soon found new partners, although they still apparently slept together occa-sionally. Lord Yarmouth took up with Madame Visconti, a former mistress of the War Minister Berthier, a woman with the right social connections. The Yarmouths renewed their acquaintance with Talleyrand, the Foreign Minister, whom they had met in London. Another of the social powerhouses who welcomed them was the celebrated Madame Récamier.

It quickly became clear that war was about to break out again, and Yarmouth urged Mie-Mie to return to London. She hesitated, and they were both arrested on Napoleon's orders and interned. General Junot had become governor of Paris, and he took her under his protection. When she became pregnant, it was widely believed that Junot was the father. Mie-Mie, however, was particularly promiscuous at this time, and among the other men who might have been responsible were an adventurer acquaintance of Talleyrand's named Count Casimir de Montrond, and Yarmouth himself, who had been allowed occasional visits. The news of her affair with Junot, and then the birth of a child, soon became known in London.* Mie-Mie, who had never been popular, was widely denounced as a traitor.

The child, a boy, was born on 18 January 1805, and christened Henry Seymour, the Hertford family name. Whatever doubts Yarmouth had about the boy he hid: he knew that Old Q would be unlikely to include him in his will if he brought ostracism on Mie-Mie for having a French bastard in time of war, and so he treated him as his son. Yarmouth had taken up with another attractive Frenchwoman, a widow named Saint-Amand. Police spies who followed them described them as a noisy couple whose drunken carousals at inns kept other guests awake.

While still Junot's mistress Mie-Mie met Montrond, a witty and penniless gambler, a handsome and prodigious womaniser. Among his conquests, says Falk, was said to be Madame Récamier. He was a noted wit, a gift that drew Talleyrand to him – the wily diplomat was said to have borrowed many of his *mots*, though those that have come down to us don't seem particularly witty. Asked to contribute to a fund for repentant prostitutes, he replied: 'If they have

---

* In 1813 Junot cut his throat and jumped out of a window, but by then Mie-Mie had long moved on.

repented, I will give them nothing; if they have not repented, I will take them the money myself.' One of the sayings Talleyrand borrowed from him was the Rochefoucauld-like witticism: 'If anything good happens to you do not fail to acquaint your friends with the news: it will make them miserable.'

Montrond was only a temporary lover as far as Mie-Mie was concerned, though for a while she was willing to pay for his virility and charm. On 10 June 1806 Lady Bessborough wrote to Lord Granville: 'Lady Y . . . remains at Paris as a fair hostage (or, as Lord Lauderdale says, a fat one) in the hands of Duroc, with whom it seems she is in love.' Geraud Christophe Michel Duroc was Grand Marshal of the Palace. Mie-Mie was cutting a swathe through the fine flower of Napoleon's generals.

In London, meanwhile, Old Q was clinging obstinately to life. In his later years it had been the task of his doctor, previously physician to Louis XV, to keep him in a fit state to perform sexually. But the fact was that Old Q, in his eighties, really was past it. His old friend Sir Nathaniel Wraxhall wrote in his *Memoirs*: 'His person had then become a wreck: but not his mind. Seeing with only one eye, hearing very imperfectly with one ear, nearly toothless and labouring under multiple infirmities . . . ' Thackeray wrote of him in old age in *The Four Georges*: 'This wrinkled, paralysed, toothless old Don Juan died the same corrupt, unrepentant fellow he had been in the most fiery days of his youth. In a house in Piccadilly there is a low window where old Queensberry is said to have sat in order to peer at passing women with voluptuous eyes.'

It was said that at this stage of his life a groom was permanently stationed at the door of the house. If a passing woman took the old man's fancy the groom was ordered to accost her, and invite her in. The Duke himself would sit on a balcony eyeing the passing beauties.

It is more likely that he was simply sunning his old bones, his mind in the past and largely unaware of passing women. There is no doubt, however, that some, attracted by his reputation, promenaded by the house in hopes of being chosen for closer inspection, if nothing more. Many a young beauty must have felt a delicious tingle at the thought of so much naughtiness within; perhaps they were disappointed that the old roué's powers had faded.

Indeed, in 1807 there was a premature report of his death, and a wag wrote some verses which caused the Duke much merriment:

> And what is all this grand to do
> That runs each street
> and alley through?
> 'Tis the departure of 'Old Q',
> The star of Piccadilly.

> The king, God bless him! gave a whew!
> 'Two dukes just dead – a third gone too,
> What! What! could nothing save "Old Q"?'
> The star of Piccadilly.

> 'Thank Heaven! Thank Heaven!' exclaims Miss Prue;
> 'My mother, and grandmother too,
> Can now walk safe from that Vile "Q",
> The star of Piccadilly.'

> The Monsieurs and Signoras too,
> Like cats in love set up their mew,
> '*Ah morto, morto, pòv'ro Q!*
> The star of Piccadilly.'

> Poll, Peggy, Cath'rine, Patty, Sue,
> Descendants of old dames he knew,
> All mourn your tutor, ancient Q,
> The star of Piccadilly.

> Old Nick he whisked his tail so blue,
> And grinned and leered and looked askew –

'Oho!' says he, 'I've got my Q'
The star of Piccadilly.

On wings of sulphur down he flew;
All London take your last adieu,
There, there away he claws Old Q,
The star of Piccadilly.

And now this may be said of Q,
That long he ran all Folly thro',
For ever seeking something new:
He never cared for me, nor you,
But, to engagements strictly true,
At last he gave the Devil his due;
And died a boy – at eighty-two,
Poor Q of Piccadilly.

Women still were as fascinated by Old Q as he by them. Such was his reputation for virility that in December 1809, when he was 84, the *Morning Herald* erroneously reported that he was about to be married: 'The Duke of Queensberry, so far from any intention of bidding this world "good night", intends to take a more pleasant course and bid "good morning" to the night-cap of a jolly dame, whom he means immediately to raise to the rank of Duchess!'

It was not until 16 January 1809, when he was 84, that he could be induced to write a will. A lawyer had waited on him day after day, hoping to help him with it, only to be driven away with curses. Once so urbane and calm, almost Olympian, Douglas's temper had not been improved by age. The dandy and diarist Thomas Raikes described him as 'a little, sharp-looking man, very irritable, and swore like ten thousand troopers'. To onlookers it seemed that the act of making a will would be an admission that the end was near, and Old Q, says Falk, 'hated being reminded of his prospective exit from the amusing scene in which, for what had seemed an incredibly long time, he had been an adroit and doughty participant'. Yet once he got down to it he found will-making fascinating: he constantly altered it until almost everyone who had deserved well of him during his long life got something. Even the poor musicians who had played as he sang snatches of operas in his pleasant voice at musical evenings in his Piccadilly mansion were remembered.

The will kept him amused in his last days. With a vast fortune to dispose of and many kindnesses to remember, it was long and complicated. Though the bulk of his estate went to Lord and Lady Yarmouth, there were many minor bequests. His old crony, the Chevalier d'Eon, who intrigued London society for years with his sexual ambiguity, was left an annuity of £100. A musician named Raselli, who lived with Old Q's greengrocer, got the same amount. Mrs Corri, wife of a musician, and Giovanni Salpietro, an old musician, were remembered with annuities of £200 and £100 respectively. The clerk at Coutts's bank in the Strand who looked after his account received an enormous £600 a year. To Nelson's mistress Emma Hamilton, whose beauty had long attracted him, and whose finances had become disordered since the hero's death, he left an annuity of £500 and £1,000 in cash.* Emma's extravagance irritated Old Q, but along with Abraham Goldsmid he did what he could to save her. Three weeks before mentioning her in his will, he wrote to Coutts's bank:

> Mr Goldsmid having informed you that Lady Hamilton is in debt to the amount of £2,500, which she has contracted since she made over her effects to the Trustees, and that if any person will advance that sum, it may be put into his hands, and that he will apply it properly, and take care that it will only go to clear those debts; I wish you to inform Mr Goldsmid that you are ready to pay him two thousand five hundred pounds (which you will charge to my account with your House) upon condition that he will see to the application of the money in discharge of Lady Hamilton's debts before

---

* Old Q annoyed Nelson by showing an interest in Emma. The hero sent her a surly note: 'As for old Queensberry, he may put you in his will or scratch you out as he pleases, I care not.'

mentioned and that if there should be any surplus that he will
return it to you on my account. It being clearly understood that
Lady H ... herself is to have no control or interference with any
part of the £2,500 which is to be applied under Mr Goldsmid's sole
direction for the payment of her above mentioned debts, and for
that purpose only.

Clearly Old Q realised Emma was hopeless with money, but she
did not live to benefit under the will.

One curious omission from the will was an apothecary named
John Fuller. According to the *Gentleman's Magazine*, Fuller
appealed in the courts for £10,000 (nearly £500,000) for 9,340
visits made in the last seven years of the old man's life, and for more
than a thousand nights in which he sat up with his patient. Whenever Old Q woke during the night he would send for Fuller, and
the faithful apothecary would sit by his bed until he dozed off
again. The court awarded him the very substantial compensation
of £7,500.

Old Q finally died in 1810 at 85 years of age, worn out by a very
full life. His reputation had kept its allure to the end. As J. H. Jesse
recounted in *Literary and Historical Memorials of London*, 'The fact is
that in December 1810, when at the point of death, his bed was literally covered with at least 70 billets doux and letters written by
women of the most varied social positions, from duchesses to
semi-prostitutes. Being unable to open and read the letters, he
ordered them to be left unopened, and they lay there until his
death.' After he died they were gathered up and burned.

For more than sixty years Old Q had contributed generously to
the upkeep of what the seventeenth-century bawd Mother Cress-
well had called the 'amorous republic'. He had outlasted all his
contemporaries of both sexes in vice. While many of the compliant young girls offered up to him by the bawds of the golden era
had gone on to independent careers as Toasts, had died and been
succeeded by others, Old Q had seemed to go on for ever. He was
less heartless than Charteris, a good and at times even a generous
friend. He had helped Emma Hamilton when she was ill and down

on her luck, having frittered away her inheritances from Nelson and Sir William Hamilton.

It was said of him that while uncommonly generous to a prostitute, he would cheat his dearest friend, and while squandering money on a favourite horse, would refuse a fellow Christian a morsel of bread. This was simply untrue, and his will showed him to be both generous and scrupulous.

By the time Old Q died he had added 35 codicils to that will. It had taken more than a year. At one stage, annoyed by some act or word of Lord Yarmouth's he had revoked his legacies, but later he changed his mind and restored them. The will was a talking point in high places for a long time. King George III, in his lucid moments, was fascinated, wanting to know all the details and, according to the diaries of the statesman George Rose, 'remarking on each legacy with the most perfect judgment'.

Because of the difficulty of ascertaining what liabilities the estate was subject to it was years before the beneficiaries of the will got their money. Some died without receiving a penny. So for years the fortune remained in the possession of the High Court, earning dividends, eventually amounting to more than a million pounds. A large part of this was cash, formerly held on deposit by Coutts; the Duke had liked to boast that he had more ready money at his disposal than any other man in the country. By 1831, when the final distribution of the assets took place, it was calculated that almost £1,500,000 had been paid out (almost £100 million).

The Yarmouths and their offspring eventually received almost a million pounds under Old Q's will. Lady Yarmouth kept the Piccadilly mansion and gave her husband the house at Richmond. Oddly enough, although they made no secret of their dislike for each other, when it came to business they put their differences aside.

Yarmouth made some half-hearted attempts to patch up his marriage to Mie-Mie, but she did not want to expose herself to the sneers of her mother-in-law, whose curious sexless but intense relationship with the Prince of Wales was making her more haughty and supercilious than ever as she approached the age of 60. And although Mie-Mie always had a dutiful lover or two in tow, she was not prepared to put up with her husband's 'dishonourable capers' which now, according to Blyth in *Old Q*, included 'a tendency towards homosexuality'. She was a good mother, and surrounded by her three children she had no intention of leaving Paris.

The Prince of Wales loved Yarmouth's company at this stage almost as much as his mother's, and he urged Yarmouth to get involved in politics. Yarmouth had been bruised by a botched attempt to negotiate with the French in 1806, in which he was involved, but was cheered by some marks of respect in the Commons. The statesman George Canning came to his aid in the winter of 1807, defending him against a government attack and saying he wished to show him 'more tenderness than has been shown by his employer, and who, I think, has acquitted himself throughout the whole of this arduous business in a manner to entitle him to the highest respect and consideration'. They were soon on opposite sides when Yarmouth's kinsman, Lord Castlereagh, challenged Canning to a duel. Yarmouth acted as his cousin's second, and the two statesmen met on Putney Heath. Canning shot a button off his opponent's coat, and Castlereagh hit Canning in the thigh. The angry statesmen were prepared to go on blazing away at each other, but Yarmouth and the other second declared the duel at an end.

The Hertfords as a family were worming their way into royal favour. During a serious illness in 1811 the Prince Regent, as he now was, would have no one else near him but Yarmouth. Falk notes that 'With his own fingers, as Thomas Grenville ruefully noted, Yarmouth bandaged the stricken royal leg.' The following spring Lord Hertford, who reacted cheerfully enough to the Prince's monopolising his wife's time, if not her affections, became Lord Chamberlain to the Prince, and Yarmouth was appointed Vice-Chamberlain of the Household.

Relations between the Prince and Yarmouth were, if anything, over-familiar. It was the Prince, usually tipsy, who overstepped the mark. One night in 1812 he 'capped his unmannerly conduct by embarrassing advances' to Yarmouth's principal mistress of the time, Fanny Wilson. (She was the sister of the notorious kiss-and-tell blackmailer Harriette Wilson, who reported in her unblushing memoirs how she slept with the Duke of Wellington among many others.)*

Yarmouth gave the Prince a violent push. The Prince, usually so prickly about his dignity, chose to overlook this insult, but someone in his household talked. The satirist John Wolcot, under his pseudonym Peter Pindar, set the episode to verse with the title 'Royal Stripes, or a Kick from Yarmouth to Wales', embellished with an offensive illustration by the brilliant caricaturist George Cruikshank. The incident made the two deeply unpopular rakes more talked about than ever. One reason the Prince overlooked the insult may have been sympathy for the way Yarmouth too was cruelly lampooned by the cartoonists: Pindar referred to the Earl as 'a red-headed whiskerandos, frolicking with wanton belles in that famed street called Chandos'. Falk comments that 'The same red whiskers proved no less a temptation to the derisory muse of Tom Moore, who pictured them flaming into a deeper red each time Yarmouth or 'Bloaters' ran into something particularly agreeable.'† In the public mind Yarmouth, a dandy, tireless womaniser, gambler and friend of the Prince Regent, was assuming the mantle of Old Q.

---

\* Six of the nine Wilson sisters were courtesans. Harriette, Amy and Fanny were known as 'the Three Graces'. When another sister, Sophia, married Lord Berwick and snubbed the rest, Harriette, who was born in Mayfair in 1786, had her revenge by taking a box directly above Sophia's at the opera and spitting down on her head. When Harriette fell on hard times she wrote her memoirs, sending copies to her many aristocratic lovers with a note demanding '£200 by return of post, to be left out'. They were listed in the index by rank: Dukes, Argyle, Beaufort, Leinster etc.; Marquesses, Anglesey, Bath, Hertford, 'and so on down through Burke's Peerage to the modest Esquire', as Lesley Blanch says in the introduction to the Folio Society edition of the *Memoirs*. One of the few to resist this blatant blackmail was the Duke of Wellington, who is said to have scrawled 'Publish and be damned' on the manuscript before sending it back.

† Smoked herrings known as 'bloaters' were produced in the east-coast town of Yarmouth.

Yet there was much more to Yarmouth than reckless hedonism. He could write Latin and Greek with ease, and he was a great connoisseur of art. For a time he bought pictures at auction for the Prince Regent, who would not think of acquiring one without the Earl's approval. Yarmouth was also a brilliant conversationist who enthralled the Prince and other guests at dinner with witticisms and a large repertoire of anecdotes, not all of them salacious. But there were drawbacks in being so closely associated with the Prince at a time when he was more unpopular than ever because of his desertion of his wife, Princess Caroline. Angry mobs hissed the Prince, shouting 'Love your wife!' Lord Hertford had all his windows smashed when he hung a banner outside Manchester House saying 'The Prince's Peace'.

With the fall of Napoleon and the occupation of Paris by the allies, Mie-Mie found herself suddenly popular. Despite her ambiguous role during the war, most of the notable English statesmen who visited Paris called on her, including Wellington, Castlereagh and Sir Robert Peel. Wellington in particular was anxious to meet the woman to whom Junot, his adversary in the Peninsular campaign, had been so kind. Lord Yarmouth came to stay, and got to know his son and heir Richard well. The boy hero-worshipped his father, and grew to be like him. In later life he could quote the classical poets, and collected works of art, though without his father's taste. (The splendid Wallace Collection, housed at Hertford House, Manchester Square, London, was largely compiled by his son, Sir Richard Wallace.) According to Falk, Richard became a cool and experienced card player, 'well able to hold his own with the doughtiest opponent and could sit the clock round without the slightest suspicion of discomforture'. He was another heartless womaniser: when a cast-off mistress attempted suicide other members of the Jockey Club turned their backs on him to show disapproval.

When Mie-Mie's father-in-law, the second Marquess of Hertford, died in June 1822, Yarmouth inherited the title and an immense fortune. Mie-Mie was now the marchioness, but she continued to live quietly in Paris. She had become fat and unattractive, her lovers had left her or died, and she was now content to live a quiet domestic life, surrounded by her family.

In 1834 Hertford's mother died. Having lived a scandalous life but with personal qualities of intellect that earned the respect of eminent men, including Sir Walter Scott, Rossini, Talleyrand and Disraeli, he now went completely off the rails. He travelled endlessly with what the diarist Charles Greville called 'a travelling harem', moving between houses in London, Paris and Milan and deliberately avoiding respectable society. His valet and steward, Nicholas Suisse, acted as his chief pander and was in charge of finding and paying for the long succession of working-class whores who passed through his bed. We catch only glimpses of him 'wallowing in sin', some of them from the memoirs of Harriette Wilson:

> Lord Hertford proposed to show us a small detached building which he had taken pains to fit up in a very luxurious style of elegance. A small low gate, of which he always kept the key, opened into Park Lane, and a little narrow flight of stairs, covered with crimson cloth, conducted to this retirement. It consisted of a dressing room, a small sitting room and a bedchamber.
>
> Over the elegant French bed was a fine picture of a sleeping Venus. There were a great many other pictures, and their subjects, though certainly warm and voluptuous, were yet too classical and graceful to merit the appellation of indecent. He directed our attention to the convenience of opening the door himself, to any fair lady who would honour him with a visit incognita, after his servants should have prepared a most delicious supper and retired to rest.

So much for the secret love nest, set among the mansions of Britain's aristocracy. What went on there? Wilson gives an intriguing glimpse. Hertford told her: 'No power on earth should induce me to name a single female worthy to be called woman, by whom I have been favoured. In the first place because I am not tired of variety, and wish to succeed again. In the second I think it dishonourable.' But on at least one occasion Hertford's sex drive got the better of his sense of 'honour'. Wilson records:

> He told us a story of a lady of family, well known in the fashionable world, whose intrigue with a young dragoon he had discovered by the merest and most unlooked-for accident. 'I accused her of the fact,' continued his lordship, 'and refused to promise secrecy until she had made me as happy as she had made the young dragoon.' 'Was this honourable,' I asked. 'Perhaps not,' said Hertford, 'but I could not help it.'

Suisse was more than generously rewarded for orchestrating his master's sex life: almost daily Hertford changed his will to add fresh sums to the already large amount Suisse would inherit. Eventually it amounted to £18,600; to this, as we shall see, was added what the servant helped himself to.

Hertford died in London in March 1842. His will was a further source of scandal, for he had written into it exactly what he thought of various relatives and friends. As a contemporary commented, 'it had the singular and original characteristic of being for the most part an instrument of defamation – a contrivance for posthumous calumny.' He also settled an old score. When he heard that Mie-Mie had received her bequest of £100,000 (about £6,000,000 today) from Old Q's estate, he deducted £700 from the income he had intended leaving her. She also got a sum of £20,000, and a bust and writing box of Charles I. He directed that she should have only such pictures and china as she could prove to have been originally her own.

There were other disappointments. The Irish politician and writer John Wilson Croker, who had acted as Hertford's devoted unpaid amanuensis and toady for nearly 25 years, was vexed to receive only £21,000. Sir Robert Peel sent him a message of sympathy: 'My chief interest in respect to Lord Hertford's will was the hope that out of his enormous wealth he would mark the sense of your unvarying and real friendship for him.'*

When an audit of Hertford's assets was carried out it was found that French securities worth 100,000 francs were missing. They were traced to Suisse, who claimed that they had been given to him by his master. Although it was clear that Suisse was prepared to tell the scandalous truth about his master as part of his defence, Croker and Hertford's heir decided to prosecute him for larceny and embezzlement.

The case was heard at the Old Bailey before Lord Abinger, the Lord Chief Baron. The revelations were sensational, and even the most staid newspapers published long accounts. The court heard how Suisse had procured women for Hertford, and paid them as much as £40,000 a year in total. Suisse's lawyer described these as 'delicate transactions'. More damaging was the evidence of Angélique Borel, a woman who had become Hertford's mistress at the age of 16 and had been left an annuity of 15,000 francs in the will. She was secretly engaged to be married to Suisse, and her evidence certainly did him no harm. She said she had once heard him tell Hertford: 'Thanks to your kindness I have become a rich man.' She also claimed that in October 1841, in Paris, Hertford had promised to buy her a house. To put pressure on him to keep his word she had threatened to leave him. He offered her some French securities, which she refused, and later in the day he gave her 211,000 francs in cash. Hertford explained that he had given the securities, which were worth 100,000 francs, to Suisse. At one stage, in an obvious dig at the sanctimonious Croker, she revealed he had dined with her and Hertford together. Croker was unable to deny this, but pointed out that on another occasion when Hertford called for Borel at her apartments in Clarge's Street, he

---

\* Hertford had intended to leave Peel his Star of the Order of the Garter, but changed his mind because he felt that Peel was not responding to his political advice. Disraeli wrote: 'He [Hertford] had left his Star of the Order of the Garter in costly brilliants with a long panegyric to Peel, as the saviour of his country and all that, and the legacy was afterwards revoked. I suppose his ghost smelt the Income Tax.' In 1878, when Disraeli returned from the Congress of Berlin, the same Star was presented to him by Hertford's grandson, Sir Richard Wallace.

had got out of the carriage rather than be seen in her company.

After a summing up from Lord Abinger apparently strongly biased in favour of Suisse, the jury found him not guilty. This brought the thunder of *The Times* about the ears of the judge. After saying how reluctant it was to comment on so entirely disgusting a subject, the paper went on:

> This picture of the last days of the Marquess of Hertford is not a pleasing one. Nor is the capacity in which Nicholas Suisse acts one which even the world ordinarily looks upon with a very favourable eye ...
>
>      And now let us hear the judgment authoritatively delivered from the bench by the Lord Chief Baron upon these services. 'The prisoner,' said Lord Abinger in directing his acquittal, 'there could be no doubt had been an invaluable servant to his master, and it was his duty to provide liberally for him under the circumstances ... Very important and valuable services had been performed since Nov. 1839, and it was only right to infer that for such services his master would reward him ... His character was described, in what the learned Counsel most properly called 'a voice from the grave of his master' [i.e. Hertford's will] as being that of 'an excellent man'. There could be no doubt of the excellence of his character.
>
>      We wish we could disbelieve our eyes when we see such a panegyric on such services proceeding from the English Bench ...
>
>      If Lord Hertford had given to Suisse or Borel, previous to these services which Lord Abinger eulogises, a bond specified to be in consideration of their expected performance, the law would have denounced that bond, as founded on a corrupt consideration, immoral and void ...

Croker and the new Marquess were abused for opening the public's eyes to scandal in high places, and Croker was accused of hypocrisy. It was pointed out that he had dined with whores at Lord Hertford's table, yet had refused to subscribe to the relief of the children of his friend Theodore Hook because they were illegitimate.

The character of the dissolute Marquess continued to fascinate. Shortly after his death three English authors introduced characters based on him into their novels – Bulwer Lytton in *Pelham*, Disraeli in *Coningsby* and Thackeray in *Vanity Fair*. Thackeray's wicked Lord Steyne is the best known, but perhaps Disraeli's Lord Monmouth is the most rounded and fair. He had known Hertford well, and his portrait of the unemotional, intellectual and shrewd aristocrat using his vast wealth for purely selfish ends rings true. Disraeli himself said: 'Lord Steyne is a mere brutal voluptuary – not the character at all. For Lord Hertford was a very clever man indeed.'

If he had a virtue it was generosity to former mistresses. Harriette Wilson recalled his kindness to her sister Fanny as she lay dying:

> He was very desirous of having her portrait painted by Lawrence to place in his apartment. 'That laughing blue eye of hers', he would say, 'is unusually beautiful' … He was the only man she admitted into her room, to take leave of her before she died, although hundreds of those of the first rank and character were desirous of doing so. I remember Lord Yarmouth's last visit to Brompton, where my poor sister died after an illness of three weeks. 'Can I or my cook do anything in the world to be useful to her?' said he. I repeated that it was too late, that she would never desire anything more, and all I wanted for her was plenty of eau-de-Cologne to wash her temples with; that being all she asked for. He did not send his groom for it, but galloped to town himself, and was back immediately.

Mie-Mie died in Paris in March 1856, aged 85, largely forgotten. But she and her husband can now be seen as links between the world of Old Q and an age of profligacy whose most famous representative, King George IV, is the subject of the chapters that follow.

# Part 5

# George IV:
# A Selfish, Unfeeling
# Dog

# Prelude

GEORGE IV DIED IN WINDSOR CASTLE at 3.15 am on the morning of Sunday 26 June 1830. He apparently cried out for his principal physician, Sir Henry Halford: 'Sir Henry, Sir Henry! Fetch him – this is death!' Halford had already joined George's last mistress, Lady Conyngham, in plundering the dying King. Three days earlier his coachman had been fined £60 (about £3,700 today) for trying to make off with furniture from the castle in his master's carriage at five o'clock in the morning. As Parissien notes in *George IV*, Halford had admitted to his wife that he had 'taken some of the gilding of the King's sick-room', including 'a swallow nest from China'. Lady Conyngham herself hurried from the deathbed with a coach laden with loot. The caricaturist William Heath pictured her loading royal silver into a chest and pushing a laden wheelbarrow from the castle, saying to her husband, 'I've taken care of myself depend on it.' The King, so long an exploiter of others, had become a helpless victim.

George, who spent his last years as a dirty, bloated, gluttonous, drunken and drugged recluse, had mostly had a bad press. Seventeen years earlier the poet and essayist Leigh Hunt was jailed with his brother John for describing George thus: 'This Adonis in loveliness is a corpulent man of fifty ... a libertine over head and ears in debt and disgrace, a despiser of domestic ties, the companion of gamblers and demireps, a man who has just closed half a century without one single claim on the gratitude of his country or the respect of authority.'

The diarist Charles Greville wrote: 'A more contemptible, cowardly, selfish, unfeeling dog does not exist than this King ... He has a sort of capricious good nature, arising however out of no good principle or good feeling, but which is of use to him, as it cancels in a moment.'

Princess Lieven, wife of the Russian ambassador, thought him 'full of vanity ... weary of all the joys of life, having only taste, not one true sentiment ...' After his death the obituarists and memorialists were if anything even more merciless. One of the King's first and bitterest biographers, Robert Huish, writing in 1830–1, said that George had 'contributed more to the demoralisation of society than any prince recorded in the pages of history'. *The Times* obituarist wrote of his 'unceasing and unbounded prodigality', his 'indifference to the feelings of others', and described his gluttony for food, wine and women as 'little higher than that of animal indulgence'. A later critic, the Victorian novelist William Thackeray, called him 'nothing but a coat and a wig and a mask smiling below it – nothing but a great simulacrum'.

George had long been an embarrassment both to himself and to the nation. In old age he skulked at Windsor, ashamed to show himself in public and afraid of his subjects. A captain in the Guards said that he was unwilling to be seen even by his own servants, and as early as 1819 George was reported as saying: 'I will not allow these maid-servants to look at me when I go in and out; and if I find they do so again, I will have them discharged.'

Apologists for George point to his taste in art and architecture, and his personal charm. But time and again the nation had to bail him out after he ran up huge debts. Tradesmen were driven into bankruptcy because he would not pay his bills. Women were by no means his only or greatest expense; he lavished fortunes on gambling, clothes, horses, works of art and, most of all, on his various homes which, as Parissien observes in *George IV*, 'were constantly rebuilt, remodelled and redecorated at vast expense'. His charm came and went. He was a fickle and inconstant lover, though perhaps no more so than many rich aristocrats of the time, but also a faithless friend. Almost none of his friendships lasted more than a year or two. His shameless abandonment of the playwright Sheridan still makes one cringe. He plotted to replace his father by becoming Regent while the King was desperately ill and appeared to be mad.

He died largely unlamented by his subjects. At his funeral at Windsor Castle in July the congregation consisted mostly of 'the servants of the household, the friends of the carpenters and the upholsterers, the petty tradesmen of the town'. The new King, William IV, behaved as though he was at a garden party, according to Parissien, 'talking animatedly and excitedly to all and sundry . . . and walked out early'. Huish said there 'seemed to be a predominant feeling not to mourn at all'. The truth is that the King had become an irrelevance. As he abandoned his friends so he abandoned his early political ideals. This one-time ardent disciple of the radical Whig Charles James Fox gradually became more reactionary, eventually opposing Catholic emancipation only to have it forced on him by the conservative Duke of Wellington. When the Act was passed in 1829, proof of the supremacy of Parliament, it was another sign that he had in effect ceased to matter. His brilliant talents had come to nothing, and a new morality was setting in which would try to expunge him from the historical record.

# *Uncommon Diversions*

T HE FAULTS OF GEORGE, PRINCE OF WALES have been blamed on his relationships with his parents. His mean-spirited mother showed him no love, so in compensation, after the first flush of youthful ardour was passed, he sought it with mother figures, ample middle-aged aristocrats, at least one of them a grandmother. His father was a pious martinet, so he sought the company of scoundrels, rakes and his father's political opponents. There is some truth in this: the three of them certainly caused each other much pain.

George was born on 12 August 1762, the first of 15 children. He was, says J. B. Priestley in *The Prince of Pleasure*, 'brought up plainly and strictly – perhaps too plainly and strictly – at the Bower Lodge at Kew'. He was educated at home, becoming a good linguist and musician. In 1771, when he was nine, a governor, the Earl of Holdernesse, was appointed for him and his brother Frederick. Horace Walpole called the Earl a 'formal piece of dullness' and he spent most of the time giving the young princes moral lectures. When Holdernesse resigned in 1776 Dr Richard Hurd, Bishop of Lichfield, became one of his teachers. The following year, asked to comment on George's progress, he is alleged to have replied: 'He will either be the most polished gentleman or the most accomplished blackguard in Europe.' The Prince was tall, handsome, already rather overweight, florid, showy. He was also intelligent.

Before drink, drugs, gluttony and incapacitating grossness made sex absurd and impossible, George was a very successful woman-iser, if not as precocious as Charles II. In 1779, at the age of 17 – when, as Christopher Hibbert asserts in *George IV, Prince of Wales*, he had already seduced, it was supposed, a maid of honour to the Queen – he fell for Mary Hamilton, a governess to one of his sis-ters. She was 23 and when she rejected him he threatened suicide, a tactic he was to use again and again. In the end she threatened to resign if he persisted, and he reluctantly agreed to address her 'by the endearing names of friend and Sister, and no longer with the impetuous passion of a Lover urging his Suit'. In the course of that suit George had admitted that he was already 'rather too fond of wine and women', and soon he forgot all about Mary as he set off in pursuit of his first great love, Mary 'Perdita' Robinson.

Mary was by common agreement one of the great beauties of the age. She was painted by the leading artists: Gainsborough, Reynolds, Romney, Zoffany, Cosway, Hoppner and Stroehling. She had married Thomas Robinson, a feckless Harrow-educated articled legal clerk, when she was only 16. When he was sent to the Fleet prison for debt she had to go too. She wrote to the Duchess of Devonshire, to whom she sent a volume of poetry she had writ-ten in prison, and the playwright Richard Brinsley Sheridan. He auditioned her after she was released and recommended her to the actor-manager David Garrick. By the time the Prince of Wales saw her in Garrick's production of *A Winter's Tale* in December 1779, in which she played Perdita, she was an established actor.

The Prince was smitten, and sent her letters signed Florizel, Perdita's lover in the play. Soon he was smuggling her into his apartments at Carlton House and Windsor for sex. He promised everlasting love, had her miniature painted and put it in a locket with the words *Je ne change qu'en mourant* (I change only by dying) and 'Unalterable to my Perdita thro' life' written on it. She left the stage and became his mistress after he signed a pledge to give her a fortune of £20,000 (about £1,800,000) when he came of age. Perhaps at the time this was a promise he meant to keep, but his promises were worthless.

The Fleet Prison. Before she became George Prince of Wales' first mistress, Mary 'Perdita' Robinson was held there with her husband for debt.

The newspapers got hold of the story, and made much of the beautiful young couple, Florizel and Perdita. The King was furious, not for the last time reminding the Prince of his duty to set a good example and pointing out that 'your love of dissipation has for some months been through ill nature trumpeted in the public papers'.

But the Prince's affections were already engaged elsewhere. With so many beautiful women to choose from he was beginning to realise it would be silly to pledge himself to one. He was attracted by the witty courtesan Elizabeth Armistead, who had emerged from a London brothel to rise vertiginously through a long string of affairs with aristocrats and would later become the beloved wife of Charles James Fox.

First he had to get rid of Perdita. He sent her a curt note saying they must 'meet no more'. She persuaded him to meet her to discuss the break, and, she told a friend, 'We passed some hours in the most friendly and delightful conversation.' But when they met by chance in Hyde Park the very next day the Prince snubbed her, she reported, turning his head to avoid seeing her 'and even affected not to know me!' The brutal abruptness of all this was characteristic. With great difficulty Mrs Robinson prised a lump sum of £5,000 and a pension of £500 a year for herself and her daughter from the Prince, who stood by complacently while she sank into poverty, illness and early death.* Yet he had the effrontery to tell the Duchess of Devonshire, the captivating Georgiana, about the split: 'Out of sight out of mind, I know, is an old proverb, and but too often the case with many people, but it is not the least, my dearest Duchess, applicable to me.'

So it was briefly the turn of Mrs Armistead. Among her first

---

* At the time of the settlement she said the £5,000 was not enough even to pay her debts. Later she wrote to the Prince describing her straitened circumstances. He promised to help, but she was rescued by the war hero Colonel Banastre Tarleton, MP and was his mistress for about 16 years. After she became paralysed from the waist down, following an illness, she became an author, writing poetry and plays. Towards the end of her life the Prince was a regular visitor to her house in St James's Place. She died at the age of 40, from 'acute rheumatic disorders . . . aggravated by pecuniary distress'.

aristocratic lovers had been the Duke of Ancaster. The *Town and Country Magazine* claimed that while they were lovers she had a child by a lieutenant in the army. Her next lover was the Duke of Dorset, who had just parted company with another great courtesan, Nancy Parsons. Nancy had first been kept by a man named Horton; Horace Walpole wrote of 'The Duke of Grafton's Mrs Horton, the Duke of Dorset's Mrs Horton, everybody's Mrs Horton'. The Duke of Grafton was the leader of the government.

Another of Armistead's lovers was Viscount Bolingbroke, known as 'Bully' and with good reason. He had been married to Lady Diana Spencer but had beaten and generally mistreated her, so she had taken a lover, Topham Beauclerk, whom she married when Bully divorced her. She regretted the new marriage almost as much, but achieved celebrity under her new name as the artist Lady Diana Beauclerk.

Armistead achieved a rare degree of autonomy for a courtesan by getting her wealthy lovers to settle large amounts on her before allowing them the use of her person. She bought two houses in fashionable Bond Street and Clarges Street, and acquired the most desirable of all trophy lovers, the Prince. In the complicated way these things were done, Armistead was still involved with Lord George Cavendish. One night, more than a little tipsy, Cavendish returned to her house. Noticing a light in a room he forced his way in, despite her entreaties not to enter. He found the Prince of Wales hiding behind the door. Summoning up more grace than the Prince could manage, he laughed, bowed and left.

Armistead found she could not really afford the Prince, who paid nothing for her favours and in fact sponged off her. Entertaining him and his friends proved too expensive, so they parted. He was probably tired of her, as he was already simultaneously wooing a 17-year-old maid of honour, Harriet Vernon, and the 'illiterate and ignorant' Charlotte Fortescue. His eye had also been caught by another courtesan, Grace Dalrymple Eliot.

Armistead left the country briefly after the split with the Prince, and the *Morning Herald* reported that 'the principal cause of her going abroad was that ill-founded patriotism, which led her to sacrifice so much of her time to the heroic members of opposition, without the receipt of a single guinea'. Eliot, who had quarrelled with her French lover the Duc de Chartres, hurried back to England to hunt this new quarry. It was later reported that she had a daughter by the Prince, a child he refused to acknowledge. (The girl overcame this snub and married into the aristocracy.)

In the summer of 1782 the swapping of sexual partners at the heart of London high society resembled an elaborate dance. I. M. Davis says in *The Harlot and the Statesman*:

> The comparative decorum of transient but temporarily exclusive pairings appeared a thing of the past ... as the Prince, his lovers and his friends entangled themselves in a network of multiple liaisons. The Grand Chain of the Cytherean dance seemed broken up into an orgy of promiscuous hands–across: the Prince and the Armistead, the Prince and Dally [Eliot]; Dally and [Lord] Cholmondeley, Cholmondeley and the Armistead; Fox ... and Perdita, Perdita and Banastre Tarleton ...

The Prince had become a conspicuous consumer of luxury goods, including sex. And in most cases he paid late, if at all. A caricature shows him being dunned by the bawd Mrs Windsor and other brothel-keepers, who are presenting him with their bills. One demands £1,000 for 'first slice of a young tit only 12 years' and £1,000 for 'uncommon diversions'. A black prostitute named Black Moll is holding out a bill itemising her services to His Royal Highness, including 'Tipping the Velvet' for £100. A young girl holds a paper asking for payment for her lost maidenhead. Thomas Rowlandson was one of several caricaturists who showed the Prince with prostitutes. In 1786 a rival artist pictured him demanding 'a brisk wench in clean straw'.

It seemed any woman was fair game. A full list would be difficult to establish now, but in addition to the professionals there were the Countess von Hardenburg, wife of a member of the diplomatic corps, women of the court including Lady Augusta Campbell, Lady Melbourne and various ladies-in-waiting, and friends' wives, including Elizabeth Billington.

His clumsy attempts to extricate himself from these entangle-ments were sometimes costly. A brief fling with the singer Anna Maria Crouch, which may, according to Joseph Farington's *Diary*, have been no more than a one-night stand, earned her a promised pay-off of 'money or Bonds to the amount of £12,000'. Her hus-band, who threatened to sue the Prince, received a pension of £400 a year. Mrs Crouch had to haggle, and in the end settled for a bag containing 1,000 guineas.

By now the Prince's debts were crushing. Pensions for current and cast-off mistresses didn't help, but the truth was that his father kept him short of money. In 1783, when he came of age, George III allowed him £50,000 a year, half what his grandfather was granted at the same age. This was a huge sum, worth around £4,000,000 today, but the Prince was expected to keep a very expensive establishment. He made no attempt to live within his income. In October 1784 his treasurer, Colonel George Hotham, informed him that he had discovered 'with equal grief and vexa-tion' that the Prince was 'totally in the hands, and at the mercy of, your builder, your upholsterer, your jeweller and your tailor'. Within three years Pitt introduced a Commons motion authoris-ing the payment of the Prince's debts, which had reached a stag-gering £210,000 (almost £18 million).

The Prince's usual reaction in these circumstances was to run away. He threatened to leave the country but his father forbade it, so instead he went to Brighton, where he would spend his happi-est years with the woman who can be called the love of his life, Maria Fitzherbert. He could not be faithful to her, but for once he almost meant his promises.

George first met Mrs Fitzherbert in 1783. She was a wealthy twice-widowed Catholic, six years older than he. Huish describes her as 'unquestionably, a beautiful woman', adding that she was 'perhaps too much inclined to fullness of figure'. She found George attract-ive and was flattered by his attention, but she was not a fool, and was unimpressed by his declarations of undying love. When she refused to become his mistress he faked a suicide attempt, even spilling some of his blood. Maria fled to the Continent, whereupon George sent her a 42-page letter. After further threats of suicide she married him in the drawing room of her Mayfair home on the evening of 15 December 1785. The marriage was clearly illegal: the Royal Marriage Act of 1772 forbade members of the royal family under the age of 26 from marrying without the sovereign's consent, and no one married to a Catholic could succeed to the throne.

Nevertheless they settled down to a kind of domestic bliss at her Brighton home and Carlton House. Maria, always rather queenly in her ways, insisted on precedence at dinner even over princesses – 'Mighty foolish this', opined John Wilson Croker, the writer, MP and busybody. Of course it couldn't last. Into George's life came the scheming beauty Lady Jersey, mother of eight and a grandmother seven years older than he, a harp-playing charmer described by the diarist Sir Nathaniel Wraxall as of 'irresistible seduction and fascination'. Huish compared her to a serpent, 'beautiful, bright and glossy in its exterior – in its interior, poisonous and pestiferous'.

Mrs Fitzherbert had long recognised the truth of Sheridan's words, that the Prince was 'too much every lady's man to be the man of any lady', and had overlooked or forgiven his minor infidelities, but she instinctively knew that Lady Jersey was more dangerous. Jersey was ambitious, sensual and heartless. The Prince had known her for some years but it was only now, when she was in her forties, that the force of her beauty struck him hard. She was the first of that line of mature, full-figured, masterly women he now preferred.

Under Lady Jersey's direction he wrote to Mrs Fitzherbert saying he would never see her again. This characteristic brutality surely refutes any claim by his supporters that he was a man of feeling. Similar cases can be quoted. Having seduced young Harriet Vernon in 1782 he showed her, in Huish's words, 'only neglect and indifference ... after she had sacrificed to him all that was most dear to her on earth', presumably meaning her virginity. She also lost her job as maid of honour, sacked by the King for her indiscretion. In 1804 the Prince had a brief affair with Marie Anne, the French wife of the Earl of Massereene, and she was soon discarded 'to make way for another whose chief recommendation was that of novelty'. According to Huish, his court was a place where 'many an ardent vow has been breathed of everlasting constancy and affection'.

George wanted Parliament to pay his enormous new debts, and he reasoned that they would do so only if he married. Naturally he discussed this with his latest mistress, and Lady Jersey was widely believed to have been behind the choice of the 24-year-old German Princess Caroline to be the Prince's bride. If the choice was hers, it was both spiteful and clever. For a man so susceptible to female beauty and good manners Caroline was a disastrous choice. John Hoppner, who painted her portrait, said her figure was 'very bad – short – very full chested and jutting hips'. Her conversation was considered indiscreet, vulgar and dirty, as was her person. On the other hand, some thought her quite pretty, with good hair and eyes; she was cheerful and kind and not stupid. With breathtaking insensitivity George appointed Lady Jersey to be one of his bride's Ladies of the Bedchamber. When Caroline found out about her, she told Lord Malmesbury, who had been sent to collect her from Germany: 'I am determined never to appear jealous. I know the Prince is *léger*, and am prepared on this point.'

Caroline's first hours in England were nightmarish. Lady Jersey, who was to escort her to London, kept her waiting for an hour, then made it plain she was 'very much dissatisfied with the Princess's mode of dress'. She made Caroline change into something less attractive, suggested she rouge her cheeks although she had a natural good high colour, and finally tried to take the best place in the carriage for the ride to London by saying that she would be sick if she sat with her back to the horses. Lord Malmesbury intervened and she had to back down.

On arriving at St James's Palace Caroline was next humiliated by the Prince, who on being introduced to her muttered: 'Harris, I am not well; pray get me a glass of brandy.' He then left the room

St James's Palace, scene of some of Princess Caroline's humiliations.

immediately, saying he was going to visit his mother. Caroline asked Malmesbury if the Prince always acted so, adding: 'I think he's very fat, and he's nothing like as handsome as his portrait.'

Nothing could have saved the marriage, but George treated the young woman, alone and far from home in a strange country, with studied rudeness. His behaviour at the wedding ceremony was unforgivable. He was so drunk he almost passed out twice, and in the carriage on the way to the chapel he told his companions, George 'Beau' Brummell and the soldier and statesman Lord Moira, of his undying love for Mrs Fitzherbert. At the altar he turned to look at Lady Jersey as he promised to love, honour and obey. When the Archbishop of Canterbury asked whether there was any impediment to the marriage the Prince burst into tears. Later he drank himself into a stupor and, according to Caroline, 'passed the greater part of his bridal-night under the grate, where he fell'.

The tragi-comedy was played out with all the predictability of a contemporary novel. The Prince had sex with his wife on three nights. He later confided to Malmesbury that Caroline showed 'such marks of filth both in the fore and hind parts of her' that he vowed never to touch her again. Evidently Caroline had ignored Malmesbury's advice to 'wash all over'. Nevertheless she conceived a daughter.

Another reason that the honeymoon was such a disaster was the presence of the Prince's friends. Part of the time the couple were at the Prince's hunting retreat at Kempshott in Hampshire. George had invited some of his drinking companions along, and it was reported that they lay about 'constantly drunk and filthy, sleeping and snoring in boots on the sofas'.

George's friends were a sore point, particularly to his parents. For obvious reasons he chose companions who were anathema to his father. The artist Benjamin Robert Haydon observed: 'The people [George] liked had all a spice of vice in their nature.' They included two of the most notorious dukes in England, Queensberry and Norfolk. Norfolk was a celebrated drunkard, ignorant and with an aversion to washing. The only time his servants could bathe him was when he was drunk. The dukes were of another generation, Norfolk being 16 years older than the Prince and Queensberry 38 years.

Worse, the King's sinister brother, the debauched Duke of Cumberland, was an intimate drinking companion of the Prince. The Duke had seduced Lady Henrietta Grosvenor and was sued by her husband. According to Horace Walpole, she had 'rendered herself too accessible' to the Duke. Cumberland's puerile love letters were a feature of the case, and Lord Grosvenor was awarded a colossal £10,000. Cumberland's other transgressions included marrying a commoner and seducing a woman whose daughter afterwards insisted on being called Princess Olive of Cumberland. When the great actress-courtesan Sophia Baddeley was on the slide he sent her a peremptory summons to a Covent Garden brothel. Sophia, who once had the wealthiest aristocrats among her lovers and could command hundreds of pounds a night, indignantly refused, retorting: 'Go and tell the Duke to send for Lady Grosvenor.'

Even more worrying for the King was his son's friendship with the leader of the Whigs, Charles James Fox. It was Cumberland who introduced the young Prince to gambling, but it was the wenching, drinking, talking, non-sleeping and gambling-mad Fox who showed him the extremes of libertine behaviour. The Prince was captivated by Fox's extraordinary charm and good nature, and impressed by the way he threw away his own fortune and the considerable sums he borrowed from his friends. Fox was a brilliant orator and a formidable statesman, but he was the worst possible role model for the weak Prince of Wales.

The son of an enormously rich man who had amassed much of his fortune while Paymaster-General of the Forces, an expected if not quite legitimate form of corruption, Fox would stay up all night playing hazard at the gambling club Almack's in Pall Mall, then go to the Commons to speak in important debates. Horace Walpole told how, before the debate on the Thirty-Nine Articles, he sat up all night gambling, and by five o'clock the next afternoon had lost £11,000 (almost £1,000,000). The following day 'he spoke in this debate; went to dinner at half past eleven at night; from thence to White's, where he drank until seven the next morning; thence to Almack's where he won £6,000.' That afternoon he went to Newmarket for the races.

His appetite for whoring was as great. A contemporary caricature, 'King's Place, or a View of Mr Fox's Best Friends' (1784), shows Perdita Robinson and the courtesan Elizabeth Armistead talking to the Prince of Wales. The bawd Mrs Windsor is saying of Fox: 'He introduced his R— H— to my house.'

When Fox eventually married and settled down it was with Armistead, the Prince's former mistress. The tale of Fox and Armistead can be told as a touching love story, only slightly tainted by the fact that they were both veterans of commercial sex who had been circling each other for years as they hopped in and out of beds. They married when Fox was 34 and she 33. By then, having lasted longer at the top of her profession than almost any other courtesan, she was competing with girls in their late teens; she was wealthy and ready for the far less demanding role of housewife, at which she was a notable success. Marriage to Fox conferred a degree of respectability equal to that achieved by her competitors Elizabeth Farren, who married the Earl of Derby, and Harriet Powell, who married the Earl of Seaforth. That is to say she was accepted in the society of Fox's male friends, but not always by their wives.

In addition to these unsuitable companions, as a young man the Prince surrounded himself with men like Richard Brinsley Sheridan, George Brummell, the artist Richard Cosway, Jack Payne, the debonair soldier Colonel Anthony St Leger and George Hanger, none of whom would have been welcome at the staid and stuffy court. His circle included a number of raffish serving officers whom he admired mostly for their worst tendencies. Sir John Lade was remarkable for drinking, for his ability to drive a coach-and-four with great skill and for marrying the harlot Letitia Smith. She had been involved with George's younger and favourite brother Frederick, and more famously with the highwayman Sixteen-String Jack Rann, who was executed in

1774. He was so called because of the silk tassels he attached to the knees of his breeches, and ever the dandy he went to his execution in a new pea-green suit, a ruffled shirt and a hat surrounded with silver rings. In his buttonhole he wore a huge nosegay. The night before his execution he was allowed to entertain seven girls in his cell. Letitia was present when he was hanged at Tyburn.

Lady Lade was also noted for driving her phaeton furiously and for swearing in public. 'He swears like Letty Lade,' the Prince once remarked of a man whose language was particularly expressive. Letitia was rumoured to have been among his conquests before her marriage in 1787, and after it she acted as his procurer. The Prince, who admired Letitia's expert and daring horsemanship, commissioned an equestrian portrait of her by George Stubbs. Huish didn't share this enthusiasm – he thought she represented 'all that was vile and despicable in woman'. She once danced with the Prince at a public assembly in Brighton, whereat the more conservative aristocratic women present, including the Duchess of Rutland, walked out and left the town.

George shared the Lades' passion for carriage driving. During the 1780s and 1790s he was often seen driving his carriage along Brighton seafront accompanied by Sir John. Thackeray recalled that the Prince once drove a carriage from Carlton House to Brighton in four and a half hours, and the Prince himself boasted of driving a phaeton-and-four 'twenty-two miles in two hours at a trot'.

In October 1795 a newspaper report caught something of the attraction of Sir John Lade for the Prince:

A curious circumstance occurred at Brighton on Monday. Sir John Lade, for a trifling wager, undertook to carry Lord Cholmondeley on his back, from opposite the Pavilion twice round the Steyne. Several ladies attended to be spectators of this extraordinary feat of the dwarf carrying the giant. When his Lordship declared himself ready, Sir John desired him to strip. 'Strip!' exclaimed the other; 'why surely you promised to carry me in my clothes.' 'By no means,' replied the Baronet; 'I engaged to carry you, but not an inch of clothes. So therefore, my Lord, make ready, and let us not disappoint the ladies.' After much laughable altercation, it was decided that Sir John had won his wager, the Peer declining to exhibit himself *in puris naturalibus*.

Such harmless high spirits kept the Prince amused for a while, and for once he showed his gratitude, granting the Lades an annual pension of £300 – this may have been partly for Letitia's services as procuress – in 1814 when Sir John emerged penniless from a debtor's prison.* But not everyone shared George's amused tolerance for Lade. Lord Thurlow, Pitt's gruff Lord Chancellor, who was also seen in the Prince's company, said on finding that he had been invited to dinner at the same time as Sir John: 'I have, Sir, no objection to Sir John Lade in his proper place, which I take to be your Royal Highness's coach-box, and not your table.'

Colonel George Hanger, a hero of the American War of Independence, was another of the Prince's boon drinking and gambling companions. Nathaniel Wraxall left this vignette:

> The Hon. George Hanger, now become an Irish baron in his old age by the successive decease of his two brothers, the Lords Coleraine, might rather be considered as a humble retainer at Carlton House than justly numbered among the friends of the heir apparent. Poor even to a degree of destitution, without profession or regular employment, subsisting from day to day by expedients, some of them not the most reputable, he was regarded as a sort of outcast from decent society.

Hanger's lifelong interest in women began as a schoolboy at Eton. In his autobiography he tells us:

---

* After George died the pension was maintained by William IV, but it was supposed his niece Victoria would cancel it when she came to the throne. However, she asked whether it was true that Lade was old and broke, and on being told that he was 78, penniless and alone – Lettie having died in 1825 – she ordered that the pension be paid until his death. He died a year later.

A carpenter's wife was the first object of my early affections; nor can I well express the nature of my obligations to her. Frequently have I risked breaking my neck in getting over the roof of my boarding house at night, to pass a few hours with some favourite grisette at Windsor.

He is frank about his later life, that of a typical if not outstanding Regency rake:

I was early introduced into life, and often kept both good and bad company; associated with men both good and bad, and with lewd women and women not lewd, wicked and not wicked; – in short with men and women of every description and every rank, from the highest to the lowest, from St James's to St Giles's [a notorious slum around the present New Oxford Street]; in palaces and night cellars; from the drawing room to the dust cart. The difficulties and misfortunes I have experienced, I am inclined to think, have proceeded from none of the above-mentioned causes, but from happening to come into life at a period of the greatest extravagance and profusion ... I could not stand the temptations of that age of extravagance, elegance and pleasure: indeed, I am not the only sufferer, for most of my contemporaries, and many of them of ten times my opulence, have been ruined.

Hanger also helped the Prince kill time, sometimes by devising what Beresford Chancellor calls curious wagers. Hanger may have been innocent or naïve, but among the Prince's circle were several professional gamblers, who successfully used such contests to fleece the royal dupe. Chancellor tells of one contest devised by Hanger, which cost the Prince thousands of pounds. During a convivial party at Carlton House Hanger suggested that turkeys could walk further in a given time than geese. The Prince, who respected Hanger's judgment, wagered a large sum on the outcome. Twenty geese were matched against twenty turkeys, and at first the latter seemed the likely winners, gaining at least two miles on the geese. But as evening drew on the turkeys flew into nearby trees to roost, and the geese won. Anyone who had looked into the matter would have predicted this result, and successful gamblers of the time, such as Lord Queensberry, were noted for their meticulous pre-contest research.

In 1803 Joseph Farington reported an example of the public behaviour of George and his cronies:

> At one of the entertainments given by the Prince, His Royal Highness filled a glass with wine and wantonly threw it in Hanger's face. [Hanger] without being disconcerted immediately filled his glass and throwing it in the face of the person who sat next to him bid him pass it round – an admirable instance of presence of mind and judgment upon an occasion of coarse rudeness.

Hanger had a touching modesty, particularly given the circles he moved in. In 1814 he succeeded his brother as Lord Coleraine, a title which gave him no pleasure. One day in Bond Street an acquaintance said to him: 'I hope I have the honour to see your Lordship in perfect health.' Hanger replied: 'What do you mean, you scoundrel, by calling a man names he is ashamed of? Whether Lord Coleraine be up there' (pointing to the sky) 'or down there' (pointing to the ground) 'I know not, or care not; but I am, as I always was, plain George Hanger.' When he was pitifully poor he once entertained the Prince, one of the royal dukes and some of their friends in his Soho lodging house. They ate baked shoulder of mutton and baked potatoes, and drank porter. The Prince, noted for serving some of the most elaborate and expensive meals ever seen in England, said he had never enjoyed a meal so much. Hanger's modesty served him in old age, when the Prince had long abandoned him for a younger, more fashionable and amusing set. He married his housekeeper, spent much of his time at a pub near his lodgings in unfashionable Somers Town telling tales of his war service in America and died in 1824, aged 72.

Another of the Prince's louche companions was Captain Jack Payne of the Royal Navy. Although he rose to be a rear-admiral and was MP for Huntingdon, he was persona non grata with the court because of his drinking and gambling. He was notoriously unreliable where money was concerned, and although the Prince proposed him for membership of Brooks's Club he was black-balled. Yet the Prince appointed him Comptroller of his household and let him use a private apartment at Brighton Pavilion. Payne was dismissed in 1796 for his support of Princess Caroline and opposition to Lady Jersey (though he later got his job back), and the Jerseys were given his house, next door to George's residence, Carlton House.

We have already met Old Q's rival Richard Barry, seventh Earl of Barrymore. In 1791, during the races at Ascot, Barrymore spent £1,785 laying on two banquets for the Prince, who attended neither. Barrymore married – at Gretna Green – the daughter of a sedan-chairman who was also the niece of Letitia Lade.

Because of his profligacy, Barrymore was known as 'Hellgate'. Wags dubbed his foul-mouthed and savage-tempered sister 'Billingsgate', his clerical brother, a compulsive gambler who was seldom out of trouble for debt, 'Newgate', and his club-footed brother 'Cripplegate', all of course London landmarks. He and his brothers and sisters got into amusing scrapes and played childish practical jokes, which greatly amused the Prince. (Indeed, successive holders of that title have shown a weakness for such behaviour.)

Brighton was the scene of many of their frolics. They would race down in their coach, says Christopher Hibbert in *George IV*, 'sometimes stopping to uproot or displace signposts, at other times screaming "Murder! Rape! Unhand me, villain!"' When they reached Brighton they raised hell, going about at night with a coffin to terrify the citizens. They called themselves the 'Merry Mourners' and knocked at doors, telling servants they had come to collect their dead masters. 'Cripplegate' charged his horse into the house of Maria Fitzherbert, up the stairs and into an attic. It was later brought down by two blacksmiths. 'Hellgate' dressed up in his cook's clothes and sang a serenade under Mrs Fitzherbert's bedroom window at three o'clock in the morning. One night they placed the open coffin, with a servant inside, outside a house, rang the bell and ran away. The terrified houseowner opened fire with a pistol, narrowly missing the servant's head.

An even more unsuitable companion for the Prince, as far as the King and others were concerned, was Louis Weltje. Weltje began his career as a cook in the court of the Duke of Brunswick. After he arrived in London he tried his luck as a street musician, then opened a gingerbread stall. When George met him he was a cook and co-owner with his brother of a cake shop in St James's Street. George had always shown an alarming tendency to treat servants as friends, and in 1828 it was reported that 'he talks to his pages with far more openness and familiarity than to anybody'. Weltje, whom the King described as a 'scoundrel', wormed his way into the Prince's confidence, performing secret services which were too sordid for the equerries. He acted as pander and bought off outraged husbands and mothers, and fobbed off creditors. Eventually he became the Prince's Comptroller at Carlton House, at the same time running an exclusive gambling club at 64 Pall Mall.

His arrogance was breathtaking. In 1778 there was an installation supper for Knights of the Bath at the Pantheon, with the Prince and the Duke of York attending. Weltje refused to do the catering, claiming that for the one thousand guineas offered he could supply only sandwiches. When he procured the *Morning Post* as the Prince's mouthpiece, *The Times* commented: 'go back to keeping your gingerbread stall ... an itinerant German music-grinder, raised from earning halfpennies ... to a great German Toad-eater who amassed a great fortune by dubious practices.'

By the early 1780s Weltje had made himself indispensable to the Prince, and in 1784 was sent to find suitable accommodation for his master in Brighton. He was heavily involved in the Prince's development of a villa that eventually became Brighton Pavilion, and for years they sought to maintain the fiction that the vastly expensive project was Weltje's.

Weltje indeed amassed a fortune, but he lost it all gambling. He died penniless in 1810, and the prince granted his widow a pension of £90 a year.

A lurid and scurrilous publication, *The Jockey Club, or a Sketch of the Manners of the Age*, depicts the Prince's friends as the 'very lees of society': 'If a man of the most depraved, the vilest cast were, from a vicious sympathy, to choose his company, it were impossible for his choice to fix anywhere else.' *The Jockey Club* attacked the Prince over Mrs Fitzherbert, his debts – 'a national disgrace' – his dissipation, extravagance and dishonesty in promising to reform. The attack on his friends was even more venomous. The rowdy Barrymores, George Hanger and Sir John Lade were described as 'creatures with whom a man of morality or even common decency' would not be seen. Lady Lade was a 'common prostitute'. The Prince's brother the Duke of York spent his time 'amongst the nymphs of Berkeley Row'. Weltje was a 'brute'. The Prince demanded that the authorities prosecute over this 'most infamous and shocking libellous production that ever disgraced the pen of man', but failed to persuade them to act.

It was his callous indifference to the fate of two of his closest friends, the dandy George Brummell, known as Beau, and the playwright Richard Brinsley Sheridan, that shows the Prince at his worst. When the Prince first appeared in society, reports Venetia Murray in *High Society in the Regency Period*, 'his magnificence was such that the arbiters of fashion were compelled reluctantly to admit that a powerful rival had come upon the scene ... His coat was pink silk, with white cuffs; his waistcoat white silk, embroidered with various coloured foil, and adorned with a profusion of French paste...' In fact this peacock style was on the way out, and Brummell did more than anyone to restrain the exuberance of dandy taste. He insisted on simplicity, cut and style, and it is no coincidence that during the Regency English tailoring won an international reputation for excellence. Brummell said: 'If John Bull turns round to look after you, you are not well dressed; but either too stiff, too tight, or too fashionable.'

He went to ridiculous lengths over minor details of dress. Another dandy, Captain Jesse, described the ritual. Brummell shaved with the smallest possible razor, then stood before a mirror naked to the waist, massaging his body with a stiff brush:

When he had done with it, as red as a lobster, he was ready for the camisole. But before dressing – or rather robing himself – Brummell took a dentist's mirror in one hand and a pair of tweezers in the other, and closely examined his forehead and well-shaved chin, and he did not lay the tweezers down till he had mercilessly plucked every stray hair that could be detected on the polished surface of his face.

Then came the main business – the tying of the neckcloth, or stock. These had been made of limp cloth, but Brummell favoured starched muslin, which was tricky to work with. As Murray notes in *High Society*, 'Brummell's dressing room was always thronged with fashionable spectators trying to see how he did it: they included the Prince Regent and the Dukes of Bedford, Beaufort and Rutland, all of whom were his personal friends.' The slightest mistake and the whole thing had to be undone and a new start made. This is how one of Brummell's friends described the operation:

> The collar, which was always fixed to the shirt, was so large that, before being folded down, it completely hid his head and face, and the white neckcloth was at least a foot in height. The first *coup d'archet* was made with the shirt collar, which he folded down to its proper size, and then, standing before the looking glass, with his chin poked up towards the ceiling, by the gentle and gradual declension of his lower jaw he creased the cravat to reasonable dimensions.

I have described this procedure in detail because it created a sensation. These young men were mostly wealthy, they had little to do all day except indulge themselves. After Brummell's fashion revolution the more dedicated dandies among them could no longer be seen in public with a crumpled stock without losing face.

The man who held sway over this constellation of rich young aristocrats was himself a commoner. Brummell's grandfather was a valet who later ran a lodging house, and one of his lodgers was the father of a future Prime Minister. Through him Brummell's father secured a job as a Treasury clerk, becoming private secretary to Lord North and acquiring a number of government sinecures. He married a beautiful and wealthy woman, mixed in the highest Whig circles, and sent his son George to Eton. When the boy left, at the age of 15, he met the Prince, who asked him what he wanted to do after studying at Oxford. Brummell said he wanted to go into the army, and the Prince promised him a commission in his own regiment, the highly fashionable Tenth Hussars.

Brummell duly joined the army, but when he was 20 sold his commission. According to legend the regiment had been posted to Manchester, social death for a dandy like Brummell, and so he resigned. He had inherited £30,000, which made him comfortably a millionaire in today's money. He was a good-looking young man with a dry wit and great charm, and soon established himself as the arbiter of taste. The Prince, who was dazzled, was said to have burst into tears when Brummell criticised the cut of his new coat. He could only have agreed with Brummell's dictum, 'A life of leisure is a most difficult art ... boredom is as depressing as an insistent creditor.'

Brummell's sayings, often repeated among the *ton*, betray his cool impudence and narcissism. Asked for the address of his hairdresser Brummell replied: 'I have three: the first is responsible for my temples, the second for the front and the third for the occiput.' When he was asked at a dinner whether he liked vegetables, he said he had never eaten any, adding, after a pause: 'No, that is not quite true – I once ate a pea.' He was said to have jilted a woman because she ate cabbage. It was of course an act, the means by which this parvenu held sway at the top of society; but it was a high-wire act, and inevitably he fell off. Making the Prince cry about the style of his coat was bad enough, but from time to time Brummell treated him with a cutting lack of respect which the touchy Prince eventually could not bear. At a ball in 1812 the Prince arrived with Lord Alvanley. He stood talking to Alvanley, pointedly ignoring Brummell. At last Brummell could stand it no longer, and called out, 'Alvanley, who's your fat friend?'

They would have fallen out sooner or later, given the Prince's tendency to tire of friends. He was probably jealous of Brummell's status as leader of the dandies, a role he felt was his, and his general popularity. But Brummell's arrogance and lacerating wit hastened the break, and those four fatal words sundered what had been a long and close friendship. They were the final insult. Brummell always denied that the real cause of the breach was his ordering the Prince on another occasion, 'Wales, ring the bell!' but there is no doubt that he annoyed him by constantly making unkind remarks about Mrs Fitzherbert. He had coined the nickname Benina for her, after the gigantic Carlton House porter known as Big Ben.

Brummell once said 'I made [the Prince] what he is and I can unmake him,' words he had long years to regret. He had made enemies, he was heavily in debt, and he failed to realise how much he owed to the Prince's support. In 1816 he fled to Calais to escape his creditors, and never returned. George helped him financially from time to time, but with such small amounts that it made little difference. On his way to Hanover in 1821 George passed through Calais but refused to visit Brummell, who had left his name in the visitors' book at the Prince's hotel as an indication that he hoped to be reconciled. Thackeray said of George's way of casting off his friends and lovers: 'On Monday he kissed and fondled poor Perdita, and on Tuesday he met her and did not know her. On Wednesday he was very affectionate with the wretched Brummell, and on Thursday forgot him.'

Brummell's end was sad. According to the *Dictionary of National Biography*, in 1837 'he began to show signs of imbecility; he held phantom receptions of the beauties and magnates of the old days. Soon all care of his person went, and from carelessness and disease his habits became so loathsome that an attendant could hardly be found for him.' This once most fastidious dandy died in a lunatic asylum in Caen in 1840.

Brummell was a minor Regency character, an insubstantial poseur who might have found it difficult to make his mark in any other milieu. Richard Brinsley Sheridan, for years George's closest political adviser, was a major figure in several fields: playwright, theatre impresario and politician. He was also a hard-drinking womaniser, a political schemer and unreliable about money.

Sheridan was born in Dublin in 1751, of a native Irish family which had converted to Protestantism and become bulwarks of the English Ascendancy. His grandfather Thomas Sheridan (1687–1738) was a close friend of Swift, and his father, also Thomas (1719–88), was a writer, a noted teacher of elocution, actor and author of a life of Swift. The family moved to Bath, Richard was educated at Harrow, and after leaving school tried writing for the theatre. In 1773 he married the beautiful opera singer Elizabeth Linley, after fighting two duels with the Welsh beau who was pursuing her, and they settled in London, living way beyond their means. In his early twenties, as Priestley notes in *The Prince of Pleasure*, he wrote 'the two best comedies of the age', *The Rivals* and *The School for Scandal*. With the exception of *The Critic* (1779), 'teeming with sparkling wit' according to the *Dictionary of National Biography*, he wrote nothing else of note.

Sheridan was a strange mixture of charlatanry and integrity, and a story told by the Regency diarist Captain Rees Howell Gronow catches this very well:

> On a Friday evening, after the second price [receipts] had been received, the treasurer of Drury Lane Theatre [of which Sheridan was the manager, later the proprietor] came to Sheridan with a woeful face, and told him there was not money enough to pay even the subordinates on the following day; and that unless a certain sum could be found he was persuaded that the house could not open on Monday. Sheridan suggested several plans for raising the wind, but all were declared by Mr Dunn to be useless. Sheridan gazed round at the thinly peopled boxes, and at length called to one of the porters in waiting, 'Do you see that stout good tempered looking man seated next a comely lady in the third box from the stage, in a front row? Immediately the play is over, go to him ... and in a loud voice enough to be heard by every one, say, "Sir, Mr Sheridan requests the honour of a private interview with him in his own room." Let every one on the way treat him with the greatest civility; and, Mr Dunn,

will you have the kindness to see that a bottle of the best port and a couple of wine glasses are placed on the table in my room.'

The order was duly obeyed. The gentleman was ushered into the presence of Sheridan with honours almost approaching those shown to royalty, and was received by him with the most cordial marks of friendship and regard. 'I am always happy to see anyone from Stafford. [Sheridan was MP for Stafford for a time] I was glad you called at my house with an order for this theatre, where I hope you will come when you please; you will find your name on the free list. I think you told me you always came twice a year to London.' 'Yes' was the reply; 'January and July, to receive my dividends.' 'You have come for that purpose now,' continued Sheridan. 'Oh, yes, and I went to the Bank of England and got my six hundred pounds.' 'Ah,' said the manager, 'you are in Consols [government stock earning an annual rate] whilst I, alas, am Reduced, and can get nothing till April, when, you know, the interest is paid; and till then I shall be in great distress.' 'Oh,' said his constituent, 'let that not make you uneasy; if you give me the power of attorney to receive the money for you when it is due, I can let you have three hundred pounds, which I shall not want till then.' 'Only a real friend,' said Sheridan, shaking his dupe by the hand with warmth, 'could have made such a proposition. I accept it thankfully.'

The following April the dupe sent to ask for the power of attorney, at which Sheridan replied: 'I never spoke of Consols in Reduced, I only spoke of my consols being reduced; unhappy is the man who does not comprehend the weight of prepositions.' The angry victim rushed to London and confronted Sheridan in his office at Drury Lane. Gronow goes on:

Sheridan, apparently not at all disconcerted, with outstretched hand and benignant smile, welcomed his victim, whose rage was at first uncontrollable; but his attack was met by the manager with an acknowledgement that, in a moment of urgent necessity he had been compelled to throw himself on the generosity of a man he had heard from everyone was a model of worth, and whose

Game of hearts: Old Q playing a game called Push Pin with the well-upholstered bawd Mother Windsor and another woman. For years Windsor supplied the Duke with young girls. On one occasion he hired three.

Betting coup: the stripped-down carriage the Duke of Queensberry had specially constructed to race at an unprecedented nineteen miles an hour. Betting was heavy, and his triumph established Queensberry as the most astute gambler of the age.

High stakes: Brooks's Club in St James's Street, where great fortunes changed hands on the turn of a card. The gambling clubs of St James's were happy hunting territory for the Duke of Queensberry.

Left: The intellectual rake: the third Marquess of Hertford, who wallowed in sin and wealth. His open marriage to the Duke of Queensberry's daughter Mie-Mie was the scandal of the age. Yet Benjamin Disraeli called him 'a very clever man indeed'.

GEORGE IV. AS PRINCE OF WALES
(STIPPLE BY BARTOLOZZI AFTER VIOLET).

Prince of hearts: George IV practised his seductive arts on ladies-in-waiting before falling
for Perdita Robinson. Eventually, as his weight and drunkenness made sex absurd, he
settled for middle-aged matrons whose girth almost matched his own.

Below: House of dreams: Carlton House by the Mall, on which George IV lavished a fortune of the nation's money. When he became king he decided it was too small and had
it pulled down. It was just one of the houses he beautified and abandoned.

King of hearts: Bertie, showing the languorous looks that some women found attractive. In fact he was pot-bellied and short and reeked of cigar smoke. As one of his biographers wrote, snobbery is a powerful aphrodisiac.

Flight of fancy: the impetuous Lady Brooke. The Prince of Wales called her his 'darling Daisy wife'. After years of mindless extravagance and affairs she became a champion of socialist ideas, but failed to convert the prince.

Class act: Lillie Langtry, the first of Bertie's official mistresses. She was the perfect Pre-Raphaelite beauty, with her columnar neck and square jaw. When she and Bertie parted she went on the stage in America and created another sensation.

acquaintance would be acceptable in the highest quarters. 'But excuse me, my dear sir,' he added; 'I am now commanded to go to the Prince of Wales, to whom I shall narrate your noble conduct. My carriage is waiting, and I can take you to Carlton House.' The eye of the provincial sparked with delight. Was it possible that he meant to take him to the Prince of Wales? It sounded something like it. He shook Sheridan by the hand, saying, 'I forgive you, my dear friend; never mention the debt again.' 'I will take care never to do so,' said the manager. The carriage came round to the door, the two friends entered it, and when they arrived at Carlton House Sheridan got out and closing the door told the coachman to drive the gentleman to his hotel. The Stafford man, with a last hope, naïvely said: 'I thought I also was going into Carlton House.' 'Another mistake of yours,' replied Sheridan. The worthy constituent returned that night to Stafford, and in future his vote was given against Sheridan.

This artful little story, if true, obviously shows Sheridan in a very bad light, and he was undoubtedly careless, to say the least, with other people's money. But another story, by the diarist Joseph Farington, redresses the balance. In August 1815 Sheridan was imprisoned for debt in the Fetter Lane sponging house. He received between £400 and £500 to obtain his release and then one of his old tenants whose own goods had been seized because of debts called on him. Farington says: 'Sheridan asked him what sum would relieve him. The man replied that £300 would restore him to his former state. Sheridan gave him the money.'

In 1778 Sheridan became the proprietor of the Drury Lane Theatre; in 1780 he was elected for Stafford, and he afterwards held some minor government posts. However, his political role as confidential adviser to the Prince was much greater. As a Whig, he was a follower and then a rival of Fox, and the three of them gambled and drank deep together. Like Fox he was a dazzling orator, and before heavy drinking made him a figure of derision he often held the Commons spellbound.

Sheridan met the Prince when the latter was just 21, at Brooks's

Club or at Devonshire House, home of Georgiana, Duchess of Devonshire. The latter had become the powerhouse of Whig politics, and Fox was a frequent guest. The Prince found the relaxed attitudes to sex, drinking and gambling there congenial, and since Fox and his friends were detested by the King he had an added reason to visit. He and Sheridan were soon close and genuine friends, sharing as Fintan O'Toole notes in *A Traitor's Kiss, The Life of Richard Brinsley Sheridan* an 'interest in drinking, music, literature and practical jokes'. But from Sheridan's point of view it was a hopelessly unequal friendship. The Prince used him and then, when he abandoned his Foxite political views, discarded him.

Sheridan led the campaign for a Regency Bill when the King seemed incurably ill in 1788. According to Parissien in *George IV*, his 'ready wit and adept political management proved invaluable to the Prince', and it was Fox whose clumsy demand in the Commons that the Prince be given unfettered powers strengthened the Pitt government's case for delaying. In the event the King recovered before the Bill could become law, but Sheridan continued to be indispensable to the Prince of Wales. As Parissien observes, 'When George heard a rumour that, in view of his recent conduct . . . his parents planned to shift the succession to the Duke of York, he asked Sheridan to negotiate with his brother.'

In the summer of 1792 they quarrelled, and George refused to speak to Sheridan for weeks. In September however he wrote his friend a touching letter of reconciliation:

> It is so long since I have either heard of you, or from you, yet I wish to know whether you are among the living. But to be serious, I wish extremely to see you . . . when there are events in this life which tease a man's feelings for a time, I think the best way is to leave them to themselves, and not to pester or plague them with officious attentions, and then perhaps when they have had a sufficient phase of time to vent their feelings, they will with more pleasure meet the cordiality of their sincere friends; such my dear Sheridan have been my ideas respecting you, and thus have I regulated my conduct towards you.

Sheridan's moment seemed to have come in 1801. Pitt resigned because of the King's obdurate opposition to his plan to give Irish Catholics full citizenship, including the right to stand for Parliament. Bizarrely, Sheridan was now in favour at court, having conducted the Queen and her daughters to safety when there was an attempt on the King's life at the theatre in May 1800. The King praised Sheridan, 'who he verily thought had a respect and regard for him', and, as Parissien notes in *George IV*, 'Sheridan's name was once more talked of in connection with government office – the Chancellorship.' The King became seriously ill again in 1804, and although Sheridan did not get high office he was still close to the Prince, acting as his intermediary with the government. Perhaps more important, in view of his pressing debts, the Prince made him Receiver of the Revenue of the Duchy of Cornwall, a sinecure bringing him at least £1,200 a year. Thanking him, Sheridan pledged that 'to the end of my Life I will strenuously employ every Faculty of my Mind in your service.'

By now Sheridan was drinking heavily.* He lost his compelling good looks and his face became red and bloated. He was usually too drunk to be an effective orator, although he occasionally reached his old heights. He had quarrelled with Fox and had stopped writing plays. His Drury Lane Theatre burned down in 1791 and was rebuilt at great expense (it was destroyed by fire again in 1809).

When George became Prince Regent in 1811 Sheridan very reasonably hoped for high office. But Fox had died in 1806 and after a show of uncontrollable grief George had quietly begun to change his politics. His old Foxite beliefs and circle became an embarrassment, and Sheridan was mortified to be directed by his royal patron to write to Spencer Percival, the Prime Minister, to

---

* It was an age of hard drinking, particularly by members of the political elite. Pitt was a heavy drinker, sometimes finishing more than three bottles of port a day. He once arrived at the House of Commons completely drunk and was sick behind the Speaker's chair. O'Toole in *A Traitor's Kiss* quotes Sir Gilbert Eliott telling his wife in 1788 that 'Fox drinks what I would call a great deal … Sheridan excessively and Grey [the Whig politician] more than any of them.'

say his Tory administration would stay in power for the time being. When Percival was assassinated, the Prince offered Sheridan a minor post in the new government; as Parissien observes, it was 'an insulting offer which [he] proudly refused'. Sheridan was a staunch supporter of Catholic emancipation, which the Regent opposed, and deciding to end his parliamentary dependence on the Court he fought Stafford in 1812, coming last in the poll. Without a seat he lost his parliamentary immunity to arrest, and in May 1814 he was held in the sponging house over a debt of £600. He was eventually released, living with his wife 'in a state of filth and stench that was quite intolerable'. It was said he called down shame on the Regent for abandoning him.

The Prince had his last glimpse of his old friend in August 1815. George was passing through Leatherhead in his coach when he saw Sheridan about thirty yards ahead, and turned to his companion, saying 'There is Sheridan.' At that point Sheridan turned aside into a lane, and the Prince made no attempt to follow or attract his attention. So parted for ever the Prince, mighty ruler of his country, and his broken friend, 'the man on whom he had depended so much for nearly forty years' as O'Toole says in *A Traitor's Kiss*. Sheridan died in June 1816.

Of all George's betrayals this was the most cruel. Just as he ignored Brummell's attempt to meet him at Calais, he passed his old friend and supporter in his last days without a hint of acknowledgement. But as we shall see, his conduct towards his own daughter was scarcely better.

# The War between the Waleses

IN JANUARY 1796 PRINCESS CAROLINE give birth to a daughter who was called Charlotte after her grandmother. The Prince wrote to his mother: 'The Princess, after a terrible hard labour, for above twelve hours, is this instant brought to bed of an immense girl, and I assure you notwithstanding we might have wished for a boy, I receive her with all the affection possible.'

The King wrote telling the Prince that he had wanted the child to be a girl. 'You are both young and I trust will have many children and this newcomer will equally call for the protection of its parents and consequently be a bond of additional union.' In view of the Prince's cold indifference towards his only daughter it is probably as well that he never had another child. He showed her little affection during her life, and after her premature death seemed to want to obliterate her memory.

The omens were bad from the start. When told of the birth he murmured 'We might have wished for a boy,' the phrase he used in the letter to his mother. Three days later he made a will leaving almost nothing to his wife or newborn daughter, but all to Mrs Fitzherbert. He insisted that Caroline 'should in no way either be concerned in the education or care of the child, or have possession of her person'. He subjected little Charlotte to a regime of petty regulations, yet seldom found time to see her. When Caroline complained to the King that her husband wouldn't let her see her daughter, George III announced that he was taking over the child's upbringing. This made the Prince 'ill with rage'. When the King gave Caroline access to her daughter the Prince hinted that the old man was insane.

Charlotte became a lively and engaging child, but inevitably in the war between the Waleses her education and her personality suffered. One of her tutors told her that her spelling mistakes would have made 'a common servant' blush. She acquired some very bad habits, swearing so strongly that one Dutch diplomat likened her to 'a mutinous boy in skirts'. Visitors were astonished that the future Queen of England had such bad manners. Like her father, she was a liar and had a monstrous temper. She stammered badly, particularly when either of her parents was present. As she grew up her father continued to ignore her. When he gave a famous fete in 1811 he did not invite her. He tried to keep her in a state of arrested emotional development, telling her official companion Cornelia Knight that Charlotte 'must lay aside the idle nonsense of thinking that she had a will of her own'. While he lived, he added, 'she must be subject to me as she is at present, if she were thirty, or forty, or five and forty'.

Inevitably Charlotte went off the rails. When she was 16 in 1812 she was believed to have had an affair with Lieutenant Charles Hesse. Matters were made worse by the suggestions that he was the illegitimate son of the Duke of York, and that the Princess of Wales had encouraged the affair to spite her husband. Charlotte later told her father that Caroline locked her in a bedroom with Hesse, saying 'I leave you to amuse yourselves.' There were rumours of other affairs, and her father thought she was 'on the brink of utter destruction and ruin in point of character'. But mostly he ignored her. She complained that he seldom visited, and she received her first letter from him on her nineteenth birthday in 1815. Its professions of affection she dismissed as 'without any meaning'.

Like so many of the Hanoverian offspring, her political affections were diametrically opposed to her father's. As he distanced himself from the Whigs she embraced them. She burst into tears when she heard her father denounce the Whigs on one of the rare occasions she was invited to a Carlton House dinner. She needled him by giving friends small busts of Fox.

The bad feelings between father and daughter grew to resemble those between him and his wife. The problem was partly that she was more popular with the public than he. In summer 1813 some of the distinguished foreigners who poured into London after the fall of Paris called on her, and in a fit of jealousy he ordered her to see less of Tsar Alexander's sister, the Grand Duchess Catherine of Oldenburg. He refused to let her visit the seaside when she was ill, chided her for spending too much on jewellery and refused to let her see her mother.

His own mother, Queen Charlotte, was also irked by her granddaughter's somewhat unwarranted popularity. She coldly refused when one of the young Princess's more sympathetic uncles, the Duke of York, suggested that she should be allowed to pass some time in London chaperoned by her aunts, because she was effectively without a mother and 'required the full support and protection of the female part of her family'.

Bad though the Prince's behaviour towards his daughter had been up to this point, when it came to the question of her marriage it became fiendish. He wanted her to marry Prince William of Orange, whom she despised, an unprepossessing short and skinny and indecisive youth known as 'Silly Billy'. George seems to have wanted to get her off his hands, and at first refused to allow a clause in the marriage contract guaranteeing her the right to return to Britain any time she wished. He gloated in telling her that he might divorce her mother and marry again, perhaps producing a male child who would replace her as heir. Charlotte refused to leave England, and after falling in love with a Russian prince told her Dutch suitor that the engagement was over. In retaliation her father spitefully sacked all her companions and all her servants but one. Among them was her 'adored' lady companion Cornelia Knight. They were replaced by what Parissien calls 'ancient pillars of respectability'.

This was too much to bear. Charlotte fled to her mother's house in Cockspur Street, only to be coldly spurned. She was reminded that her father had absolute power over her until she was 21, and her mother asked her to leave the house. Crushed, feeling she had scarcely a friend in the world, she went back home.

She was rescued by a German princeling, Leopold of Saxe-Coburg-Saalfeld. He was good looking and a distinct improvement on Silly Billy. They met when he came to London in 1814 as an officer in the Russian army. In February 1816 her father gave his reluctant consent, and after the marriage the young couple settled down at Claremont in Surrey, in a house built for Clive of India. They were unusually happy, and she invited all her friends to what she called 'Liberty Hall'. The painter Sir Thomas Lawrence recalled:

> His address to the Princess was 'my dear Charlotte' and she always called him 'My Love' – Their manner to each other was affectionate, and it was manifest that by the equality of [Leopold's] temper and his good sense he had great influence over her, which he used with discretion, never directly showing it, but always at a time to have an effect in a gentle manner.

Charlotte's relations with her father improved, and she spent the Christmas of 1816 at Brighton Pavilion. By the following spring she was pregnant. Her labour, the following November, lasted 46 hours before a still-born male baby was born. Later that day the Princess died after falling into 'a strange lassitude'. Her blameless *accoucheur*, Sir Richard Croft, shot himself the following February.

The outpouring of grief that followed Charlotte's demise has inevitably been compared to the death of another Princess of Wales. She had lived her life in seclusion, and few people had any knowledge of her whatsoever. Nevertheless, as Stephen Berendt observes in *Royal Mourning and Regency Culture*, her death focused people's thoughts on their times, on her father, and among women, on 'that most common of Regency women's experiences, death in childbirth'.

Charlotte's husband was prostrate but her father reacted with his usual shocking self-centredness. Lawrence reported him as saying 'nobody could so feel the loss which himself and the public had sustained so deeply as himself'. Yet within a month of his daughter's death he was entertaining lavishly at Brighton Pavilion, where the celebrated chef Antoine Carème was now installed. When the public raised an enormous sum for a monument to his daughter the Prince pocketed the lot. The Duchess of York raised another £12,000 (more than £500,000) for a monument to be sited in Hyde Park. There was an outcry when the Prince announced it would be erected, not in London, but in St George's Chapel at Windsor Castle, effectively inaccessible to the public. But he got his way.

While the doomed Princess lived, the war between the Waleses raged on. Caroline won one important victory. In June 1796, after months of pressure by the Princess, Lady Jersey was dismissed from her position at court. This simply gave her more time to spend with the Prince, who moved her into Jack Payne's former house adjoining Carlton House. But the Prince was already tiring of her overblown charms, and his thoughts were turning again to Mrs Fitzherbert.*

By the summer of 1800 they were again 'inseparable', although she refused to have sex with him. In any case, the Prince's ardour was not what it had been. He was almost 40, corpulent and lazy. He ate and drank too much, wept easily, was prickly and petulant. However, for the moment they were happy. Mrs Fitzherbert told a friend: 'He is much improved ... all that was boyish and troublesome before is now become respectful and considerate ... We live like brother and sister.'

Mrs Fitzherbert must have had a capacity for self-delusion

---

* Lady Jersey refused to go quietly. When the Prince sent Edward Jerningham to tell her the affair was over, and that the Prince would not see her again, she said: 'Damn you! I wish you well of your new trade.' George was soon demonising her. He warned his daughter's servants against 'all the wickedness, perseverance, and tricks of that infernal Jezebel Lady Jersey and all her Jacobinal set of connections'.

almost equal to the Prince's. After their reconciliation he had a series of minor affairs which she ignored, meanwhile wisely getting him to raise her annual pension from £3,000 to £6,000. A more formidable rival came on the scene in the ample and matronly form of Lady Hertford, very wealthy, handsome and haughty, an arch Tory and a grandmother. The Whig grandee Lord Holland thought her 'stately, formal and insipid'. The social commentator Mrs Calvert, while admitting her residual beauty, called her 'the most forbidding, haughty, unpleasant-looking woman' she had ever met. Lady Hertford's husband, the easy-going Marquess, was on excellent terms with the Prince, sharing his collector's passion for fine furniture and works of art. His son, Lord Yarmouth, was, as we have seen, one of the Prince's cronies.

If George was hoping for the sexual passion Mrs Fitzherbert presumably still denied him, he was disappointed. Behind the bony corsets of the frigidly virtuous Lady Hertford beat a heart of ice. George may have been impotent by now, and simply wanted mothering. But this did not stop him playing the lovesick suitor, a role by now second nature to him. He wrote letters to her endlessly, sometimes staying up all night. He lost his appetite and grew thin, making himself ill. Not for the first time, some of those around him wondered if he was mad.

This loss of weight was very temporary, and when he recovered George was a monstrous figure. The essayist Charles Lamb painted a devastating word picture of the amorous old gent:

> Not a fatter fish than he
> Flounders round the polar sea.
> See his blubbers – at his gills
> What a world of drink he swills ...
> Every fish of generous kind
> Scuds aside or shrinks behind;
> But about his presence keep
> All the monsters of the deep ...
> Name or title what has he?
> Is he Regent of the sea?

By his bulk and by his size
By his oily qualities
This (or else my eyesight fails)
This should be the Prince of Whales

This makes even more absurdly amusing a story told by Lady Bessborough about his distracted love for Lady Hertford. In a letter she related to her lover, Lord Granville Leveson Gower, how the Prince had thrown himself on her in a frenzy of misdirected passion:

Such a scene I never went through ... [he] threw himself on his knees, and clasping me round, kissed my neck before I was aware of what he was doing. I screamed with vexation and fright; he continued sometimes struggling with me, sometimes sobbing and crying ... Then mixing abuse of you, vows of eternal love, entreaties and promises of what he would do – he would break with Mrs F. and Lady H., I should make my own terms!! I should be his sole confidante, sole adviser – private or public – I should guide his politics, Mr Canning should be Prime Minister (whether in this reign or the next did not appear); ... then over and over and over again the same round of complaint, despair, entreaties and promises, and always Mr Canning ... and whenever he mentioned him it was in the tenderest accent and attempting some liberty, that really, G., had not my heart been breaking I must have laughed out at the comicality of having [Canning] so coupled and made use of – and then that immense, grotesque figure flouncing about half on the couch, half on the ground.

Mrs Fitzherbert's final quittance from the Prince was humiliating. At a dinner at Carlton House in 1811 she was placed not as usual on the Prince's right but far down the table. When she questioned this she was told: 'You know, Madam, you have no place.' She left immediately. Afterwards she behaved with dignity and was widely liked and admired, no doubt consoled by her guaranteed pension. When George died she showed genuine grief.

Lady Hertford's time as the Prince's favourite was also coming to an end. Her size had been a gift to the brilliant caricaturists of the day, but the woman who next caught George's eye was simply fat. Elizabeth, Lady Conyngham, a fading beauty, was 50 years old in 1820, eight years younger than George. Some years before she had been part of that elaborate game of hearts at the centre of the aristocracy, her lovers including Lord Ponsonby – a former lover of Lady Jersey – and, it was rumoured, the future Tsar Nicholas I.[*] When she visited Paris during the brief Peace of Amiens the French deemed Lady Conyngham the most beautiful woman in the city, but by the time George fell for her charms her amplitude had made her an unlikely object of desire. A wag wrote of the two of them behaving like young lovers:

> 'Tis pleasant at seasons to see how they sit,
> First cracking their nuts and then cracking their wit:
> Then quaffing their claret – then mingling their lips,
> Or tickling the fat about each other's hips.

According to Parissien in *George IV*, by the time of George's coronation in 1821 his affair with Lady Conyngham was being conducted in public: 'Mrs Arbuthnot [the Duke of Wellington's confidante] was disgusted by the kisses they sent one another in the middle of the coronation ceremony.' In February 1821 Countess Granville noted: 'He is jealous of her as a boy of fifteen would be, and pouts and sulks if she does not follow him from room to room.' Lady Conyngham was on the make, and 'through his wife's personal friendship with the Prince Regent', her husband was created viscount, earl and marquess.

In 1820 George III died, blind and hopelessly insane. The Prince Regent's coronation, planned for August of that year, was postponed until 1821, first because he was ill, and then because of his fruitless attempt to divorce Caroline, who was now Queen.

---

[*] The Tsar, who was very much a ladies' man, muttered aside when introduced to Lady Hertford: 'She is mighty old.'

Caroline heard of George III's death while in Italy. Worn out by the constant feuding with the Prince, she had been granted leave to travel on the Continent. She left in August 1814 and soon the courts of Europe were agog with gossip about her outrageous sexual misbehaviour. After she moved on to Italy her affair with the Milanese Bartolomeo Pergami was conducted in the glare of public scrutiny. The Regent ordered British diplomats to gather evidence for a divorce.

Pergami, described by one of George's spies, Count Ompteda, as 'a sort of Apollo, of a superb and commanding appearance, more than six feet tall', was appointed Chamberlain to Caroline. He accompanied her to Naples where, according to Ompteda, she 'raped' the King, Joachim Murat, Napoleon's former marshal. This was just the sort of thing the Regent wanted to hear. He sent a commission to gather evidence against her and in 1819 they presented their findings. They gave him compelling evidence, including accounts of Pergami joining Caroline in her (rare) baths. George began divorce proceedings, which however were so unpopular they had to be abandoned.

Caroline hurried back from Italy, making it clear that she expected to be crowned at the same time as her husband. When the coronation ceremony finally took place at Westminster Abbey on 19 July she tried to get in but was repeatedly turned away by burly guards, some of them prize-fighters hired to keep her out.[*] The radical writer William Cobbett wrote indignantly: 'When she got to the door and made an attempt to enter, she was actually thrusted back by the hands of a common prize-fighter.' The Queen then tried to get into Westminster Hall and had the doors slammed in her face. The crowds gathered outside were surprisingly hostile, given the degree of support she had recently been shown. Farington recorded that 'Her reception was generally unfavourable. "Shame, shame" and "Off, off" was the general cry

---

[*] For the new King, George IV, the occasion was an unsurpassed opportunity to dress up. His costume cost £24,704 8s 10d. The Treasury later estimated that the coronation cost a sum equal to about £12 million in today's money. Of this more than half was paid out of the war reparations imposed on the French in 1815.

though a few cried "Queen".' Many people were sympathetic, but felt she was spoiling a great national occasion.

Within weeks she was dead. She became ill at Drury Lane Theatre on 30 July and died on 7 August. She had told the statesman Henry Brougham, her long-time supporter: 'I am much better dead for I be tired of this life.' She also remarked: 'They have killed me at last!'

George, who was about to set out for Ireland, ordered some perfunctory mourning and then spoiled the effect by landing dead drunk at Howth. He was heard singing songs and seen drinking glasses of whisky. The previous May, when Napoleon died, he had been informed that 'his greatest enemy' was dead, and promptly replied, 'Is she, by God!'

Early in his reign George's tendency to withdraw from the public became marked. He was now grossly overweight. Farington had noted that in December 1797 George weighed 17 stone 8 pounds, and his weight continued to increase inexorably. But this was just one reason for not wishing to be seen in public. Another was fear for his own security. He immured himself at Windsor, seldom visiting London. In August 1827 Prince Pückler-Muskau visited Windsor and recorded that the King had 'had several roads cut, for his own special and peculiar use, through the most interesting parts' of the park. He decided he didn't like Carlton House and the Pavilion being so close to roads. Carlton House, on which he had lavished so much money, was demolished and in March 1827 he visited the Pavilion for the last time. Parissien notes the Duke of Wellington's gleeful repetition of a rumour that George abandoned the Pavilion because of a 'quasi-Biblical admonition' etched on one of its windows by a disapproving local.

He had already begun to create another architectural fantasy nearer home. In December 1823 the Treasury approved his request to rebuild the Royal Lodge in the middle of Windsor Great Park. George had already spent a fortune on it: as long ago as 1812 the Treasury had agreed to the architect John Nash's plan to provide a small 'cottage ornée' at a cost of £2,750, but by 1816 it had cost more than £30,000, with no end in sight. The furniture alone had cost an extra £17,000. As Parissien observes, 'By the time of George IV's death it had become one of the largest "cottage" ever seen, virtually a Gothic counterpart to the Brighton Pavilion.' Yet the Treasury never seemed to learn. In 1825 they approved another £8,000 for further alterations – the actual cost was more than twice that. The lodge was largely demolished after George's death.

In this bloated fantasy of the simple life George created a court even duller than his father's. It consisted of Lady Conyngham and a few other ladies. Charles Greville reported that Lady Conyngham 'looks bored to death, and she never speaks, never appears to have one word to say to the King, who however talks himself without ceasing'.

George enjoyed fishing, and in 1825 the Treasury authorised the construction of a Chinese fishing temple at Virginia Water in Surrey. The firm of Crace and Company, who had helped decorate the Brighton Pavilion, put in an estimate of £500 for work on the temple. Within a week this had risen to about £1,600. There were other follies all over the park, and shortly before George's death an MP complained that the Treasury was paying £20,000 annually to furnish the park 'with the silly gewgaws resulting from the bad taste of a High Personage'.

All this time Windsor Castle was being remodelled at a cost, it has been estimated, of more than £60 million today. Then George changed his mind. In September 1829 the Whig politician and diarist Creevey reported that the King had now decided 'never to live in the Castle, which considering the hundreds of thousands of pounds which have been expended upon it inside and out is amiss. He says it is too public ... ' It is clear that his death in 1830 saved the nation a great deal of money.

It is tempting to compare George IV to Charles II. They both loved women, were intelligent and amusing. But where Charles was warm-hearted, made lifelong friends and was surprisingly tolerant of criticism, George was fickle and touchy and needed the kind of sickening sycophancy provided in great dollops by Sir

Walter Scott.[*] Charles was as generous as limited funds allowed; George was profligate but stingy. Charles had experienced battle; George, not for want of trying, never heard a shot fired in anger. His father refused to allow him an active army command during the Napoleonic wars, so he constructed a fantasy in which he led a charge at Waterloo. He would call on Wellington to corroborate these claims, and the great soldier would murmur, 'So you have often told me, Sir.' When the King described leading a charge down a slope, Wellington said: 'Very steep, Sir.' Charles's dying thoughts were for others – 'Let not poor Nelly starve.' George's were for himself.

After Victoria came to the throne there was an inevitable re-action against the House of Hanover. The great nationalist frescoes by Daniel Maclise which decorate the walls of the new Palace of Westminster contain no references to the four Georges or William IV, last of the Hanoverians. Victoria distanced herself from George IV's legacy, disposing of the Brighton Pavilion and building her own royal residences, where her life with Albert and their growing family established a model of cosy and virtuous domesticity the middle classes were keen to embrace and emulate. But the Hanoverian strain had not quite died out. Her son Albert Edward, the next Prince of Wales, displayed what she regarded as some of the worst characteristics of her wicked uncle George.

---

[*] When George died Scott wrote that his 'gentle and generous disposition, and singular manners and captivating conversation, rendered him as much the darling of private society as his heartfelt interest in the general welfare of the country and the constant and steady course of wise measures by which he raised his reign to such a state of triumphal prosperity, made him justly delighted in by all his subjects'!

# Part 6

# Bertie and the

# Age of Hypocrisy

# Prelude

RESPECTABLE SOCIETY IN THE VICTORIAN PERIOD took its cue from the court, where for two decades the busy little Queen and her dutiful, dull husband Prince Albert set almost impossible standards of decency and sobriety. Meanwhile, however, some almost unbelievably wealthy and powerful aristocrats behaved as they pleased. The result was a level of hypocrisy in sexual matters difficult to imagine today. Middle-class fathers imposed a kind of censorship in the home in which it became impossible to mention sex. Young women, whatever their feelings, had to pretend to innocence. There was a lot of blushing and resort to smelling salts, although I have never found documentary evidence of the covering up of piano legs.

It was Edward, Prince of Wales, known as Bertie, who led the assault on Victorian values. His own attitudes to sex with actresses, high-class whores and the wives of friends spread through the upper reaches of society, as had those of Charles II. As Anita Leslie says in her book *Edwardians in Love*: 'Albert Edward, Prince of Wales, would personally dictate the code of social behaviour for the next fifty years, and it would be unique in history.'

It was important that this code did not lead to a general break-down of morals. Sex with young unmarried women of the upper classes was taboo. Their reputations were beyond price, and just the suspicion that they had dallied too long in the conservatory might blight their chances of finding a suitable husband. The reason was that men were *beasts*, and given the chance would take advantage of any woman. Anita Leslie, herself from an upper-class Irish background, wrote that all Victorian mamas took care to prevent loss of their daughters' reputation as well as loss of the real thing. Men were odd creatures, and if rumour spread that a girl had disappeared for an hour or so it meant that something could have happened. Potential suitors then evaporated . . .

Wives, however, were fair game in certain circumstances. They first had to provide their husband with a nursery well stocked with potential heirs. After that husband and wife were free to pursue their separate sexual interests, so long as they didn't create a scandal. In the case of the wife this simply meant not getting caught, and particularly not getting into the newspapers.

When the society beauty Lady Colin Campbell transgressed this unwritten code, she found herself at the centre of one of Britain's most sensational divorce cases. After her husband, the son of the Duke of Argyll, gave her syphilis, Lady Colin started a series of affairs. She was seen on a train with Lord Blandford, already notorious for his part in another Victorian scandal, the Aylesford Affair, and a newspaper claimed that they had run away together. Although this was untrue, they were indeed having an affair, and Lady Colin then abandoned herself to what one reporter called 'the unbridled lust of Messalina and the indelicate readiness of the common harlot'. Blandford visited her frequently at her house in Cadogan Place; the Campbells' butler testified that he had found Blandford and Lady Colin, whose dress was disordered and her face flushed, together on a sofa. During the 18-day divorce hearing in 1886 Blandford said the reason for their friendship was a common interest in literature.

Another frequent caller at the house was Captain Shaw, chief of the Metropolitan Fire Brigade. A second butler told the court that through a keyhole he had seen Lady Colin lying on the floor with Captain Shaw. He was asked: 'Did you see her bust?' and replied: 'I certainly saw more than that.' A third lover was Tom Bird, a surgeon who was attending her husband, but whom Lord Colin eventually banned from the house. The couple accused each other of adultery, but the jury decided there was no proof.

After Lord Colin died of syphilis in 1895, his wife, shunned by society, tried to make a living as journalist and writer. She was confined to a wheelchair by the effects of syphilis, and died of the disease at the age of 53. Leslie calls Lady Colin a 'glamorous nymphomaniac', and says her naked portrait by Whistler was torn to pieces by Blandford's outraged wife. But the manifest unfairness of all this didn't matter. By offending against the code, Lady Colin had made herself a pariah.

When, after 'months of glances, sighs, blushes, protestations and trembling assignations', upper-class men and women decided to have an affair there came the difficult business of arranging a consummation. The rules under which a man might visit a woman who was not his wife were strict. Though it was quite proper for a woman to invite a man to tea, he might not leave his tall hat, gloves and stick in the hall, but had to lay them on the drawing-room floor as if he had called as an afterthought and was ready to go at any moment. Servants could usually be relied on not to enter the drawing room unless called, but the case of Lady Colin reminded wives that they might be spied on by their servants.

The Edwardians solved this social dilemma with carefully organised invitations to their country houses. If the hostess approved of the liaison, and was expert in the distribution of rooms, the couple would be allocated bedrooms near enough in those 'interminable, icy, creaking corridors' to make midnight trysts risk free. At the same time the husband would be invited to another country house, where he might be sealing another such promise or just killing the wildlife. There is no better description of this business than Virginia Sackville-West's in her novel *The Edwardians*:

> The name of each guest would be written on a card slipped into a tiny brass frame on the bedroom door. This question of the disposition of bedrooms always gave the duchess and her fellow-hostesses cause for anxious thought. It was so necessary to be tactful, and at the same time discreet. The professional Lothario

would be furious if he found himself in a room surrounded by ladies who were all accompanied by their husbands. Tommy Brand, on one such occasion, had been known to leave the house on the Sunday morning ... Then there were the recognised lovers to be considered: the duchess herself would have been greatly annoyed had she gone to the same party as Harry Tremaine, only to find that he had been put at the other end of the house ... It was part of a good hostess's duty to see to such things: they must be made easy, and not too obvious.

Given a sympathetic hostess this should have been easy to manage, but there are many stories of men blundering into the wrong bedroom and the wrong bed. Anita Leslie in *Edwardians in Love* tells of the rake Sir Charles Beresford tiptoeing into a dark room which he thought was occupied by the impulsive Daisy, Countess of Warwick. He flung himself into the bed shouting 'Cock-a-doodle-doo.' A trembling hand lit a paraffin lamp and he found himself between the Bishop of Chester and his wife. Beresford, who told this story himself, found the situation too difficult to explain and left the house before breakfast the next morning. At Windsor Lord Palmerston, pursuing his 'affectionate relations' with one of the Queen's Ladies of the Bedchamber, found himself in the wrong bedroom, the occupant of which raised the alarm. And Bertie's role in the matter is fixed by Hilaire Belloc's unpublished verses about Edwardian bed-hopping:

> There will be bridge
> and booze 'till after three
> And after that a lot of them will grope
> Along the corridors in *robes de nuit*,
> Pyjamas, or some other kind of dope.
> A sturdy matron will be sent to cope
> With Lord —, who isn't quite the thing,
> And give his wife the leisure to elope,
> And Mrs James will entertain the King!

Envoi
Prince, Father Vaughan will entertain the Pope,
And you will entertain the Jews at Tring,
And I will entertain the larger hope,
And Mrs James will entertain the King.

# My Naughtie Little Man

IT WAS IN THIS MORALLY AMBIGUOUS ATMOSPHERE that the Prince of Wales, Albert Edward, had his first sexual experience in the summer of 1861. The naturally sensual princeling was 19 and clearly eager. He had been sent to the army camp at the Curragh in Ireland for a ten-week course of infantry training, almost his first opportunity to mix with men of his own age. His father wanted to make him 'the most perfect man', and his education had been rigorous, almost pitiless. At the age of five he had three governesses who taught him French, English and German; at seven he was given a team of tutors who taught him five subjects six days a week. Experts warned his father that it was all too much, but the well-meaning pedant persisted, even when the little boy began to have uncontrollable tantrums. As Anita Leslie observes in *Edwardians in Love*, there were no magic hours fishing with bent pins, like other boys. Every minute of every day had to be organised and accounted for.

By 11 the Prince was studying six or seven hours a day, six days a week. He was not allowed to mix with other children, and continued to have fits of 'nervous unmanageable temper'. But as soon as he was allowed into the company of girls anything like his own age he showed a distinctly amorous side. When he was 16 he went on a trip to Germany with three tutors, and on the very first evening he kissed a girl after dining rather well. One of his companions reported the incident to William Ewart Gladstone, and the great statesman, who also had a weakness for kissing beauties, was shocked. 'Evidently the Prince of Wales has not been educated up to his position,' he commented. He was missing the point.

During his time at Oxford University the Prince was not allowed to reside in college like other undergraduates, but had to rent rooms and live with an equerry. He had special instruction from professors with six selected companions. So when at the age of 19 he was sent to Ireland and mixed with young officers who all kept mistresses, he couldn't help being envious. The young men took pity on him and smuggled an 'actress', Nellie Clifton, into his bed nightly.* What should have been a simple rite of passage for a young man turned into a delicious scandal, for Nellie went to London and boasted. Already widespread in army circles in Ireland, in November 1861 the story reached the ears of the Prince's father.

The royal parents already had a poor opinion of their son. The Queen complained that he was 'a very dull companion' and that in his dislike of clever books he was like a caricature of herself. Her husband went further: 'Bertie's propensity is indescribable laziness. I never in my life met such a thorough and cunning lazybones.' When he heard the rumours of the Curragh escapade he wrote to Bertie 'with a heavy heart upon a subject which has caused me the greatest pain I have yet felt in this life'. Bertie apologised, saying he had yielded to temptation, but refused to name the officers who had brought about his downfall. This was a gesture his father warmly commended, and he was forgiven. Condemning the 'evil deed', Prince Albert urged Bertie to fight 'a valiant fight' against what was, in truth, to be the great interest of his life, sex with beautiful women. Albert thought the way out was to pluck a bride for his son, young though he was, from the vortex of royal entanglements in Europe.

A few days later Albert was seriously ill. He wrote to his eldest daughter: 'I am at a very low ebb. Much worry and great sorrow

---

* Nellie was later a fairly high-class street prostitute at Burlington Arcade in London.

(about which I beg you not to ask questions) have robbed me of sleep during the past fortnight.' On the night of 14 December he died of typhoid fever.

The Queen blamed Bertie for her husband's death, and said she could hardly bear to have him in the same room. At 42 she retired into deep mourning, so stunned and distraught that she may have been a little mad. However, although it was a long time before she completely forgave him, she was to stand by Bertie through all the scrapes of the coming years.

The Queen's disapproval changed nothing. She wanted her son to be a paragon but she gave him little in the way of official business to do; like many of his aristocratic friends, he was rich but idle. When George III, who refused to allow the Prince of Wales an active command in the army, upbraided him for his lifestyle, the Prince replied: 'I find, Sir, however late I rise, that the day is long enough for doing nothing.' His grand-nephew, an amiable sensualist who loved women and was loved by them, was to devise a way of life that proved a safety valve for men and women who found the smothering moralising of court, church, newspapers, morals reformers and politicians unbearable.

That way of life involved unsuitable friendships with men as well as women. Three of those companions had been his contemporaries at Oxford and were later part of his drinking and gambling set. Harry Hastings, the fourth and last Marquess of Hastings, has been compared to the Earl of Rochester. Sir Frederick Johnstone was a gambler and ladies' man. Henry Chaplin was a vastly wealthy magnate. They were just the kind of idle pleasure-seeking young men whom the Queen despised.

Hastings was more than a little eccentric. He once emptied a bag of rats among the dancers at Mott's, a kind of exclusive night club which was also a resort of high-class harlots. This is how D. Shaw, author of *London in the Sixties*, depicts the scene: 'To describe what followed is impossible. Two hundred men and women and two hundred sewer rats compressed within the compass of forty feet by thirty, and in a darkness as profound as any that was ever experienced in Egypt.' Hastings was also a man of legendary generosity: 'Six cases of champagne invariably formed the first order' as he treated all and sundry. Ronald Pearsall in *The Worm in the Bud* describes Hastings as a Regency buck thirty years out of his time. After breakfasting on mackerel fried in gin, and caviar on toast, he would seek a companion for the day's revels. A specimen of his febrile conversation is recorded by Pearsall:

By Gad, old man, I'm damned glad to see you! To begin with you must dine with me at eight – here. I've asked Prince Hohenlohe and Baron Spaum, and young Beust and Count Adelberg, and if you'll swear on a stack of bibles not to repeat it, I expect two live ambassadors – it's always as well to have a sacred person or two handy in case of a row with the police. First we go to Endell Street – to Faultless's pit. I've got a match for a monkey with Hamilton to beat his champion bird, The Sweep, and after that I've arranged with a detective to take us the rounds in the Ratcliffe Highway.[*]

Hastings and Henry Chaplin both fell for the Lady Florence Paget, daughter of the Marquess of Anglesey. She accepted Henry's proposal and the wedding was set for the end of summer 1864 at St George's, Hanover Square. Had it taken place it would have been the society wedding of the year. But just a fortnight before the wedding Florence went shopping in Marshall and Snelgrove's in Oxford Street. She went in by a side entrance and shortly afterwards emerged from the front entrance with Harry Hastings, and married him that same day at St George's. (Three years later Hastings ruined himself by betting against Chaplin's colt Hermit in the Derby. He died, broken and bankrupt, at the age of 26.)

Society was shocked. The Queen was outraged. She had reason to remember an earlier scandal involving the Hastings family, although the fault was all on her side. Lady Flora Hastings had been lady-in-waiting to Victoria's mother, the Duchess of Kent. Because of some obscure domestic infighting the Queen had

[*] The Ratcliffe Highway was on the riverside east of Wapping, famous for its sailors' brothels and general lawlessness. The police went there only in groups.

come to dislike her. At Christmas 1838 Lady Flora, who was 27, felt unwell and consulted the Queen's physician Sir James Clark. He noticed that Lady Flora's figure looked unusually full for an unmarried woman, and speculated unwisely to one of the Queen's ladies that she might be pregnant. The Queen got to hear of this and wrote in her journal: 'We have no doubt that she is – to use the plain words – with child.' The Queen insisted on Lady Flora being medically examined. Two doctors testified that she was not pregnant. News of the affair got out and there was a public scandal. Flora's brother Lord Hastings wrote to the *Morning Post* to clear her name. Four months later Lady Flora died and the cause of the swelling was revealed: she had incurable liver disease.

Perhaps it would be too much to expect public remorse from a sovereign. The Queen certainly remembered that she had lost face because of the Hastings family, and now told her son that she was disgusted that he was mixing with such people.

In March 1863 Bertie married the 18-year-old Princess Alexandra of Denmark, whose parents 'were not as rich as most London shopkeepers', according to Jane Welsh Carlyle, wife of the historian and sage. Her family had already been warned about his indiscretion on the Curragh. Alexandra didn't care. She told the Prince's elder sister: 'You may think I like marrying Bertie for his position, but if he were a cowboy I would love him just the same, and would marry no one else.' Alexandra was unquestionably beautiful, and photographs show that she became if anything more so, reaching her peak in the 1880s. She showed a touching loyalty to her husband in spite of everything, and recalled: 'He loved me the best.'

She had much to put up with. While in the next seven years she bore six children, Bertie was making profligacy in high places acceptable again, having taken to horse racing with gusto.[*] He borrowed money from the international financiers Hirsch and

---

[*] And with some success, unlike George IV. In *The Worm in the Bud*, Pearsall says his stallions brought in £269,495 in stud fees, and his horses won £146,345 in prize money.

Cassel, wrote indiscreet but possibly naïve letters to young wives, and had affairs with a long series of lovely women, very few of them however quite as lovely as his wife. She unfortunately became increasingly deaf. She also had a limp, but this proved no disadvantage, as great ladies took to imitating her, just as the Chesterfield House set adopted a drawl round the Devonshires as a kind of badge of caste. When practised by these ladies it was known as the 'Alexandra limp'. She was not very bright, but this carapace of stupidity may have helped her cope. Queen Victoria, who liked her, remarked 'Very clever I don't think she is,' and Theo Aronson says in *The King in Love* that 'She had very little brain.' She could not help knowing of Bertie's many betrayals, but it was public humiliation rather than private torment that hurt her most, and unfortunately she often had to meet the royal mistresses in public. Nevertheless, 'my naughtie little man' was apparently the strongest reproof she ever issued.

Although he was an affectionate father Bertie was not often *en famille*. He craved company, preferably wealthy men with attractive wives. He lived at a frantic pace, constantly in search of new amusements, which were either sexual or childish. He was easily bored, could not stand intellectual talk or pursuits, disliked serious music or art, and hated anything that could be regarded as work.

His friends were drawn from a wider social range than any other Prince of Wales before or since. Women had to be beautiful and interesting, men to be very rich, certainly rich enough to afford the ruinous cost of entertaining him. The Queen disapproved of his Jewish friends, but they had money. In December 1873, the Bishop of Peterborough wrote after a visit to Sandringham: 'We are a curious mixture. Two Jews, Sir Anthony de Rothschild and his daughter; an ex-Jew, Disraeli; a Roman Catholic, Colonel Higgins; an Italian duchess who is an Englishwoman, brought up a Roman Catholic and now turning Protestant; a set of young Lords and a bishop ... '

Bertie discovered that he could seduce, or be seduced by, almost any woman he chose. His unimpressive looks – low stature, weak chin, heavy-lidded slumbrous eyes, portly figure – were no

disadvantage. As one of his biographers wrote, snobbery is a powerful aphrodisiac. Word got about that the Prince of Wales was
sleeping with attractive women in high society and there was a
sudden loosening of morals as well as stays. Twenty-five years of his
mother's gloomy matriarchy had made such women wary of
expressing their natural high spirits. Now a 'Fast Set' emerged in
which Bertie's behaviour was copied in a discreet and well-
organised way. At its heart was Louisa, Duchess of Manchester, a
beautiful and domineering woman. She had upset the Queen and
been discouraged from attending court, so she held a court of her
own at Manchester House in London. Manchester House became
synonymous with 'fast' behaviour.

As a young married woman Louisa had extorted a promise from
the Earl of Derby that if he ever became Prime Minister he would
make her a Mistress of the Robes at court. When he did achieve
that high office Louisa insisted he keep his promise, and he did. The
Queen, who already disapproved of the heavy gambling and loose
behaviour at Manchester House – how like George III's attitude to
the goings-on at Devonshire House – heard of this and refused to
invite the Duchess to her son's wedding, an unprecedented insult
for a Mistress of the Robes. But Louisa was already entrenched at
the heart of high society. She was the lover of the leading Liberal
Lord Hartington, 'Harty Tarty', who had previously kept as mistress
the celebrated courtesan Catherine Walters, known as 'Skittles'.
Through her husband, whom she obliged with five children before
becoming Harty Tarty's acknowledged mistress, and later wife, she
was wealthy, had splendid homes and a commanding position in
society. Some men said in private that she was stupid, but she had
considerable political pull. Although older than Skittles she had
enough sexual allure to win and hold Hartington for more than 30
years; she married him when her husband died and he had succeeded to the title of Duke of Devonshire, so earning herself the
nickname of the Double Duchess. And she had a strong streak of
independence: when Bertie fell out with Lord Randolph
Churchill and let it be known that he and the Princess would boycott any house where the Churchills were received, Louisa told

him to his face: 'I hold friendship higher than snobbery.'

Hartington was a friend of Bertie's, and despite his political eminence was not spared the childish and sometimes cruel jokes the members of his set played on one another – but not of course on the Prince, who was touchy where his dignity was concerned. In 1876, when the Duchess of Manchester had triumphed in her struggle with Skittles for proprietary rights to Hartington, the Prince played a joke on him which we can all enjoy, as it was without malice. During a tour of Coventry he informed the mayor that Hartington should be shown a bowling alley, as he was particularly interested in the game. Hartington was baffled, until the mayor pointed out: 'His Royal Highness asked especially for the inclusion of this alley in the tour in tribute to your lordship's love of skittles.'

## Bertie in love

One of Bertie's early affairs was with the French actress Hortense Schneider; many others followed, as Pearsall recounts in *The Worm in the Bud*. There is not enough space to mention all Bertie's conquests, however famous they were at the time: until he was 35 he enjoyed a long string of brief affairs without ever becoming deeply involved emotionally. In 1877 that changed when he met Lillie Langtry, who was to become the first of his official mistresses. She arrived in London from Jersey, the daughter of the dean of the island, penniless and with a husband.* She had however great assets – high intelligence, an eye for the main chance and marvellous beauty. Even rivals admitted she was, in the current parlance, a stunner. Daisy, Countess of Warwick, her successor as 'official mistress', paid fulsome tribute: 'How can words convey the vitality, the amazing charm, that made this fascinating woman the centre of

---

* The dean was a notorious lecher. Lillie said of him: 'He was a damned nuisance, he couldn't be trusted with any woman anywhere.' The dean was once ambushed by Colonel Knatchbull and Admiral de Saumarez as he emerged from church with their wives – both noted beauties – on his arms. The husbands belaboured him with their walking sticks, but the dean managed to slip away leaving the furious men fighting each other.

any group that she entered?' Because her looks accorded with the artistic ideal of the time, including the very pronounced jaw, she was much in demand by fashionable painters – she was known as the Jersey Lily after a painting by John Everett Millais, in which she is shown holding the flower.

Apart from the jaw she was broad-hipped, full-breasted and walked with an animal grace, exuding sexual allure. Like many people who become suddenly famous, you wonder why they were not spotted sooner. Lillie certainly wondered, as she and her husband spent a friendless and obscure first year in London. Then by chance she met Lord Ranelagh, an old roué whom she had known in Jersey, and she was invited to an evening at-home given by the bohemian hostess Lady Sebright at her house in Lowndes Square. Among the guests were the artist and conversationist James McNeill Whistler, Millais and the actor Henry Irving. The women were bejewelled and expensively dressed. Lillie had no jewels – 'I owned none', she recalled – and wore a simple black dress made by a Jersey dressmaker. She was a sensation.

In her autobiography *The Days I Knew* Lillie wrote: 'Fancy my surprise when I immediately became the centre of attention and, after a few moments, I found that quite half the people in the room seemed bent on making my acquaintance.' Millais took her down to supper. He would later say of her: 'Lillie Langtry happens to be, quite simply, the most beautiful woman on earth.' Before long her hall table was heaped with invitations. Lillie had arrived.

Bertie met Lillie at a party in May 1877. He subjected her to his practised and successful form of insidious seduction – caressing looks, compliments, the implication that she was the only woman in the room who mattered. By the time she said goodnight with a curtsey there was an unspoken understanding. Soon they were lovers and as word leaked out beyond aristocratic circles, her beauty drew crowds whenever they appeared together in public. Margot Asquith, who later married the Liberal Prime Minister, recalled the effect she created:

Mrs Langtry was new to the public and photographs of her in the shop windows made every passerby pause to gaze at them. My sister, Charlotte Ribblesdale, told me that she had been in a London ballroom when several fashionable ladies had stood upon their chairs to see Mrs Langtry come into the room.

In a shining top-hat and skin-tight habit, she rode a chestnut thoroughbred of conspicuous action every morning in Rotten Row [in Hyde Park]. Among her adorers were the Prince of Wales and the Earl of Lonsdale. One day when I was riding I saw Mrs Langtry – who was accompanied by Lord Lonsdale – pause at the railings in Rotten Row to speak to a man of her acquaintance. I do not know what she could have said to him, but after a brief exchange of words Lord Lonsdale jumped from his horse, sprang over the railings and with clenched fists hit Mrs Langtry's admirer in the face. Upon this a free fight ensued, and to the delight of the surprised spectators, Lord Lonsdale knocked his adversary down.

Leslie reveals that the adversary was Sir George Chetwyn, who was complaining that Mrs Langtry should have been riding with him. The angry rivals were separated by the Duke of Portland and Sir William Gordon-Cumming. (In those days there was usually a duke around when you needed one.) Asquith went on:

The 'Jersey Lily' ... had Greek features, a transparent skin, arresting eyes, fair hair and a firm white throat. She held herself erect, refused to tighten her waist [wear stays]...The Princess of Wales, the Empress of Austria, Lady Dalhousie, the Duchess of Leinster, Lady de Grey, Lady Londonderry, Mrs Cornwallis-West, Mrs Wheeler ... [the list of Amazonian belles continues] dazzled every London drawing room.* But with the exception of Georgiana, Countess of

---

* Mrs Cornwallis-West was a 'professional beauty', the equivalent of a modern celebrity. They advertised various commodities – Maud Branscombe appeared in adverts for toothpaste with the slogan 'nun nicer' – their photographs were sold and they appeared in plays, not acting but lounging around and looking lovely. As Pearsall recounts in *The Worm in the Bud*, Gladstone, the grand old man of politics, was once caught kissing Mrs Cornwallis-West. The young daughter of an estate worker once saw the Prince of Wales lying on top of Mrs Cornwallis-West in some woods. She told her father, who struck her a violent blow, saying she would be killed if she repeated the story.

Dudley, no one in my lifetime has excited the same excitement and attention as Mrs Langtry.

Bertie was fascinated by his beautiful young conquest, and too infatuated to be discreet. He began to appear with her in public, and hostesses soon realised that if they wanted him to accept invitations they had to invite Lillie too. This created a certain tension. Some straight-laced hostesses were prepared to overlook Bertie's reputation in exchange for the social cachet of having him grace their dinner parties, but Mrs Langtry wasn't even of the right class. When eventually they got the opportunity they cut her.

By the beginning of 1880 Lillie had achieved a rare degree of celebrity, for her beauty and for her mind. Her friend Oscar Wilde said: 'Lillie's beauty has no meaning. Her charm, her wit and her mind – what a mind – are far more formidable weapons.' However, she knew her social acceptability was fragile – it largely depended on Bertie. The doors of the highest aristocracy remained closed to her, and the wealthy parvenus who welcomed her would mostly close their doors too if Bertie dropped her. And he would drop her eventually, she knew. He was too fickle, too easily bored, too attractive to too many young beauties for the affair to last. Lillie had only to consider the long list of Bertie's discarded lovers to read her fate.

Bertie too was a realist in love. Not for him the world-well-lost attitude of his grandson, Edward VIII, who would give up the throne for his great passion, Mrs Wallis Simpson. Bertie was genuinely in love with Lillie Langtry but he realised it wouldn't last. These things didn't, did they? Her beauty, her rare independence of spirit, her wit and the quality of her mind had captivated him for a time, but the clamorous throng of beauties present at all functions at Marlborough House, his London residence, could not be ignored for ever. However, for about two or three years she monopolised his thoughts and his bed. When they were apart he wrote her chatty letters, once confessing almost in surprise that he was not flirting with the society beauties at Cowes.

Their relationship had another kind of consummation in May 1878 when Lillie was presented to the Queen at Buckingham Palace. This otherwise meaningless ceremony implied a high degree of social acceptability. With the grinning Bertie looking on Lillie approached the grim old woman. The Queen extended her hand 'in a rather perfunctory manner' as Lillie remembered, and showed no interest in her whatever, staring past her into the distance. Dancing with Lillie that evening at a Marlborough House Ball, Bertie told her that the Queen had simply wanted to see her. It was sheer curiosity that led Queen Victoria, in some ways one of the most powerful women in history, to countenance her son's official mistress, a mere clergyman's daughter. The homage of one celebrity to another.

But Lillie had already had to endure Bertie spending more and more time with other women, including another professional beauty, Mrs Luke Wheeler, and the actress–courtesan Sarah Bernhardt.

Bernhardt came to London in 1879 to appear in *La Dame aux Camellias*, but not everyone shared the Prince's enthusiasm for the French beauty. Lady Frederick Cavendish, sister of the Duke of Devonshire, wrote: 'London has gone mad over the principal actress of the Comedie Francaise, a woman of notorious, shameless character. Not content with being run after on the stage, this woman is asked to respectable people's houses to act, and even to lunch and dinner; and all the world goes. It is an outrageous scandal!'

Bertie asked Ferdinand de Rothschild, one of his rich Jewish friends, to give a midnight supper party for Bernhardt so that she could meet the Duc d'Aumale. Some grand English ladies went too, because Bertie wished it, but they had no intention of actually speaking to the actress. Sir Charles Dilke, himself involved in a sensational divorce case, left an amusing account of the evening.[*] 'It

---

[*] The case was so hilarious that it became the basis for a play. Dilke was a member of a Gladstone government and was regarded as a politician of great promise, despite being a radical and at one stage a professed republican. He was also a philanderer who left a trail of affairs. He was cited in an action brought by a Mr Donald Crawford, and the following exchange is said to have taken place between Crawford and his wife Virginia:

was one thing to get them to go, and another to get them to talk when they were there; and the result was that, as they would not talk to Sarah Bernhardt, and the Duc d'Aumale was deaf and disinclined to make conversation on his own account, nobody talked at all, and a reign of the most absolute and dismal silence ensued.'

Lillie too was beginning to stray. She had a secret lover, Arthur Jones, and as she realised her grip on Bertie was weakening she became less discreet about other affairs. Daisy, Countess of Warwick, who would have a long and intense affair with Bertie, told how in her first season she was being courted by a lordling who professed undying love. Then one night she heard him making an assignation with Lillie Langtry, whom he called 'my darling'. 'Naturally I was furious, and never looked at him again', wrote Daisy.

In March 1880 Lillie met Prince Louis of Battenberg, a handsome 25-year-old naval officer who was distantly related to Bertie, and like him was a successful womaniser. Unlike the Prince of Wales he was tall, well-built, good-looking and intellectual. Lillie introduced him to many of the 'leading cultural personalities of the time'. With their shared interests it was probably inevitable they should have an affair. By the autumn Lillie was pregnant. Louis told his parents and they sent a flunkey to pay her off, while the Admiralty sent him away on a long voyage.

It is a pity to usher the amusing Mrs Langtry out of the story for the moment, but Bertie had finally lost interest in her and was

---

'Virginia, is it true that you have defiled my bed? I have been a faithful husband to you.'
'Yes, it is true, it is time that you should know the truth. You have always been on the wrong track, suspecting people who are innocent, and you have never suspected the person who is guilty.'
'I have never suspected anybody except Captain Forster.'
'It was not Captain Forster. The man who ruined me was Charles Dilke.'

With ready-made dialogue like this it is no wonder the case was turned into a play. *The Right Honourable Gentleman* was staged at Her Majesty's Theatre in 1965 and starred Anthony Quayle and Coral Browne. The case ended messily: Mr Crawford was first granted a divorce, but a later jury decided it had been improperly obtained. Dilke was finished as a major politician. In 1886 he lost his seat in Parliament as a consequence of the case, although he later won another seat and returned to public life, organising the Labour MPs into an effective party.

ready for his next official mistress. Lillie's pregnancy closed the doors of the great to her sooner than she expected. She went on the stage and was hugely successful, amassing a fortune during a tour of America. She continued to enjoy an exuberant love life, among her conquests being Crown Prince Rudolf of Austria and King Leopold. Other lovers included the hyper-wealthy George Alexander Baird, a hard-drinking, brawling young American who showered her with presents and beat her up. After blacking her eye he bought her a £100,000, (more than £6,500,000) 220-foot steam yacht which was twice the size of the Prince of Wales's yacht *Britannia*. Baird died in 1893 after another brawl, at the age of 32. Among his legacies to Lillie were several racehorses, and Lillie took up the sport seriously. She had some success, bought a house near Newmarket and through the sport was eventually to make contact with Bertie again.

## Daisy Warwick: the great game

After he and Lillie Langtry parted Bertie had another breathless series of affairs, both at home and abroad, before his eye fell on Frances 'Daisy' Maynard, a beautiful young heiress. For the second time in his life he was completely captivated. In his many letters he called her 'his own little Daisy wife', his 'own adored little Daisy wife' and 'his own lovely little Daisy wife'. He had chosen another strong and intelligent woman, and it is to his credit that with his own limited intellect he fully appreciated her qualities. In appearance Daisy, who was born in December 1861, was the antithesis of Lillie, slight, golden-haired, sharp-featured. Aronson says in *The King in Love* that she needed elegant clothes and carefully coiffured hair 'to show off her more subtle looks'.

Daisy was born in December 1861. When she was three her father, the Hon. Charles Maynard, died and left her an enormous fortune and the palatial Easton Lodge near Dunmow in Essex.[*]

---

[*] When the will was read her Maynard relatives were so incensed at the amount of Daisy's inheritance that they threw pats of butter at the portrait of her late father.

Her mother married Lord Rosslyn, a favourite of Queen Victoria. In *Afterthoughts*, her second book of memoirs, Daisy would later claim that he was the only man who could get away with telling the Queen risqué stories. 'I have been at dinner in Windsor Castle and heard Lord Rosslyn spinning a daring yarn to the Queen, while the Princess Beatrice [one of the Queen's daughters] looked as though she were sitting on thorns, and other guests were quaking. I have seen the Queen's lips twitching with suppressed laughter and ... I have seen her most gracious Majesty shaking like an agitated jelly.'

Daisy married Francis Greville, Lord Brooke, heir to the Earl of Warwick, although she had been intended by her parents and Queen Victoria to marry the Queen's son Leopold. Leopold didn't love her, and suggested she turn him down in favour of Brooke, whom she said she did love. Daisy agreed – not the last time she upset the Queen – and the wedding at Westminster Abbey in April 1881 was described as 'the most brilliant wedding of a dozen seasons'.*

The unthinking hedonism of the upper classes suited Daisy, who threw herself into an endless succession of balls, parties, and especially, hunts – she was a fine horsewoman. For the moment the great social injustices of the time made no impression on her or her friends.

From time to time the Brookes met the Prince of Wales at great country house parties. On one occasion Bertie danced with Daisy, but his thoughts were elsewhere. 'He spent most of the evening with Mrs Cornwallis-West, then in the zenith of her beauty,' Daisy wrote in *Life's Ebb and Flow*. Like other society women Daisy took her cue from the Prince, and began to have affairs. 'From the beginning of our life together, my husband seemed to accept the inevitability of my having a train of admirers,' she wrote. 'I could not help it. There they were. It was all a great game.' Her husband thought a good day's fishing or shooting 'second in point of pleas-

---

* Leopold, a haemophiliac, married Princess Helen of Waldeck-Pyrmont. Two years later he was dead from an internal haemorrhage, having knocked his knee on some stairs.

ure to nothing on earth'. Daisy said she found the long house parties where the men went off in pursuit of such pleasures, leaving the women to make their own amusement, 'intolerably boring'. One way of making the time pass was to have affairs, and the most serious Daisy had before she became Bertie's mistress was with the dashing naval commander Lord Charles Beresford.

Beresford, who would later blunder into the Bishop of Chester's room mistaking it for Daisy's, was a highly successful adulterer. The bored wives of the country house party set could not resist this handsome war hero. Lord Charles was often a guest of the Brookes at Easton Lodge, and by 1886 he and Daisy were lovers. She was 25 and had already provided her husband with a nursery full of heirs; Beresford was 39. Daisy was a generous but tempestuous and reckless beauty who was inclined to throw caution to the winds when she fell in love.

One day while Lord Charles and his plain wife were staying at Easton Lodge, Daisy went to Lady Beresford's room, told her of the affair and said she was going to elope with Lord Charles. Lady Beresford was furious. Thus began a fight over Lord Charles. As Margaret Blunden explains in her biography *The Countess of Warwick*, he was anyway already losing interest in Daisy, having discovered that she was 'not content with his attentions alone'.

Late that year Daisy heard that Lady Beresford was pregnant. As far as she was concerned, this meant that Lord Charles had been unfaithful to her with his own wife. She wrote him a letter, the kind that only an angry and irrational lover can write. She told him he had no right to get his wife pregnant, that he must leave her at once and join Daisy on the Riviera, and that one of her children was really his.

When the letter arrived at Lord Charles's home he was away, and it was opened by his wife. She passed it to George Lewis, a solicitor who specialised in the follies of the rich and powerful. Lewis wrote to Daisy, warning her against causing any further trouble. Daisy demanded the return of her letter, claiming it was her property – it wasn't, it belonged to Sir Charles, to whom it had been addressed.

Daisy turned for help to a man she hardly knew, the Prince of Wales, a close friend of Sir Charles. She went to see him at Marlborough House, his London residence. They sat in his study. 'He was charmingly courteous to me,' she said afterwards, 'and at length he told me he hoped his friendship would make up, in part at least, for my sailor-lover's loss. He was more than kind.' Much more. Suddenly Daisy noticed him 'looking at me in a way all women understand'. What the Prince had in mind was obvious, but first he had to deal with the matter of the letter. Although it was late at night he went straight to see Lewis, who was so impressed by his visitor that he showed him the letter. However, he was not prepared to destroy it, as the Prince wanted, so Bertie went to see Lady Beresford.

She laid down strict terms for returning the letter. Lady Brooke had to agree to stay away from London for the entire season. This was too drastic for Daisy, who again appealed to Bertie for help. Fired by his growing passion for her, he went back to Lady and issued an ultimatum: if she didn't part with the letter he would have her frozen out of society. Even this blatant social blackmail didn't move Lady Beresford, and Bertie began his campaign by seeing to it that the Brookes were invited to the same houses as himself. Daisy wrote: 'And when that sign of the Prince's support didn't stop the angry little cat, the Prince checked her in another way. She had been put down as one of the house party of a great lady to meet him. He simply cut her name out and substituted mine for it . . .'

Lord Charles had been trying to persuade his wife to return the letter, but the Prince's threat to ostracise her angered him. In January 1890 he called on the Prince. In the furious scene that followed he called Bertie a blackguard and pushed him. The corpulent Prince sat down heavily on a sofa. As London rang with tales of *lèse-majesté*, Beresford went off to sea, leaving the Prince and his inamorata to carry on a grand affair.

For some time Lady Beresford was snubbed. She wrote to Lord Salisbury about the Prince, 'he has cast all sense of decorum to the winds and probably prompted by the now victorious lady, who thinks that during Lord Charles' absence I am defenceless – he has now proceeded to boycott me in the most open manner.' After a decent interval the letter was returned to Lady Brooke.

The letter affair had made Daisy appear ludicrous. In fact she was an intelligent woman with a growing social conscience which would eventually lead her to socialism. Bertie, not a particularly intelligent man, nevertheless liked women whose conversation was not limited to the social trivia of their immediate circle. He was enchanted and soon deeply in love with her. He began writing letters to her, sometimes three times a week.[*] One which he wrote from Chatsworth, Derbyshire home of the Duke of Devonshire, ends: 'Now my loved one and I bring these lines to a close, as I must dress and breakfast. God bless you, my own little adored daisy wife ... Your only love.' He liked giving her presents; these included a gold ring his parents had given him, inscribed 'To Bertie from his affectionate parents A. and V. R. July 1860'. Daisy later recalled: 'He had manners and he was very considerate, and from a woman's point of view that's a great deal. Then he was remarkably constant and adored me exceedingly. I grew to like him very much. I think anybody would have been won by him ... ' It is interesting that she does not mention love.

They were seen together everywhere. Bertie took her sailing with him at Cowes and to horse racing meetings around the country, and he insisted she be invited to all the balls and house parties he attended. She became one of the adornments of the set surrounding Bertie at Marlborough House, and she was thrilled, as she describes in *Afterthoughts*: 'I can still feel something of the same sense of enchantment, in recalling it, that children experienced when they watched the transformation scene at the pantomime. For them, the girls in their spangles were beautiful fairies, and the scene a glimpse of fairyland ... ' In London they could stay at Daisy's town house or, if the Princess of Wales was away, at Marlborough House. As Aronson reveals in *The King in Love*, some of

---

[*]  Having dissipated her huge fortune in philanthropic schemes, Daisy eventually sold Bertie's love letters to settle her debts. They were published after his death.

the best London restaurants had private rooms 'where the touch of a button would part the panelling to reveal a double bed'. Wherever they went, Bertie's formidable sex drive had to be considered. Daisy found him 'a very perfect, gentle lover', but also a frequent one, and the question of contraception was important. By the 1880s crêpe rubber condoms were being widely used, a great improvement on the uncomfortable sheaths Boswell had written about.* A popular brand bore portraits of Queen Victoria and Gladstone on the box. How piquant for Bertie.

Daisy often entertained Bertie at her country home, Easton Lodge. Lord Brooke took it all with good humour, writing later of the Prince without apparent irony:

> He delighted in performing kind actions, they may be said to have been his hobby; and while as a host he could anticipate every possible want of his guests, as a guest he was most affable, courteous and responsive. He appreciated everything that was done for his comfort, and had the gift of setting everybody, whether prince or ploughman, at their ease.

Perhaps an element in Lord Brooke's complacency was his own weakness for beautiful women. Once when he invited the novelist Elinor Glyn to inspect a rose garden at Easton Lodge, he astonished her by putting his arms around her and telling her she was the 'fairest rose' in the garden. When she complained to her husband he chuckled: 'Did he, by Jove! Good old Brookie.'

The Prince's love of clothes, if not equalling that of his ancestor George IV, was great – he managed to hide his growing bulk to some extent with immaculate tailoring. This meant that he travelled with a large retinue of servants, who had to be accommodated. They included a gentleman-in-waiting and a couple of equerries, two grooms for his horses, two loaders for his guns if he was shooting and two valets. His father had complained that the

---

* Boswell describes using condoms in his journals, but they gave him little satisfaction.

only thing Bertie was interested in was clothes. Perhaps it would be more accurate to say that the only thing he was more interested in than clothes was sex.

Entertaining him could be ruinously expensive. It might be said that the price of friendship with Bertie was to provide lavish and expensive entertainments. Daisy could afford the expense, but others could not. She wrote: 'I could tell stories of men and women who had to economise for a whole year, or alternatively get into debt that they might entertain Royalty for one weekend.' As we shall see, his friend Christopher Sykes was almost driven into bankruptcy and had to retire to his country estate. Bertie seemed not to notice that his hosts and hostesses were practically bankrupting themselves to make the hours press less heavily on his sensitive soul. After he became king a visit to a country house for the first time would often involve the owners in extensive redecorations and refurnishing, what estate agents now call refurbishment. Anita Leslie recounts one such visit in *Edwardians in Love*. On the first morning the hostess asked the King if everything was satisfactory. Bertie, who hadn't noticed that the hangings and fabrics were all new, considered for a moment. 'You might put a hook for a dressing gown on the bathroom door,' he ventured. The hostess was shattered.

Daisy's parties for the Prince were lavish. A list of the guests had first to be shown to him for approval, and he would sometimes add the names of friends. If the guest list was long enough Daisy would hire a special train from London, laying on transport from the station for the guests and their mountainous luggage. (Eventually she had a special railway station built at great expense.) She would hire extra servants and an orchestra, and order special food. The Edwardians didn't invent gluttony, but many of them practised it to destruction, including Bertie. A chef would be brought in from London to prepare these dishes – perhaps Bertie's friend Rosa Lewis.

In the summer of 1891 Daisy Brooke was publicly received by the Princess of Wales at Marlborough House. This could be seen as a kind of seal of approval on her status as official mistress. By one bitter woman, however, it was seen as one humiliation too many. Lady Charles Beresford had followed accounts in the newspapers of Daisy's triumphs with growing fury. Having continued to send a stream of angry letters to her absent husband about Bertie's continuing snubs, she eventually goaded him into writing a particularly intemperate letter in which he threatened to destroy the Prince by publicity. He dispatched the letter to his wife, telling her to send it to the Prime Minister, Lord Salisbury. With it she enclosed a letter of her own warning this busy public servant that her sister, Mrs Gerald Paget, had written a pamphlet about the affair between the Prince and her enemy, Daisy Brooke. There were people, she continued, who wanted to 'make use of the story at the next General Election for purposes of their own'. What she wanted was a public apology from the Prince of Wales for making her a social pariah.

Lord Salisbury wrote to both the Beresfords pointing out that the 'social laws of our class' made it impossible for a gentleman to act in a way that would disgrace his mistress. This seems to have calmed Lord Charles, but Mrs Gerald Paget began circulating her pamphlet, which was an exposé of Daisy Brooke's affair with the Prince of Wales. It was called *Lady River*, according to Aronson in *The King in Love*, a hostess had only to announce a public reading of it for her drawing room to be crowded.

Eventually news of the pamphlet reached the Princess of Wales. Deeply hurt by yet another of her husband's infidelities becoming public, she decided not to return from holiday for Bertie's fiftieth birthday in November 1891 but instead went to visit the Russian Tsarina. Before Bertie could get over this obvious snub from his wife, Lord Charles Beresford issued another ultimatum. Unless Bertie apologised in public to Lady Beresford, and unless Daisy Brooke withdrew from society for a year, Beresford would call a press conference and publish the full details of Bertie's private life. We have become used to royal scandals, but a full and frank exposé of the fabulous fornicator would have been truly sensational.

Lord Salisbury, who had an empire to run, nevertheless involved himself in frantic negotiations between the various parties and, it was rumoured, Queen Victoria herself. They ended with Daisy temporarily withdrawing from court and Bertie and Beresford exchanging conciliatory letters. The crisis seemed to be over.

Now another of the wronged parties unexpectedly acted. Just as Alexandra could not take any more, for the present anyway, Lord Brooke was rumoured to want a divorce, and to have been ready to name 14 of his wife's lovers, including Bertie, Beresford, Lord Randolph Churchill and the Duke of Marlborough. In the end it all blew over – perhaps Brooke was too much of a gentleman to drag his wife through the divorce court.

Bertie's love for Daisy outlasted all these trials, and it was Daisy herself who began to make impossible demands of it. In the spring of 1892 she met the crusading journalist William Thomas Stead, standard bearer for a new kind of frank, conviction journalism. As editor of the *Pall Mall Gazette* he conducted a campaign against child prostitution, and to get the age of consent for girls raised from 12 to 16. There were powerful interests ranged against him. In 1885, in a series of sensational articles called 'The Maiden Tribute to Modern Babylon', Stead exposed the excesses of the trade. Then, in a silly stunt, he 'bought' a young girl from her mother to show how it could be done and was jailed for three months. The ruling class was by and large outraged by the tone of the articles, and the fact that they were written at all, but the public bought the papers in unprecedented numbers and the law was changed.

Stead, his ardour for good causes burning as bright as ever, became editor of the *Review of Reviews*. He saw in Daisy Brooke a chance to further a pet project – reforming the Prince of Wales's character. He had written an article about Bertie, which suggested that if he had been given a real job to do 'he might have developed somewhat more of his father's virtues'. Daisy read it and told Bertie it was 'very just', and that it gave him 'good advice and was very fair'. She had been nourishing vague philanthropic yearnings, and when Stead suggested to her that she might recruit Bertie for good causes she enthusiastically agreed.

Bertie was very unpromising material for reform. He had no interest in social issues and little sympathy for the working classes, as Hibbert explains in *Edward VII: A Portrait*, warning against 'the lower classes getting the upper hand'. But he could be touched by personally witnessing the squalor of London's slums. After a tour of the deplorable tenements of Holborn he made a speech in the House of Lords attacking these 'perfectly disgraceful' conditions. At the same time he admitted that some of the London property he owned through the Duchy of Cornwall was just as bad. However, while he was capable of such gestures, he couldn't understand Daisy's growing commitment to socialism.

Her father-in-law died in 1893, and she became the Countess of Warwick. Her ardour for good causes was undimmed. She brought Stead and Bertie together over lunch, hoping contact with the charismatic journalist would inflame the Prince with some of his zeal, but he really wasn't very interested. In fact the Prince was no longer very interested in Daisy, either. By 1898, fickle Bertie was 'finding his sexual satisfaction elsewhere', and was also ready for a new relationship. He and Daisy continued to be warm friends, and since she too was craving love elsewhere this suited her. She had never been in love with Bertie, and even found him a bit of a bore. She had always wanted to be a woman of importance, and now, with socialism, she thought she had found a new and better route to it. The affair had lasted about nine years, marred but not destroyed by Daisy's growing advocacy of feminism and socialism. When in 1898 she became pregnant by another man it was obvious to everyone that it was over. Within a short time they both found solace elsewhere.

Bertie's was to be a long and happy relationship; Daisy's new love would be short and sad. At the age of 36 she fell for a man five years younger. Joseph Laycock was a wealthy army captain of the same landed class as the Duchess, with what Aronson in *The King in Love* describes as 'a strong animal magnetism' that made him attractive to women, and Daisy 'worshipped' him. But the terms of this affair were very different from that with Bertie. Like many an older woman she now found herself clinging to a love that was slipping away. Her biographer, Margaret Blunden, contrasts the affairs: 'If with the Prince of Wales he had been the captive, she the conquering, he the adoring, she the adored, the reverse was nearer the truth with Laycock. Lady Warwick could still be imperious, was seldom less than demanding, but Laycock was ultimately in the happy position of being the one most desired, the one more loved than loving.'

After Laycock was hurt in a hunting accident he was nursed by a younger beauty, Lady Kitty Downshire. They fell in love and the Marquess of Downshire sued for divorce. Daisy wrote imploring, incoherent letters beseeching Laycock not to marry Kitty, an 'ill-fated, impossible marriage' as she put it. 'Joe, my Joe', one letter ran, 'if you could see how my hand shakes when I write your name ...' In October 1902 in desperation she dragged Bertie into it: 'My darling ... only to say that the King more than nice to me – agrees about it all – only he says (as we do) you must go away for a bit then "things will be alright" and "a pity a man's life should be ruined" etc. (He is very down on poor Lady D, but I can tell you ...)'

In November Laycock married Kitty. Daisy found some consolation in her good works for trade unions, the physically handicapped, progressive education. She worked for an Anglo-American alliance and tried to interest Bertie, but he was more interested in an entente cordiale with France. All this time he was writing to Daisy, letters which, she said, revealed 'qualities that are none too common in any class, but rare indeed in Royalty'. In 1899 he sent her 'a charming letter reminding me of the tenth anniversary of our friendship'. By then Bertie was in love with Alice Keppel, his last official mistress.

## Mrs Keppel, La Favorita

Bertie met Alice Keppel early in 1898, he was 56 and she 29. They were introduced by the writer Anita Leslie's grandfather; as she recounts in *Edwardians in Love*, he said there was no mistaking the look in the Prince's eyes as they 'travelled over Mrs George Keppel's lovely face and fashionably curved figure'. Alice was voluptuous rather than beautiful, and she certainly had 'It', as defined by Elinor Glyn. Her large blue-green eyes, piled-up chestnut hair and flawless skin exuded sex appeal. According to Aronson, she was proud of her small hands and feet. She had Greek blood, and men saw in her a Mediterranean sensuousness. She was high-spirited and vivacious and like Bertie's other mistresses, Lillie Langtry and Daisy Warwick, she had been a tomboy. She was good-natured and without malice, and she was known for her witty turns of phrase. Bertie found her wholly irresistible.

King's mistresses are powerful people, but after Bertie became monarch in 1901 Alice seems to have used whatever power she had wisely. Diaries of the time are by and large kind to her. Lord Harding of Penshurst, head of the Foreign Office, wrote in his private file:

> I used to see a great deal of Mrs Keppel at that time, and I was aware that she had knowledge of what was going on in the political world. I would like here to pay a tribute to her wonderful discretion and to the excellent influence which she always exercised upon the King. She never utilised her knowledge to her own advantage, or to that of her friends; and I never heard her repeat an unkind word of anybody. There were one or two occasions when the king was in disagreement with the Foreign Office, and I was able, through her, to advise the king with a view to the policy of the government being accepted. She was very loyal to the king, and patriotic at the same time. It would have been difficult to find any other lady who would have filled the part of friend to King Edward with the same loyalty and discretion.

The whole of England knew about the affair. Once Mrs Keppel summoned a hansom cab to her home in Portman Square to take her to a railway station. 'King's Cross,' she told the cabby. He is said to have replied: 'Is he? Oh dear.'

If Alice Keppel had a flaw, people said, it was that she was a little 'grasping', but perhaps this was because she had never had any money. Certainly her husband, the Hon. George Keppel, third son of the Earl of Albemarle, brought none to the marriage. He had other qualities – he was six feet four of handsome manliness, a magnificent figure in his Gordon Highlander's uniform. But the lack of money was a problem, and Mrs Keppel set about getting it like some other desirable but impoverished women in the Marlborough House set. It was rumoured that the father of her first daughter, Violet, was the wealthy future Lord Grimethorpe. (As Violet Trefusis she would become notorious for her turbulent affair with Vita Sackville-West.)

If George Keppel was jealous he never showed it. He behaved with dignity, even complacency, in what to most men would have been a humiliating situation. He had to 'go into trade' to earn enough to support a lifestyle commensurate with his wife's high office as the Prince's mistress. Sir Thomas Lipton, the tea magnate, received a 'high class Victorian order' for making Keppel his agent and sending him to America.

Alice was the perfect mistress for Bertie in every sense except one. There were rumours of other lovers, that George was not the father of either of her two daughters. Lady Curzon wrote to her husband in September 1901: 'Mrs Favourite Keppel is bringing forth another questionable offspring! Either Lord Stavordale's or H. Sturt's!!' Aronson points out that Alice did not have another child, and so probably this was just gossip.

Bertie was by no means faithful, either, but his relationship with another woman he met at about the same time as Alice Keppel will always be a little mysterious. Miss Agnes Keyser was forceful, attractive and intelligent, and what we would now call a career woman. She was the daughter of a wealthy stockbroker, but decided to make nursing her career, and like Florence Nightingale was admired and respected. Forty-five when she met Bertie, she was rather bossy and intimidating, but these qualities fascinated him. Her house in Grosvenor Crescent was a haven of calm and sense after the amusing fripperies of his normal milieu. Agnes gave him good advice about his health, which was not good. More important, she gave him wholesome food, including Irish stews. They would dine together by the fire, and as Agnes was a good bridge player she and her sister would sometimes join Bertie and

Alice for an evening's cards.

Like Florence Nightingale, Agnes did not like women, and preferred men when they were ill or otherwise at her mercy – sick, wounded, dying. When the Boer War broke out and Agnes and her sister wanted to run a nursing home for officers, Bertie had a whip-round among his wealthy Jewish and banker friends. Money poured in from Nathaniel Rothschild, Sir Ernest Cassel, Arthur Sassoon, Lord Sandwich, the banker Hambro and Lord Iveagh, and the Keyser sisters' large house became the King Edward's Hospital for Officers.

For 12 years Bertie visited Agnes at her house, which was conveniently close to Buckingham Palace. There the King found peace and quiet reassurance from a woman who cared nothing for the high-pressure social life that took up so much of his time. He was the only man in her life, and her obscure devotion was touching. Mrs Keppel was too discreet to say what she thought of all this.

Were they lovers? Most people who knew them thought not. Bertie, one of the great lovers of the age – Henry James called him 'Edward the Caresser' (Hibbert, *Edward VII*) – had more than enough opportunities, and may have welcomed a friendship that was simple and emotionally undemanding. Probably Agnes Keyser gave him something that had been missing in his life, a caring mother figure.

After many years of servicing exciting young actresses and horizontal grandes dames, sex still had a hold over him. However, his health was poor, Edwardian indulgence in eating and drinking had taken a toll on his heart, and the effort was disproportionate to the sensual reward. He still had an eye for a pretty face and a good figure, and as Leslie says, 'he was indeed still unfaithful all round.' But most of the time now he wanted quieter joys, and these two women provided them.

There was another remarkable woman in the life of Edward VII, although again it is not known whether they were lovers. Rosa Lewis is probably best remembered today as the model for Lottie Crump, proprietress of the louche Shepheard's Hotel in Evelyn Waugh's novel *Vile Bodies*. In reality this former skivvy ran the extraordinary Cavendish Hotel in Jermyn Street from 1902 until after the Second World War, and for much of the time it doubled as a comfortable if eccentric love nest for members of the aristocracy.

Lewis was born in Leyton in 1867 and began in domestic service when she was 12. She became a celebrity cook, travelling round great houses and preparing multi-course meals for large numbers of guests at house parties. At different times she cooked for Bertie and the Kaiser. Her services were far from cheap and she became rich.

In 1902 Rosa bought the lease of the Cavendish Hotel, on the corner of Jermyn Street and Duke Street. There were suggestions that a cabal of aristocrats including Bertie had persuaded her to take over the hotel so they would have somewhere to conduct their amours, but although Bertie had a suite there he probably didn't use it much. As Anthony Masters puts it in *Rosa Lewis, An Exceptional Edwardian*: 'Her rich clients regarded the Cavendish as a naughty nursery where they sowed their spurious wild oats and tippled their champagne, managed all the while by Rosa, their amoral nanny.'

There were no bars. Guests would drink in their own rooms, and the more intrepid would make their way to Rosa's own parlour where some heavy drinking went on. Those who drank most did not necessarily pay. In her increasingly eccentric way Rosa would charge those she thought best able to afford it. Waugh's *Vile Bodies* describes the system.*

When Bertie died Rosa, greatly distressed, reacted in typically eccentric fashion. First she served champagne to guests at her hotel, who raised their glasses to a portrait of the King. Then she led them down to a special wine cellar where she kept a selection of great vintages reserved for the King's table at country house par-

---

* Rosa, who never lost her Cockney vulgarity, was furious with Waugh, and barred him from the hotel with the words 'Take your arse out of my chair.' In his biography of Waugh, Christopher Sykes says Rosa used to screech in rage: 'There are two bastards I'm not going to have in this house. One is that rotten little Donegall [a gossip columnist] and the other is that little swine Evelyn Waugh.'

ties. There was Veuve Clicquot 1904, Château Pontet-Canet 1895 and Schloss Johannisberg Cabinet 1893, 80-year-old brandies and vintage ports. Afterwards she locked the door of the cellar and refused to allow it to be opened again during her lifetime; it remained a curious shrine to her beloved Bertie.

# *The Age of Scandal*

LATE VICTORIAN SOCIETY was shaken by a series of high-society scandals, some of the worst involving Bertie. The response of the aristocracy was to don a mask of imperturbable sang-froid. In 1897 the Duke and Duchess of Devonshire gave a great ball in Devonshire House to celebrate the Queen's Diamond Jubilee. The richest and most powerful aristocracy in the world gave a demonstration of its wealth and insouciance which was breathtaking, particularly in view of the earthquakes, political and social, shaking English society. Bertie attended in the costume of the Grand Master of the Knights of Malta. The Duke was dressed as the Emperor Charles V and the Duchess as Zenobia, Queen of Palmyra. Princess Henry of Pless came as the Queen of Sheba, Joseph Chamberlain as Pitt the Younger. Mr Asquith came as a Roundhead, appropriately enough – it was in 1911 during his premiership that the House of Lords lost the power to veto legislation passed by the Commons. Photographs of the ball show us the aristocracy serenely confident of its divine right to be rich and profligate whatever happened, still dreaming its fantasy of moral and financial invulnerability. It was the face the aristocracy, and the man at the apex of that rather impenetrable society, liked to show to the world. But from time to time the curtain was drawn aside and the world saw a different picture.

The scandals for which Bertie is remembered were not really of his own making, but usually involved an unwise choice of companions and a habit of writing indiscreet letters to pretty young married women. In 1870 Sir Charles Mordaunt, a prominent society figure, sued his wife for divorce on the grounds of her admitted adultery with, among others, Sir Frederick Johnstone and Viscount Cole. He had pressed her to name her lovers and she had replied: 'With Lord Cole, the Prince of Wales, and others, often, and in open day.' Lady Mordaunt was almost certainly insane, at least temporarily. She had given birth to a blind son, and was torn by remorse. The father of the child, she said, was Viscount Cole.

Bertie had written a dozen letters to Lady Mordaunt, and although these were dismissed as innocuous by the Lord Chancellor, the Prince was served with a subpoena to appear as a witness in the divorce proceedings.

The Lord Chancellor felt that the Prince's appearance in court even as a witness in a divorce case would be 'as bad as a revolution'. Until the freedom of the press to report fully the details of divorce cases was curbed early in the last century, newspapers gave them maximum publicity, sometimes treating them as high farce.* The Queen, who despite evidence to the contrary was beginning to

---

* The law was changed after a 1925 divorce case in which Ian Onslow Dennistoun in effect sold his wife to a senior army officer in exchange for promotion. Dorothy Dennistoun had become the mistress of General Sir John Cowans, quartermaster-general of the army, during the First World War, while her husband, a captain in the Grenadier Guards, became a colonel with safe jobs out of the front line and a seat on the Supreme War Council. Cowans, an extravagant womaniser, died in 1921, and four years later Dorothy, who had by then divorced her husband, sued Dennistoun for money he had borrowed from her. By then he was wealthy, having married the Countess of Caernarvon, widow of the discoverer of Tutankhamun's tomb. Nevertheless he refused to pay up and the whole sordid story came out. Her counsel told the court: 'Colonel Dennistoun was prepared to accept from his wife that she should pass into a condition of adultery with the General – a relation from which he proposed to profit, as he had done.' The court heard that on one occasion Dennistoun met his wife at the Paris Ritz and inspected the suite she was to share with the general.

Neither Dennistoun nor Dorothy came well out of the case, and she did not win any money. The judge said that such cases 'do not in any way represent the general way of life of well-to-do people in England. They give a wholly false impression of English social and family life.' Shortly afterwards Parliament passed a law restricting the reporting of matrimonial cases (Wilkes, *Scandal*).

think Bertie was rather a decent man though with a regrettable weakness for pretty women, told him she had every confidence in his innocence but advised him to be more circumspect in future. In a letter to the Lord Chancellor she was less sanguine:

> The fact of the Prince of Wales's intimate acquaintance with a young married woman being publicly proclaimed will show an amount of imprudence which cannot but damage him in the eyes of the middle and lower classes, which is most deeply to be lamented in these days when the higher classes, in their frivolous, selfish and pleasure-seeking lives, do more to increase the spirit of democracy than anything else.

In the event Bertie escaped lightly. He was in the witness box for only seven minutes, where he denied that he had committed adultery. The formidable barrister William Ballantine did not grill him and the most unpleasant aspect of the day from his point of view was being booed in the street.

His next brush with scandal was potentially more damaging. In October 1875 the Prince went to 'show the flag' in India, the kind of pleasant but unimportant official duty the Queen allowed him. Among the party of 18 people he took with him was Lord Aylesford, known as 'sporting Joe'. Four months into the mission Aylesford received a letter from his wife telling him that she intended to elope with Lord Blandford, brother of Randolph Churchill. Bertie was incensed, and referred to Blandford as 'the greatest blackguard alive'. Naturally, he overlooked his own womanising.

The scandal seemed to be fizzling out, with Lady Aylesford drawing back from the brink of divorce, when Churchill stepped in. He believed that the Prince had taken Aylesford to India in order to leave Lady Aylesford free to commit adultery. As he sought to bring pressure on the Prince to prevent a divorce, he learned that Lady Aylesford had given her lover a bundle of letters written to her by Bertie – that embarrassing letter-writing habit again. These were passed by Blandford to Lord Randolph, who declared to friends that he had the Crown of England in his pocket.

Randolph – father of Sir Winston Churchill – was a powerful politician, once widely expected to become leader of the Tories and Prime Minister. He was also impulsive and hot-headed, and according to Anita Leslie he gave his wife syphilis. He called on the Princess of Wales and drew her attention to the letters. They were of 'the most compromising character' and his lawyer said they would unquestionably result in another subpoena for Bertie.

Lord Chancellor Cairns, asked for his opinion, said the letters were fairly harmless, but contained 'foolish and somewhat stupid expressions'. Bertie had been flirting with attractive young married women again. He was making a stately progress back to England, and when he heard of Churchill's treachery in bringing his wife into the matter he was incensed. His court jester, Beresford, was sent to arrange a duel between Churchill and the Prince of Wales. Churchill dismissed the idea as absurd. The Aylesfords separated quietly, and Churchill apologised, although it took more than ten years for the rift between him and Bertie to be healed. Lady Aylesford lost the custody of her children and was banished from society for ever.

Whatever his intentions may have been, Bertie's relations with the young correspondents who got him into so much hot water were probably innocent. However, it was a fact notorious throughout Europe that he had many, many affairs, some of them long lasting, with women of his own class. There were as well shorter affairs with actresses and brief encounters, particularly in Paris, with courtesans. His favourite Paris brothel was the exclusive Le Chabanais, while the chanteuse Mistinguett and the courtesan Emilienne d'Alençon were among the notables who claimed in their memoirs to have shared a bed with *le roi Eduard*. La Goulu, the red-stockinged dancer of the Moulin Rouge painted by Lautrec, apparently once welcomed him to the music hall with a shout of ''Ullo Wales!' The Prince roared with laughter, and ordered champagne for the musicians. And his letter writing got him into trouble again with Giulia Barucci, one of the *grandes horizontales* of the Second Empire, who referred to herself as 'the greatest whore in the world'. He bought back his indiscreet letters to her.

His abundant sexual energy found outlets nearer home, too. The King of the Belgians, no stranger to such places, was shocked to hear that Bertie frequented a notorious London night spot, the Midnight Club. Aronson in *The King in Love* says that at the same time he was being asked for money by Lady Susan Vane Tempest, who was about to bear his child.

When Bertie entered a room and showed interest in a woman the other men, including her husband, were expected to withdraw. If the lady acquiesced, and many did, the affair that followed could not be kept secret. Bertie was fairly reckless in his amours, but lucky. Out of gratitude that he had made discreet high-class sex acceptable again, the people of his circle stayed silent. Keith Middlemass in his biography *Edward VII* wrote: 'Edward's activities did not mould a new high society, but they simply bestowed the patronage of royalty on the fringe of the aristocracy which had scarcely bowed to the middle-class ethic of morality and which looked for tradition to the eighteenth-century style of "fast" living.'

Bertie did not have to obey the rules. He could call on a woman and leave his carriage outside for hours, while midnight suppers with great ladies were passed over in silence. The deference of Fleet Street towards those in high places had begun. *The Times* had thundered against George IV, but while most journalists knew Bertie to be an enthusiastic fornicator they went 'into fits of righteous indignation', as Pearsall puts it in *The Worm in the Bud*, when his reputation was challenged. In May 1870 a magazine called *The Tomahawk* leapt to his defence:

But when we know the stories to be lies, to be based upon prurient fancies, and to be uttered by poisonous tongues, then indeed is our conduct contemptible – then indeed is our manhood our curse, our chivalry a sound – meaning nothing!... The Prince of Wales may not be a milk-sop or a Saint, but he is the Heir Apparent to our Throne, the son of our Queen, and the husband of Alexandra. As such his honour should be as precious to us as our own.

There was speculation about the exact relationship between Jennie, Lady Randolph Churchill, and the Prince. Anita Leslie says that she 'nibbled away like a detective' and came to the conclusion that the friendship was 'on platonic lines'. In 1886 Bertie told his son that he wanted to patch up the ten-year quarrel with Churchill, 'though we can never be the same friends again'. In May 1886 Bertie finally dined at the Churchills' home, a grand gesture of reconciliation. Churchill was now Secretary of State for India and soon to be Chancellor of the Exchequer and Leader of the House of Commons, Jennie was 'at the height of her beauty' at the age of 32. The dinner went off well, and whatever the Prince thought of Randolph Churchill he was more than happy to renew his friendship with Jennie.

At about this time, says Leslie, Randolph caught syphilis, and was no longer sleeping with his wife. She began an affair with the Hungarian Count Charles Kinsky, who admitted in old age that it had been the supreme love of his life. This makes it unlikely that she would have wanted an affair with Bertie, but as many a woman who entertained him alone discovered, you just didn't know what was likely to happen. Incidentally, the behaviour of the belligerent and overbearing Randolph may have been made yet more erratic by his illness – he threatened to resign, and was forced to make good his threat, ending his political career.

Bertie's last brush with public scandal did not for a change involve a beautiful woman, but it was all the more damaging, although again he was not directly involved. In September 1890 he went to stay with Arthur Wilson, a ship owner, at his home, Tranby Croft, for the Doncaster races. There was some card playing, including baccarat, which was illegal, and one of the guests, Sir William Gordon-Cumming, was accused of cheating. The host and four other men went to Gordon-Cumming and told him that they had seen him cheat: he must sign a paper swearing never to play cards again. Gordon-Cumming denied cheating, but agreed to sign on condition that the five swore to keep the matter secret. When Bertie was told of the affair he added his name to those of the witnesses. Next day Sir William left the house. Bertie contacted Lord and Lady Brooke, who were on their way to a funeral, and asked them to stop off at York station to see him. He told them what had happened; when the story leaked out it was assumed Daisy had talked, and she was referred to as 'the babbling Brooke'.

But the other men in the affair had also talked. The secrecy promised Gordon-Cumming had been betrayed, and he found himself being cut in his London clubs. He brought a libel action against his original accusers. The case came to court in June 1891, and Bertie was subpoenaed as a witness. The revelation that the heir to the throne had been involved in a sordid gambling scandal, however incidentally, was a sensation. Queen Victoria wrote to her eldest daughter: 'This horrible trial drags along, and it is a fearful humiliation to see the future King of this country dragged (and for the second time) through the dirt, just like anyone else, in a Court of Justice.'

Gordon-Cumming's solicitor gave Bertie a hard time in court, accusing him of illegal gambling and breaking Article 42 of Queen's Regulations, which specified that an officer who witnessed dishonourable conduct by another had to report it to the culprit's commanding officer. Bertie was a senior army officer in an honorary capacity, and so was in breach of the regulations. But he firmly stated that he had every confidence in Gordon-Cumming's accusers, and as a result Sir William lost his case. He was dismissed from the army and expelled from his clubs. When Bertie, who suffered an enormous loss of public popularity, let it be known that anyone who even mentioned him would no longer be asked to Marlborough House, the press turned on him. He wrote to his sister: 'The Press have been very severe and cruel, because they know I cannot defend myself.' He wrote to his son George: 'Thank God! the Army and Society are now well rid of such a damned blackguard. The crowning point of his infamy is that he, this morning, married an American young lady, Miss Garner (sister to Madame de Breteuil) with money!' Even more galling than all this was a letter from the Kaiser to Queen Victoria, protesting that his uncle (i.e. Bertie) who held the honorary rank of colonel of Prussian Hussars, should have been involved in a gambling scandal with men young enough to be his sons. The Kaiser did not like his uncle.*

The Gordon-Cummings were totally ostracised. They lived at Gordonstoun (later a school at which Prince Charles, Bertie's great-great grandson, was one of the pupils), in an estate of 40,000 Scottish acres, which became a vast desert of social leprosy. One of their children wrote that 'the vengeance was thorough'.

The Prince was now fat from gluttony, from too much whisky, wine, brandy and liqueurs, short-winded from too many cigars and cigarettes. Edwardian upper-class consumption of food was impressive, and Bertie, a compulsive eater most of his life, would happily demolish three vast meals a day, starting with an enormous breakfast. When in the country he would fit in a fourth, of scones and cake, and if at midnight supper with a lovely woman, often an actress, a fifth. There were snacks in between.† His energetic pursuit of sex seemed to make him hungrier but not fitter.

And so Bertie's aimless and pointless life went on. Then suddenly, in late middle age, and without any real training, he was launched on to the world stage.

---

\*   They quarrelled over many things, but what Bertie found really unbearable was the Kaiser's attitude to his moral shortcomings. He was furious that his nephew had not stopped the German press from attacking him over the Tranby Croft affair. A cartoon had been printed changing the motto of the Prince of Wales from *Ich Dien*, 'I serve', to 'I deal'.

†   Edwardian meals were not to be taken lightly. There might be a choice of 30 different dishes for breakfast, including porridge, bacon, ham, sausages, poached and scrambled eggs, devilled kidneys, haddock, tongue, pressed beef and ham, cold roast pheasant, partridge, grouse, ptarmigan, fruit, scones and toast. For the toast, marmalade, honey and jam. To drink, coffee, Indian and China tea and cold drinks. Lunch would consist of at least eight courses. In mid-afternoon there would be a break for tea, sandwiches, bread and butter, toast, jam, cakes, and if the Prince of Wales was there, lobster salad. Dinner was particularly formidable: 12 rich courses might consist of soup, fish, two consecutive entrees, joint, game, sweet, savouries, bread and cheese, mustard and cress, dessert, fruit, nuts and cheese. All these were served with appropriate wines, but the serious drinking began after dinner for the men. (This made a pleasant contrast to eating with Queen Victoria. She ate very quickly, and the servants had instructions to whip all the plates away as soon as she was finished.) Finally, for those who had stayed the course and were not working off some of the calories in a distant bed, at about 2 am there would be devilled chicken, sandwiches, whisky and soda.

## Twilight of the gods

Queen Victoria died in January 1901. Winston Churchill wrote to his mother: 'So the Queen is dead ... A great and solemn event: but I am curious to know about the King. Will it entirely revolutionise his way of life? Will he sell his horses and scatter his Jews or will Reuben Sassoon be enshrined among the crown jewels and other regalia? Will he become desperately serious?...Will Keppel be appointed First Lady of the Bedchamber?'

Bertie was king at last, as Edward VII, 11 months before his sixtieth birthday.* When he was crowned in August, the nation had one of its outbursts of enthusiasm for royalty. The poet Wilfred Scawen Blunt, for long a tortured and hopeless lover of Skittles, wrote in his diary: 'Popular enthusiasm knew no bounds, and a mighty roar of continuous cheering echoed from the Palace to Westminster.'

Inside the Abbey during his coronation several of Bertie's lovers past and present were housed in the King's special box, dubbed by a wit 'the loose box'. As Pearsall states in *The Worm in the Bud*, the occupants included a Mrs Hartmann, Lady Kilmorey, Sarah Bernhardt, Mrs Arthur Paget and the reigning royal favourite, Mrs Keppel. Others were Mrs Ronnie Greville, Lady Sarah Wilson, Feo Sturt 'and that ilk'. One of Alexandra's ladies-in-waiting thought the King's parading of his conquests was 'the one discordant note in the Abbey – for to see the row of lady friends in full magnificence did rather put my teeth on edge – La Favorita of course in the best place ... 'The King was not distracted by his duties from the display of feminine beauty. After Alexandra had been crowned, the peeresses 'in one graceful, fluid, simultaneous movement' placed their coronets on their heads. As Aronson notes, the King remarked afterwards that 'their white arms arching over their heads' resembled 'a scene from a beautiful ballet'. The ceremony was, as usual, long and tedious, trying the patience and bladders of the elderly courtiers. Louisa the Double Duchess, now in her

---

* He announced that he would drop his father's name rather than rule as King Albert – there could only ever be one, saintly Albert.

seventies, tried to find a lavatory as soon as the royal procession left, and found her way barred by a line of Grenadier Guards officers. With a queue of peeresses building up behind her she spoke angrily to the officers, then tripped in trying to push past them. She fell down a flight of steps and rolled, a furious ball of ermine and velvet, to the feet of the Chancellor of the Exchequer. He 'stared paralysed' at this apparition, but the Marquis de Soveral had more presence of mind and lifted her to her feet. Margot Asquith was meanwhile pursuing Louisa's coronet, which was bouncing away among the stalls. She retrieved it and replaced it on the Double Duchess's head.

The cobwebs of the old Queen's court were blown away by the jaunty new King and his entourage. Rooms at Buckingham Palace which had remained cocooned in mourning were suddenly full of the chatter of pretty, beautifully dressed and coiffed women. Bertie's Jewish friends, City financiers and business magnates paced the luxurious new carpets, as if in answer to Winston Churchill. He didn't want the company to be too challenging: in a letter to her husband, published in *Lady Curzon's India: Letters of a Vicereine*, Lady Curzon commented that Bertie was 'miserable in the company of any but his few bridge friends as he feels so hopelessly out of it with intelligence or intellect – on the whole he has begun badly'.

Certainly Bertie was no intellectual, and he had no conversation. A dozen words were the most he could put together at a time. Aronson calls the tone of the new court 'somewhat philistine'. In many ways Bertie was a child, easily bored and needing constant entertainment and distraction. This accounted for his weakness for practical jokes, another sign of his essentially vulgar streak. He enjoyed playing them, and enjoyed those of others. Jennie Churchill played a particularly elaborate one which delighted him. At a dinner party she claimed she was wearing a Jubilee bustle which played 'God Save the Queen' every time she sat down. Actually there was a servant hidden under her chair with a musical box.

There was no subtlety about royal humour. 'If anyone caught his foot in a mat, or nearly fell into the fire or out of the window the mirth of the royal family knew no bounds', commented one observer. As Aronson notes, why bother thinking up witty remarks when a finger caught in a door will bring gales of laughter?

His friends never knew where Bertie would strike next. When Christopher Sykes became hopelessly drunk at a ball and had to be put to bed, Bertie arranged for a dead seagull to be put beside him. The following night a trussed rabbit shared Sykes's bed. Apart from sousing him with his own brandy, Bertie liked to play a painful joke, if so it can be called, on his friend. Bertie would call, 'Come here, Christopher, and look at the smoke coming out of my eyes.' As Sykes looked into his eyes Bertie would 'pretend' to burn him with his cigar.[*] (A similar joke used to be played on children. No child fell for it twice, but they didn't have Sykes's dog-like devotion to their torturer.) Masters lists in *Rosa Lewis* some of the now-forgotten tricks these wealthy idlers played when the stultifying conversation flagged: 'Booby-traps, apple-pie beds, slapstick, horseplay were never very far away ... ' Incidentally, the sycophantic and ridiculous Sykes beggared himself in his efforts to amuse his royal master. For ten years he had entertained Bertie at his Yorkshire house and in London with a succession of magnificent dinners and house parties. Eventually Sykes could no longer afford to entertain Bertie at all. His near bankruptcy seems to have angered Bertie – going broke was an unforgivable solecism. Nevertheless he tried to help.

With this unthinking callousness went extreme touchiness. One night at Sandringham, Bertie's old friend Sir Frederick Johnstone (one of the co-respondents in the Lady Mordaunt divorce case) became very drunk. Bertie said: 'Freddy, Freddy, you're very

---

[*] However cruel Bertie's jokes were, he never went as far as his friend Robert Bristowe. Pearsall relates one example in *The Worm in the Bud*. To get rid of two servants who would not accept that they had been sacked, Bristowe once let a jaguar loose in his house in Clarges Street. He rang for the servants and then locked himself in the dining room. The servants, terrified of the animal, refused to answer his calls. Bristowe then bored a hole in the dining-room door and took pot shots at the jaguar with a revolver, finally killing it after an hour.

drunk,' and suggested that he go to bed. Johnstone pointed to the Prince's mighty belly and replied: 'Tum-Tum, you're very fat.' He was, says Pearsall, out of the house before breakfast the next morning; Bertie's dignity counted for more than old friendships. Once at billiards with an acquaintance he played a poor shot. 'Pull yourself together, Wales,' the man joked. The Prince promptly sent for the man's carriage.

Years before Bertie's death, rumours circulated that he was impotent and that his parade of virility was a sham. The courtesan Skittles told Wilfred Scawen Blunt that sexual overindulgence could not have hastened his death, because 'the King has been impotent for the last fifteen years'. Yet although he had to be discreet in England now that he was King, when travelling abroad without his wife or Alice Keppel he 'flung himself into amorous adventures with as much gusto as ever', as Aronson puts it. The Liberal Prime Minister Sir Henry Campbell-Bannerman, who holidayed with him at Marienbad, complained, 'I got so mixed up with the King's incessant gaieties, for which his energy and appetite are alike insatiable' that after the King had left, the statesman's doctor ordered him to bed for 48 hours' rest. Of course we cannot know what the King got up to when he was behind closed doors with the lovely young woman who caught his fancy, but an officer on the royal yacht once heard from the porthole of the King's cabin the royal voice saying: 'Stop calling me Sir and put another cushion under your back.' However, it would be strange if there had been no diminution in his once awesome powers. Lillie Langtry paid tribute to them by reporting that after he complained, 'I've spent enough on you to buy a battleship,' she replied, 'And you've spent enough in me to float one.'

There was a great gulf between Bertie's private world, where he let his hair down and enjoyed childish pranks, and his public life. He had an almost majestic dignity which belied his portly lack of stature. Gradually he came to be seen as a bastion of stability in an uncertain world. Gladstone had objected to his dabbling in politics, condemning his 'total want of political judgment, either inherited or acquired', but as king he took on at least the appearance of gravitas. George Dangerfield wrote in *The Strange Death of Liberal England*: 'He represented in a concentrated shape those bourgeois kings whose florid forms and rather dubious escapades were all the industrialised world had left of an ancient divinity; his people saw in him the personification of something nameless, genial and phallic.'

However, from 1905 on there were clear signs that Bertie's self-indulgent lifestyle was killing him. Bronchial attacks became more frequent, and in 1909 he collapsed during a state visit to Berlin. That year he met Lillie Langtry for the last time, shortly after his horse Minoru won the Derby, their shared love of racing bringing them together again briefly. Bertie spoke to her in the Jockey Club enclosure at Newmarket, and suggested that he visit her next day at Regal Lodge, her large mock-Tudor home nearby. They sat in her boudoir and reminisced over chilled hock and peaches.

In 1910 he went to Biarritz for a 'cure', but at 69 he had lost his old resilience. In May he insisted on inspecting some crops in pouring rain, and a severe bronchial attack followed. Queen Alexandra rushed back from Corfu, and the whole family hurried to Buckingham Palace. On 6 May the Queen reluctantly invited Alice Keppel to join the family at the King's deathbed before he sank into a coma. There was a widespread belief that this was a touching gesture by the Queen, but the royal doctor, Sir Francis Laking, and Wilfred Scawen Blunt in his secret diary tell a different story: one of near blackmail by Alice to force the Queen to invite her, of Alexandra's distaste when the King insisted she kiss Alice, of the Queen later hissing 'Get that woman away.' But shifting Alice was far from easy. Having become hysterical and shrieking, 'I never did any harm, there was nothing wrong between us. What is to become of me?' she was carried to a nearby room where she remained for several hours. James Lees-Milne in *The Enigmatic Edwardian* reports a comment on the incident written by Lord Esher, Bertie's trusted confidant: 'Altogether it was a painful and rather theatrical exhibition, and ought never to have happened.'

The contrast between the reactions of the nation to the deaths of the two playboy kings, George IV and Edward VII, could not be starker. A quarter of a million people filed past Bertie's coffin as it lay in state in Westminster Hall, and huge crowds lined the route of the funeral procession on 20 May. Many people recorded their sense of loss and shock. Asquith, the Prime Minister, sailing home through the Bay of Biscay, wrote:

> I went up on deck and the first sight that met my eyes in the twilight before dawn was Halley's comet blazing in the sky ... I felt bewildered and stunned ... We had lost, without warning or preparation, the Sovereign whose ripe experience, trained sagacity, equitable judgment and unvarying consideration counted for so much.

Wilfred Scawen Blunt took a cooler view:

> Today the King was buried, and I hope the country will return to comparative sanity, for at present it is in delirium. The absurdities written in every newspaper about him pass belief ... In no print has there been the slightest allusion to Mrs Keppel, or any of the 101 ladies he has loved, or to his gambling or to any of the little vices which made up his domestic life. It is not for me or perhaps any of us to censure him for these pleasant wickednesses, but his was not even in make-believe the life of a saint or an at all virtuous or respectable man, and according to strict theology he is most certainly at the present moment in hell. Yet all the bishops and priests, Catholic, Protestant and Non-conformist, join in giving him a glorious place in heaven ...

It would have been a brave clergyman who spilled the beans. As Sir Edward Grey, the Foreign Secretary, wrote: 'He became intensely and increasingly popular and when he died the unprecedentedly long-drawn-out procession to pass the bier of State in Westminster Hall was a manifestation of genuine and personal sorrow as well as national mourning.'

There was real grief that good old Bertie was no more. The portly old roué had been genuinely popular. When his horse won the Derby in 1909 the crowd roared 'Good old Teddy' and sang 'God Save the King'. There was a jingle at the time about 'The monarch to make things hum, the King, the runabout King'. Although he may not have merited his reputation for influencing Britain's foreign policy, there is no doubt that his enormous popularity in France was a considerable factor in bringing about the entente cordiale in 1904, and he had done what he could to ease tensions with Germany. He had given his name to an age, and it would be a long time before the nation felt as self-confident again.

Of course upper-class men didn't suddenly become moral just because Bertie had died. But the new king, George V, was a dull nonentity, and the Fast Set had lost its leader. Upper-class sex became more furtive in a more democratic age. Two world wars dispelled for ever the carefree hedonism of a class that had felt itself to be somehow above society.

# Appendix: The Royal

## Mistresses

THE MISTRESSES OF CHARLES II AND EDWARD VII mostly led interesting and more or less scandalous lives after the kings died. I have chosen to continue their stories here, rather than interrupt the flow of the main narrative.

### The mistresses of Charles II

At the time of his death Charles had been about to make a noble if not an honest woman of Nell Gwynn, with the title of Countess of Greenwich. Before he died Charles had implored his brother, 'Let not poor Nelly starve.' James had often been the butt of Nell's wit. She had nicknamed the pompous and serious-minded Duke 'dismal Jimmy'. Nevertheless, when he succeeded as James II he paid off most of her debts and gave her a pension. Like all the other pensioners of the Court she had difficulty getting her money, and had to plead for it. She told James, in words presumably deliberately echoing those of Cardinal Wolsey: 'Had I suffered for my God as I have done for your brother and you, I would not have needed either of your kindness and justice to me.' She died of a stroke two years later at the age of 35.

When James II fled England in 1688, Hortense Mancini lost her pension of £4,000 a year and was plunged into poverty. She died in 1699 in a Chelsea lodging house, her end hastened, said John Evelyn, 'by the intemperate drinking of strong spirits'.

The Duchess of Portsmouth, whom James always disliked, had taken refuge with the French ambassador in London. James refused to let her return to France until she had paid her debts and returned some of the Crown jewels. He refused to confirm the pension Charles had promised her and denied her son, the Duke of Richmond, the post of Grand Equerry which he had been guaranteed. The Duchess was so disgusted that she used 'plain words', Louis XIV was told.

After she retired to France she found herself in trouble with Louis for criticising his mistress Madame de Maintenon, and he was with difficulty dissuaded from sending her into exile. He gave her a generous pension, but her ungovernable extravagance – she was a reckless gambler – meant that she slowly sank into poverty. Time and again she asked Louis to stop her creditors pursuing her, and time and again he obliged. She lived to be 85, and Voltaire, who saw her when she was a very old woman, said that she was still a beauty. According to Saint-Simon, she died 'very old, very penitent and very poor'; she would have hated two-thirds of this description.

Lady Castlemaine had many further adventures. Robert 'Beau' Feilding was at least ten years younger than her. He was also known as Handsome Feilding, and it was said that he had 'passed like an inundation over the fair sex'. The same fair sex was 'his seraglio' and he appealed alike to the willing chambermaid or the haughty baroness. When he took his place in church a murmur went round and all the women gazed at him. He drove round the town in a coach emblazoned with the spread eagle, accounted for by his claim to descent from the counts of Habsburg, and dressed in magnificent if old-fashioned clothes. To the small mob of urchins who ran behind his coach he would call out 'Good bastards, go to school ... I am loath to hurt you, because I know not but you are all my own offspring ...'

Feilding, who was distantly related to the Villiers family, had married two heiresses and was now a widower. He and Lady Castlemaine were Catholics and supporters of James II, in whose army he had served, and when her husband Roger died in 1705 he wrote her a proposal:

> Madam, It is not only that nature has made us two of the most accomplished of each sex, and pointed to us to obey her dictates in becoming One; but that there is also an ambition in following the mighty persons you have favoured. Where Kings and heroes, as great as Alexander, or such as could personate Alexander, have bowed, permit your General to lay his laurels.

In November 1705, when Lady Castlemaine was 64, they were married. Feilding moved into her house in St James's and began to beat her and plunder her fortune. He would have taken everything if her grandson, the young Duke of Grafton, had not discovered that Feilding had married a Mrs Wadsworth only a fortnight before his wedding to the Duchess. Lady Castlemaine flew into one of her famous rages, at which Feilding broke into her safe and stole £100, thrashed her and threatened to kill her. When she cried for help to the crowd that gathered outside, Feilding fired a blunderbuss. He was arrested and held briefly in Newgate. In retaliation he published an advertisement warning tradesmen 'upon no account whatever to trust, or give credit to the said Duchess, whose debts he will in no wise satisfy'.

He went on trial for bigamy at the Old Bailey in December 1706 and it emerged that he too was the victim of a confidence trick in marrying Mary Wadsworth. He had really been after a widow named Anne Deleau, who was worth £60,000 (almost £8,000,000), and had paid a hairdresser, Charlotte Villars, £500 to introduce him. Instead she dressed Mrs Wadsworth, who had recently been released from the Bridewell prison, in mourning and took her to Feilding's lodgings. He had hired an opera star to sing love songs as he showed her round before marrying her.

Feilding's marriage to Lady Castlemaine was declared invalid. He received a pardon from Queen Anne, lived apparently happily with Mary Wadsworth and referred to her in his will as his 'dear and loving wife'. However, his last years were clouded by debt; he spent some time in the Fleet prison and 'ended his dolors in a garret'.

Barbara Castlemaine retired to Chiswick, where she died of dropsy in October 1709. She had dissipated her great fortune, and had little to leave to the Duke of Grafton. Her greed had been almost boundless. When the body of Bishop Robert Braybrook, who died in 1440, was exhumed, it was found to be remarkably well preserved. The Duchess is said to have gone to see it and asked to be left alone. Afterwards it was noticed that the penis was missing. As related by Brian Masters in *The Mistresses of Charles II*, a document in the British Museum quotes a witness: 'and though some ladys of late have got Bishopricks for others, yet I have not heard of any but this that got one for herself'.

## The mistresses of Edward VII

When Alice Keppel went to Marlborough House to sign the book of condolence for Edward VII she was prevented from doing so on the order of the new king, George V. Realising that she now faced ostracism by the royal family, Alice concocted a fantasy about Bertie's last moments, of how Alexandra 'had fallen upon her neck and wept with her', and how she had promised that the royals would look after her. In fact Alexandra had told Sir Francis Laking that she would not have let Keppel kiss her cheek had it not been the King's wish. But for a while Alice's version prevailed.

To avoid publicity (not creditors, as has been suggested – Bertie had made her a wealthy woman), the Keppels left their home in Portman Square overnight and moved in with friends. Sonia Keppel, their younger daughter, was nine years old at the time. As she relates in her book *Edwardian Daughter*, she asked her father: 'Why does it matter so much, Kingy dying?' George Keppel, generous as ever, told her: 'Poor little girl, it must have been very frightening for you. And for all of us, for that matter. Nothing will ever be quite the same again. Because Kingy was such a wonderful man.'

Alice thought it would be best if she left the country for a while, and decided the family should go to the Far East. When her daughters asked her why she wanted to visit Ceylon, she replied: 'In my opinion, no young lady's education is complete without a smattering of Tamil.'

Two years later the Keppels returned to London and became the centre of one of London's liveliest social sets. Sonia recalled as many as 70 sitting down to lunch. The First World War, when George joined his regiment and Alice helped run a hospital in Boulogne, dimmed the gaiety somewhat. A greater upheaval in a personal sense was caused by her daughter Violet's three-year affair with Vita Sackville-West.

In 1927 the Keppels moved to a villa in the hills above Florence where the writer Sir Harold Acton was among their neighbours. In *More Memoirs of an Aesthete* he left an unforgettable portrait of the ageing grande dame, now white-haired and magnificent rather than voluptuous:

> A fine figure of a woman, as they used to say, more handsome than beautiful, she possessed enormous charm, which was not only due to her cleverness and vivacity but to her generous heart. Her kindnesses were innumerable and spontaneous. Altogether she was on a bigger scale than most of her sex; she could have impersonated Britannia in a tableau vivant, and done that Lady credit.

When Italy entered the war in 1940 the Keppels returned to London. They lived in the Ritz Hotel for the duration, and Alice became, according to Acton, 'empress of the Ritz'. Her sense of humour was as sharp as ever. Once she asked the Bishop of Bath and Wells what his favourite reading was. He thought for a moment and then said his idea of a perfect afternoon was 'to relax on that sofa with my favourite Trollope'. This story lost nothing in her frequent retellings.

Several writers refer to Alice's drinking. The politician and diarist Chips Channon recalled in his diary that he once gave a dinner party at which Alice was the 'showpiece'. He wrote, 'she is so affectionate and grande dame that it is a pity that she tipples, and then becomes garrulous and inaccurate in her statements ... ' As Aronson recounts in *The King in Love*, during these years Alice was often to be seen 'holding uproarious court to gatherings of equivocal young men in London pubs', a sight hard to imagine. By the time the Keppels returned to their Tuscan villa in 1946, Alice was 77 and beginning to suffer from liver trouble. She died in September 1947 and was buried in the Protestant cemetery in Florence. She had outlived Bertie by almost forty years, and also his other official mistresses, Lillie Langtry and Daisy Warwick.

In 1925 Lillie published her very unrevealing autobiography, *The Days I Knew*. Although clearly proud of her 'friendship' with Bertie, she gives no hint that they had loved each other deeply in the flesh. She died at her Monte Carlo home in February 1929, aged 75, and her body was buried with her parents in Jersey near the rectory where she had grown up.

Daisy Warwick had gone on doing good works and getting deeper and deeper into debt. In 1914 she owed friends and moneylenders about £90,000 (more than £5,000,000). Warwick Castle had been let, her valuables sold or mortgaged, attempts at journalism did not produce nearly enough income. Facing bankruptcy, she turned to Bertie's love letters.

Bertie had left instructions in his will that all his private letters were to be destroyed, and most were. This made his letters to Daisy all the more valuable. It was unthinkable, of course, that she would publish them, but could she bluff someone into paying her £90,000 not to publish?

She began a complicated game with the Palace. At the last moment, after the King's advisers, who had no intention of paying her a penny, had stalled as long as possible, Daisy threatened to publish her memoirs, including the letters, in America. The Palace then had her served with an injunction preventing publication, a move they had long planned. It was the day before the outbreak of the First World War, and she had been completely outmanoeuvred.

Fifteen years later Daisy published her anodyne memoirs. There is no mention of the attempted blackmail, only pious declarations

# Bibliography

Acton, Harold, *More Memoirs of an Aesthete*, Methuen, 1970

Alcock, Thomas, *The Famous Pathologist or the Noble Mountebank*, Nottingham University, 1961

Anon, *Life, Adventures, Amours and Intrigues of . . . Jemmy Twitcher*, 1770

Anon (a monk of the order of St Francis), *Nocturnal revels, Or, The History of King's Place and other Modern Nunneries*, 2vols, M. Goadby, 1779

Archenholz, Baron J. W. von, *A Picture of England*, 1789

Aronson, Theo, *The King in Love*, Corgi, 1989

Ashe, Geoffrey, *Do What You Will*, W.H. Allen, 1974

Ashley, Maurice, *Charles II: Man and Statesman*, 1971

Aubrey, John. *Brief Lives*, Folio Society, 1975

Berendt, Stephen C., *Royal Mourning and Regency Culture*, Macmillan, 1997

Blunden, Margaret, *The Countess of Warwick*, Cassell, 1967

Blyth, Henry, *Old Q, The Rake of Piccadilly*, Weidenfeld & Nicolson, 1967

*The High Tide of Pleasure*, Weidenfeld & Nicolson, 1970

Burford, E. J., *Royal St James*, R. Hale, 1988

Burnet, Gilbert, *History of my Own Time*, 1724–34

*Some Passages in the Life and Death of John Earl of Rochester: Written by his Own Direction on his Deathbed*, 1680

Carswell, John, *The Old Cause*, Cresset Press, 1954

Chancellor, E. Beresford, *The Lives of the Rakes*, 6 vols, Philip Allen, 1925

Chapman, Hester W., *Great Villiers*, Secker & Warburg, 1949
    *The Tragedy of Charles II*, Cape, 1964

Clarendon, Edward Hythe, First Earl of, *The History of the Rebellion and Civil Wars in England*, Folio Society, 1967

Coke, Mary, *Letters and Journals*, Kingsmead Reprints, 1970

Cole, Edward, *History of the English Stage*

Curzon, Lady, *Lady Curzon's India: Letters of a Vicereine*, Weidenfeld & Nicolson, 1974

Dangerfield, George, *The Strange Death of Liberal England*, Constable, 1936

Davis, I.M., *The Harlot and the Statesman*, Kensal Press, 1986

Evelyn, John, *Diary and Correspondence*, ed. William Bray 1850

Fairfax, Brian, *Memoirs of the Life of George Villiers, Duke of Buckingham*, 1758

Falk, Bernard, *Old Q's Daughter*, Hutchinson, 1951

Farington, Joseph, *The Farington Diary*, ed. James Greig, 8 vols, Hutchinson, 1922–8

Fraser, Antonia, *King Charles II*, Phoenix, 2002
    *The Weaker Vessel*, Mandarin, 1993

Fuller, Ronald, *Hell-Fire Francis*, Chatto & Windus, 1939

Goldsworthy, Cephas, *The Satyr, An Account of the Life and Work, Death and Salvation of John Wilmot, Second Earl of Rochester*, Weidenfeld & Nicolson, 2001

Greene, Graham, *Lord Rochester's Monkey*, Bodley Head, 1974

Hamilton, Elizabeth, *The Illustrious Lady*, Hamish Hamilton, 1980

Hanger, George, *The Life, Adventures and Opinions of Col. George Hanger, Written by Himself*, 1801

Hawkins, Sir John, *Life of Samuel Johnson*, 1787

Hearne, Thomas, *Remarks and Collections*, 1885–9

Hibbert, Christopher, *The Roots of Evil*, Sutton, 2003
    *George IV, Prince of Wales*, Longman, 1972
    *Edward VII: A Portrait*, Allen Lane, 1976

Hill, C. P., *Who's Who in Stuart Britain*, Shepheard-Walwyn, 1988

Huish, Robert, *Memoirs of George the Fourth*, 2 vols, 1831

Jesse, J. H., *Literary and Historical Memorials of London*, 1847

Jesse, *George Selwyn*, J. C. Nimmo, 1901

Johnson, James William, *A Profane Wit, The Life of John Wilmot, Earl of Rochester*, University of Rochester Press, 2004

Johnstone, Charles, *Chrysal*, Dutton, 1908

Keppel, Sonia, *Edwardian Daughter*, Hamish Hamilton, 1958

Langtry, Lillie, *The Days I Knew*, Hutchinson, 1925

Lees-Milne, James, *The Enigmatic Edwardian*, Sidgwick & Jackson, 1986

Leslie, Anita, *Edwardians in Love*, Hutchinson, 1972

Linnane, Fergus, *Encyclopedia of London Vice and Crime*, Sutton, 2004

  *London the Wicked City*, Robson, 2003

Macky, John, *Memoirs of the Secret Service*, 1733

Magnus, Philip, *King Edward VII*, John Murray, 1964

Martelli, George, *Jemmy Twitcher*, Jonathan Cape, 1962

Masters, Anthony, *Rosa Lewis, An Exceptional Edwardian*, Weidenfeld & Nicolson, 1977

Masters, Brian, *The Mistresses of Charles II*, Blond and Briggs, 1979

McCormick, Donald, *The Hell-Fire Club, The Story of the Amorous Knights of Wycombe*, Jarrolds, 1958

Middlemass, Keith, *Edward VII*, Weidenfeld and Nicholson 1972

Moreton, Maria, *Memoirs of the Life of the Duke of Queensberry*, 1810

Murray, Venetia, *High Society in the Regency Period*, Penguin, 1999

O'Toole, Fintan, *A Traitor's Kiss, The Life of Richard Brinsley Sheridan*, Granta, 1997

Parissien, Steven, *George IV, The Grand Entertainment*, John Murray, 2001

Peakman, Julie, *Lascivious Bodies*, Atlantic Books, 2004

Pearsall, Ronald, *The Worm in the Bud*, Pimlico, 1993

Pepys, Samuel, *Diary, 1660–8*, ed. Robert Latham and William Matthews, HarperCollins, 1995

Pike, Luke Owen, *A History of Crime in England*, 1873-6

Porter, Roy and Hall, Leslie, *The Facts of Life*, Yale University Press, 1995

Priestley, J.B., *The Prince of Pleasure*, Heinemann, 1969

Rodger, N.A.M., *The Insatiable Earl*, HarperCollins, 1992

Shaw, D., *London in the Sixties*, 1908

Swift, Jonathan, *Journals to Stella*, Methuen, 1901

Thackeray, W.M., *The Four Georges*, 1879

Thomas, Peter D.G., *John Wilkes, A Friend to Liberty*, Clarendon Press 1996

Uglow, Jenny, *Hogarth, a Life and a World*, Faber and Faber, 1997

Walker, Captain C., *Authentic Memoirs of the Life of the Celebrated Sally Salisbury . . .* , 1723

Walpole, Horace, *Memoirs of the Reign of George III*, Yale University Press, 1999

   *The Last Journals of Horace Walpole During the Reign of George III*, 2 vols, 1910

Ward, Ned, *The History of The London Clubs*, 1709

   *The London Spy*, Folio Society, 1955

Warwick, Frances, Countess of, *Life's Ebb and Flow*, Hutchinson, 1929

   *Afterthoughts*, Cassell, 1931

Wilkes, Roger, *Scandal: A Scurrilous History of Gossip*, Atlantic Books, 2002

Wilson, Harriette, *Memoirs*, Folio Society, 1964

Wraxall, Sir Nathaniel, *Historical Memoirs of my own Time*, 1772–84

   *Posthumous Memoirs*, 1884

# Index

Note: page numbers in **bold** refer to illustrations and where the letter *n* prefixes a page number it refers to the text in the footnote on that particular page